TEACHING PSYCHOLOGY
Information and Resources

Third Edition

BPS
BOOKS

Published by
The British Psychological Society

First published in 1993 by The British Psychological Society, St Andrews House, 48 Princess Road East, Leicester LE1 7DR, UK.

A catalogue record for this book is available from the British Library.

ISBN 1 85433 102 7 paperback

Designed by DFP – Design For Publishing
Printed in Great Britain by BPCC Wheatons Ltd, Exeter

CONTENTS

AUDIOVISUAL AIDS

Rosemary Westley

❏ *off-air recording • video formats • information sources and publications • films and videos: distributors and libraries, societies and associations • selected audiovisual materials • subject index • addresses*

Audiovisual materials are extensively used by teachers of psychology at all levels. All institutions have limited facilities for producing their own materials, overhead transparencies being the most popular, while some have fully equipped television studios and are able to produce films for their teaching staff. However most teachers will at some time need to hire or purchase audiovisual aids.

Whether you need films, videos or cassette tape/slide programmes, there is a very wide range of commercial material available to suit all budgets. The widespread use of videos has considerably reduced the cost of showing films. Many libraries transfer new films onto video cassettes, keep the film copy as the original and hire out the video version with savings on handling and postage. Video cassettes can also be purchased at a reasonable cost, and this is a realistic alternative to hiring them.

The main problem posed by the use of commercial products is the time it can take to find the right material. Because a range of subject areas is relevant to psychology courses, useful material may be catalogued under a number of headings. The main ones are children and child development, psychology, social psychology, medicine, mental health, social problems, health and safety, education, mental and physical handicap. However, there is a great deal of overlap in the criteria used for the classification of materials in distributors' catalogues and it is very easy to miss suitable items.

This chapter is designed to save time and effort in locating material by providing a guide to what is currently available. There is information on where to get advice and assistance, video formats and off-air recording, distributors and their range of topics, charities that have audiovisual programmes and a selection of relevant materials from current catalogues. The chapter ends with a comprehensive subject index for easy reference and a list of names, addresses and telephone numbers of the companies and organizations that are referred to.

OFF-AIR RECORDING

The new Copyright, Designs and Patents Act 1988 enables an educational establishment to record, off-air, any radio or television programme for educational purposes (except those made by the Open University, for which there is a separate licence scheme) subject to the acquisition of a licence from the Educational Recording Agency Ltd (ERA). There is at present no licensing scheme to cover cable and satellite broadcasts and therefore you may record them under the Act. Programmes recorded after 1st August 1989 can be retained indefinitely.

Television and radio are valuable teaching resources and you can now build up a recording library of suitable materials for teaching. You can lend videos to and borrow videos from other educational establishments provided they are licensed by ERA.

VIDEO FORMATS

Three video cassette formats are used by distributors in education. Before hiring or purchasing video tapes check which format your video recorder uses. It will be one of the following.

Betamax   Originally designed by Sony, but no longer manufactured. The Betamax system uses cassettes that contain half-inch tape.

VHS   VHS (Video Home System) is now the dominant video cassette system in the UK.

U-matic   High quality video cassette which holds three-quarter inch tape. This system is now used in a variety of modes for production purposes.

INFORMATION SOURCES AND PUBLICATIONS

When selecting audiovisual material, it can be difficult to decide on its suitability for your teaching needs when the only information available is an uncritical description in a distributor's catalogue. Although you may be able to get recommendations from other teachers on suitable materials there are also several organizations that can provide help in locating materials, that publish reviews and appraisals and can provide preview facilities.

British Film Institute   The BFI holds the nation's film archives. It has production, distribution and information divisions.

PUBLICATIONS:
British Film Institute Film and Television Yearbook lists all production companies, exhibitions and distribution organizations,
and gives information on the film industry and BFI services.

    British National Film and Video Catalogue provides a com-
plete record of short non-fiction films, video cassettes and
16mm feature films released for non-theatrical distribution in
the UK. The catalogue has been published since 1963 in quarterly issues with annual cumulated volumes.

British   BUFVC exists to promote the production, study and use of
Universities Film films, television and related media in higher education and
& Video Council research. The Council provides the following facilities:

INFORMATION SERVICE: deals with enquiries by members relating to the production, availability, and use of audiovisual
materials in higher education. It has a small reference library,
catalogues of over 500 UK and 100 foreign distributors and a
file of appraisals on audiovisual materials currently available
in the UK. Membership is by subscription.

AUDIOVISUAL REFERENCE CENTRE: holds audiovisual materials
produced in institutions of higher education which can be
previewed in the BUFVC offices.

HIGHER EDUCATION FILM AND VIDEO LIBRARY: contains specialized films and video cassettes in all subjects. This material
would not normally be available in the UK (for example,
films made in the course of research). The films and video
cassettes are suitable for degree-level and research work.
Distribution is handled by Concord Film Council.

PUBLICATIONS:
BUFVC Catalogue. Programmes in this catalogue can be found
at present on microfiche (1990 edn). In future they will be
made available online via JANET and on CD-ROM. Some
6,000 video cassettes, films, tape/slide programmes, audio
cassettes, slide sets, computer programs and videodiscs are
fully described, with subject and title indexes. Many of the
programmes were produced in institutions of higher education; others have been recommended for use in degree-level
teaching and research. Television programmes and sound
tapes from new Open University courses are now included.
Appraised items are marked, as are those available for preview at the BUFVC'S Audiovisual Reference Centre. The
addresses and telephone numbers of more than 500 UK distributors are also listed. Further information can be obtained
from the library and database manager, Marylin Sarmiento.

    Interpersonal Skills: A Guide to Film and Video Resources
(1987). This 40-page booklet lists 170 programmes which
demonstrate counselling and communication techniques. An
appendix lists organizations that provide training and advisory services.

Higher Education Film and Video Library Catalogue. Some 400 films and videos for use in degree-level teaching are listed. They include materials produced abroad, and research and teaching materials produced in institutions of higher education which would not otherwise be easily available to teachers elsewhere. (Hire and sale.)

View Finder is the BUFVC magazine that is published three times a year, once each term. It contains information and reviews on audiovisual materials and publications and articles on recent developments in the film and television industry.

Distributors: The Guide to Video and Film Sources for Education and Training. A subject guide to audio and audiovisual catalogues. Includes entries from more than 650 sources in over 100 subject categories.

The Researcher's Guide to British Film and Television Collections. Lists details of collections of film and television materials in the UK which are not normally available for viewing outside the premises where they are held.

Mental Health Film Council

MHFC is an educational charity founded in 1963 to promote the making and use of films in mental health training and education. The Council provides the following facilities:

SEMINAR SCREENINGS: regular seminars and screenings on various themes concerning mental health and well-being.

INFORMATION SERVICE: advice and information on media concerning people's well-being.

PUBLICATIONS:
Media for Wellbeing (annual). Hundreds of films and videos from over 60 distributors are listed alphabetically. Entries give production and distribution details and brief synopses of content. The subject index contains three main categories: mental handicap, mental health and mental disorder. Other subjects include professional training, conflict and violence, legal and statutory aspects and self-help.

Mediawise. For an annual subscription the quarterly magazine provides news, information, comment and features on media concerning mental health.

Other Information Sources

Other publications that include reviews or appraisals are:
Audio Visual Directory published by EMAP, PO Box 109, 19 Scarbrook Road, Croydon CR9 1QH.

Independent Media published monthly by DVA, 7 Campbell Court, Bramley, Basingstoke RG26 5EG.

Journal of Educational Television published by the Carfax Publishing Co., PO Box 25, Abingdon, Oxfordshire OX14 3UE. The journal provides reviews and discussion and reports on developments in the expanding field of the use of television and related media in teaching, learning and training.

FILMS AND VIDEOS: DISTRIBUTORS AND LIBRARIES

The following pages list the main distributors and film libraries that supply materials relevant to psychology. The range of topic areas covered is listed in each case, so as to help teachers decide which companies are worth contacting. The entries are numbered and these numbers are used instead of page references in the index at the end of this chapter. For titles, descriptions, prices and running times, individual catalogues should be consulted. Alongside each entry, the type of media they supply is indicated as shown below:

Video	Video cassettes
Film	16mm film
Slide	Slide sets
Audio	Audiotapes
Tape/slide	Audio and slide programmes
OHT	Overhead transparencies
Learning packages	Learning packages

Availability (that is hire, sale, loan) is also indicated.

1. Aleph One

CATALOGUE: *Data Sheet 3* consisting of books and audio cassettes on lifestyle training recorded by Dr Robert Sharpe.

Audio
Sale

TOPICS:		
	assertiveness	relaxation
	fear	sleep
	interviewing	smoking
	phobias	study skills

2. British Broadcasting Corporation

The BBC has more than 2,000 programmes available for educational and institutional use. Current material can be recorded if you work in an educational establishment which has a licence from the Educational Recording Agency.

CATALOGUE: *BBC Enterprises Programmes for Education and Training Central Reference Catalogue*. Details of the relevant materials available in your subject area supplied on request.

Video
Film
Hire & Sale

TOPICS:		
	addiction	mental handicap
	ageing	obesity
	animal behaviour	physical handicap
	birth	police and judicial
	the brain	issues
	child development	relationships
	crime	religion
	death	social issues and problems
	health services	wildlife

3. Brook Production

Selected programmes from television productions suitable for educational use.

CATALOGUE: *Programmes from Brooks*

Video
Sale

TOPICS: artificial intelligence   psychoanalysis
          philosophy   psychology

4. BSIP Europrofile

The BSIP produces educational audiovisual material in sciences dealing with brain and behaviour for teaching and research. Topics listed below such as perception include subtopics, for example, depth perception (visual cliff), optical illusions (ambiguous figures) and the biological basis for behaviour.

CATALOGUE: *BSIP Catalogue*

Video
Film
Slide
Audio
Tape/Slide
Hire & Sale

TOPICS: brain damage   perception
          learning   sleep
          nervous system

5. Central Independent Television

The Video Resources Unit has films available for educational institutions and individuals.

CATALOGUE: *Video Resources*. Booklets covering business, housing and social, geography, science and the environment, history and politics, art, literature and music.

Video
Sale

TOPICS: child abuse   mental illness
          crime   physical handicap
          mental handicap   rape

6. CFL Vision

CFL Vision has a wide variety of films for education.

CATALOGUE: *Video Collection, leaflets on specific subjects*

Video
Film
Hire & Sale

TOPICS: alcohol abuse   education
          blindness   paediatrics
          child development   parenting
          deafness   rehabilitation
          drug abuse   young people

7. Concord Video & Film Council

Now one of the largest educational film libraries in the UK, its list covers documentaries, animated films and feature-length productions concerned with contemporary issues. It is registered as a charity and distributes films for many other bodies (see section on societies and associations). The films are selected primarily to promote discussion for instruction and training. Concord also acts as a distributor for the British Universities Film and Video Council (Higher Education Film and Video Library). For further details see entry in the Information Sources and Publications section in this chapter.

CATALOGUES: *Concord Video and Film Catalogue* (1993–95)
800 Video and Films for the Caring Professions (1985–87) catalogue lists all 16mm films

Video
Film
Hire & Sale

TOPICS:

abortion	genetics
addiction	handicap
adolescence	health education
age	human rights
aggression	learning
alcohol abuse	medicine
animal behaviour	mental health
behaviour	mother–child
blindness	interaction
child behaviour	perception
child care	personal relationships
child development	physiology
communications	psychology
community care	rehabilitation
deafness	sex education
drug abuse	smoking
ecology	social problems
education	sociology
encounter groups	wildlife
family planning	young people

8. Edward Patterson Associates

Edward Patterson hold a wide variety of materials selected by advisers in health education, safety training, and for all subject areas of education.

CATALOGUES: *Health and Safety Catalogue* (including medical) lists films and videos.
Slide/Tape Multimedia Programmes Catalogue lists slides, tapes and slide/tape programmes on communications, human behaviour, health, social studies, sciences. Preview service for sales.
Education Film and Video Catalogue

Video
Film
Slide
Audio
Hire & Sale

TOPICS:

ageing/dying	family problems
aggression	mental handicap
alcohol abuse	mental health
animal behaviour	occupational therapy
anxiety	parenting
attitudes	peer groups
behaviour therapy	personal conflict
brain and behaviour	personal construct
child care	therapy

child development	personality
child behaviour	physical handicap
communications	Piaget
conformity and	prejudice
individualism	retirement
deafness	self-image
depression	smoking
disability	stress
drug abuse	teenage
family planning	communications

9. Educational Media Film & Video Ltd

Educational Media have a range of videos covering health and education.They distribute videos for the Film Board of Canada.

CATALOGUES: *Health Videos*
Educational Videos

Video
Sale

TOPICS:

addiction	death
ageing	education
aggression	genetics
behaviour	institutional care
biology	learning
child care	mental and physical
crime	handicap

10. Focal Point Audio-Visual

Focal Point sell videos, slides and tape/slide programmes for social sciences and science.

CATALOGUES: *Art, Design and Social Science Catalogue*
Science–Geography Catalogue

Video
Slide
Tape/Slide
Sale

TOPICS:

addiction	psychiatric centres
community care	rehabilitation
crime	stress
health education	wildlife
nervous system	

11. Glenbuck Films

Glenbuck has a large selection of documentaries covering a wide range of contemporary and educational titles. There is a preview service for sales.

CATALOGUES: *Film Hire Library Catalogue*
    Video for Sale Catalogue, and leaflets on specific topics, including health and safety, social and legal studies.

Video
Film
Hire & Sale

TOPICS:

alcohol abuse	drug abuse
black culture	juvenile delinquency
children and their	marriage
relationships with	suicide
each other	welfare
communal life	women's liberation

12.Graves Medical Audio-Visual Library

Graves is a non-profit making educational charity which produces audiovisual materials for use in medical education.

CATALOGUE: *Graves Medical Audio-Visual Library Catalogue* contains videos, tape/slide programmes, slide sets, audio tapes, computer software and booklets on all medical subjects. Entries arranged under more than 50 subject headings. Each entry includes technical details, a brief description, author, producer, date and an indication of audience level.

Video
Slide
Audio
Tape/Slide
Hire

TOPICS:

abortion	neuroticism
addiction	occupational
adolescence	psychology
adoption	occupational therapy
ageing	parenting
aggression	phobias
alcohol abuse	psychiatry
anxiety	psychology
autism	psychosexual
battered wives	problems
bereavement	psychosomatism
child abuse	rape
child development	rehabilitation
child welfare	relaxation
communication	residential care
deafness	schizophrenia
death	shock
dementia	sleep and sleep
depression	disorders
drug abuse	social problems
dyslexia	speech and speech
examination fears	disorders
family problems	stress
geriatric psychiatry	strokes
handicap	suicide
homosexuality	terminal care
hysteria	tranquillizers and
menopause	antidepressants
mental illness	violence
nervous system	vision and voice

13. Hertfordshire School Library Service

Specializes mainly in the production of teaching materials for use in schools and places of further and higher education. There is a preview service.

CATALOGUE: *Video Programmes for Education and Training*

Video
Sale

TOPICS:

assessment	interviewing
computers	language
education	remedial assessment
handicap	study skills

14. Lawrence Erlbaum

Lawrence Erlbaum supply five videos for teaching cognitive neuropsychology.

CATALOGUE: *Titles in Neuropsychology*

Video Sale

TOPICS: Cognitive neuropsychology

15. National Film Board of Canada

The Film Board of Canada has over 1,000 films. Main distributors are Concord Video & Film Council and Educational Media Film &Video Ltd.

CATALOGUE: *Film Loan Library Catalogue: Films available from the Film Board*

Video Film Hire & Sale

addiction	genetics
adolescence	greed
ageing	institutional care
aggression	learning
alcohol abuse	love
attitudes	mental illness
prejudice	mental and
battered wives	physical handicap
behaviour (emotional	mother–child
social, sexual,	interaction
violent)	perception
child development	personality
cognition	prostitution
communication	rape
crime	relationships
death	(social and
depression	interpersonal)
dreams	self respect
education	sexual behaviour
fear	social control
friendship	social psychology
gambling	

16. Open University Educational Enterprises

The OUEE Ltd sells resource materials produced by the Open University. It also manages the Open University Off Air Recording Scheme which allows members, for a fee, to record and retain Open University broadcasts for educational use.

CATALOGUE: *The Catalogue of Learning Resources*

Video Audio Sale

TOPICS:

addiction	learning
ageing	learning difficulties
autism	memory
behaviour	personality
biology	play
biology of behaviour	Piaget
brain	politics

communication	poverty
death	psychology
deafness	social care
decision-making	social problems
development	social science
dyslexia	social welfare
education	sociology
genetics	statistics
health care	stress
intelligence	violence

17. Oxford Educational Resources

International distributors of audiovisual teaching materials. Incorporating Camera Talks, Didactic Films, Marine Audio-Visual Instructional Systems and Highline. Detailed synopses from their database on any title can be supplied, preferably on computer disc (IBM-compatible computers reading WordPerfect files).

CATALOGUE: *Title List of Audio-Visual Programmes*. List of titles supplied to cover the subject area requested.

Video Tape/Slide Hire & Sale

TOPICS:

adoption	health education
alcohol abuse	mental health
anxiety	neurology
battered wives	phobias
biology	psychiatry
care for the elderly	sexual problems
child abuse	speech therapy
child development	social problems
deafness	stress
drug abuse	violence
epilepsy	wildlife
handicap	zoology

18. Philip Harris

Slides, learning packages and overheads for teaching.

CATALOGUE: *Philip Harris Biological Catalogue*

Slide OHT Learning packages Sale

TOPICS:

addiction	genetics
animal behaviour	human biology
drugs and health	smoking

19. Psychology News

Makes documentaries for ITV and Channel 4 which are often of interest to psychologists and their students.

CATALOGUE: *Psychology News Video Catalogue*

Video	TOPICS:	child abuse	stress
		drugs	why people make
		mental health care	false confessions
		psychiatric hospitals	
		(Soviet)	

20. Scottish Central Film & Video Library

Part of the Scottish Council for Educational Technology, the Library supplies neuropsychology educational and documentary films and videos for hire and purchase.

CATALOGUES: *Health Education Films and Video Catalogue.* Films and videos only available for distribution in Scotland.
Social Subjects on 16mm Film and Video Catalogue. Mainly suitable for social sciences.
Science Catalogue includes wildlife and biology films.

Video	TOPICS:	addiction	mental health
Film		age	mother–infant
Hire & Sale		alcohol abuse	interaction
		aggression	nursery schools
		animal behaviour	perception
		behaviour	physiology (nervous
		child behaviour	system and the
		child care	senses)
		child development	smoking
		genetics	social problems
		handicap	sociology
		learning	therapy
		marriage problems	wildlife

21. Tavistock Publications

Provides video cassettes which address issues encountered by medical practitioners, nurses, psychiatrists and therapists.

CATALOGUES: *Tavistock Videotapes* lists video programmes which concentrate on the importance of interpersonal skills in medical practice.

| *Video* | TOPICS: | behavioural | psychiatry |
| *Sale* | | psychotherapy | |

22. Univ. of Aberdeen

Video
Hire & Sale

	TOPICS:	anxiety	cognition
		aptitude	intelligence
		child assessment	personality
		children's problem-	phobias
		solving	psycholinguistics
		children's thought	visual perception

23. **Univ. of Birmingham**

The University's Television and Film Unit produces programmes designed to teach some of the elementary principles of medical interviewing to undergraduates in psychiatry and the behavioural sciences.

CATALOGUE: *Videos in Psychiatry* produced by Dr Tim Betts.

Video
Sale

TOPICS:
epilepsy	relaxation and
interviewing	biofeedback
psychosexual	stress
counselling	

24. **Univ. of Manchester**

The University's Department of Psychiatry has a series of self-teaching video tapes which are relevant to psychiatry.

Video
Sale

TOPICS:
behaviour	psychotherapy
EEG	relaxation
family therapy	schizophrenia
interviewing skills	stuttering

25. **Univ. of Newcastle**

CATALOGUE: *AVC Video Catalogue*

Video
Hire & Sale

TOPICS:
child development	medicine
infant social	
behaviour	

26. **Viewtech Audiovisual Media**

One of the distributors for the National Film Board of Canada (see separate entry), Indiana University Audio-Visual Centre, Gateway Educational Media, Marsh Film, Rank Aldis and Walt Disney Productions. Educational videos can be hired under a multi-user or single-user licence price.

CATALOGUE: *Video and Film Catalogue – Education*

Video
Film
Audio
Learning packages
Hire & Sale

TOPICS:
animal behaviour	handicap
biology	nervous system
care of elderly	psychology
child abuse	social problems
child development	(including alcohol
drug abuse	abuse and divorce)
genetics	stress

FILMS AND VIDEOS: SOCIETIES AND ASSOCIATIONS

This section lists some charitable societies and associations that produce or sponsor audiovisual materials in an effort to publicize their cause. Many of the films can be useful for teachers of psychology. These organizations quite often supply booklets and notes to go with their audiovisual materials. They can sometimes provide a speaker if there is a branch near you. The entries are numbered, and these numbers are used instead of page references in the index at the end of the chapter.

27. British Agencies for Adoption and Fostering

Video
Film
Tape/Slide
Hire & Sale

TOPICS: guidance on adoption and fostering

DISTRIBUTION: Concord Video & Film Council

28. British Assn for Counselling

Video
Film
Audio
Hire & Sale

TOPICS: counselling techniques, assessment of behaviour, psychotherapy

DISTRIBUTION: Concord Video & Film Council

29. British Epilepsy Assn

Video
Film
Hire & Sale

TOPICS: medical and social aspects of epilepsy and its treatment

DISTRIBUTION: Concord Video & Film Council

30. Disabled Living Foundation

Video
Hire & Sale

TOPICS: occupations and activities of the disabled, activities of the elderly

DISTRIBUTION: Concord Video & Film Council

31. Dr. Barnardo's

Video
Hire

TOPICS: adoption, fostering, child abuse, residential care

DISTRIBUTION: Dr. Barnardo's Film Library

32. The Family Assn

Video
Hire & Sale

TOPICS: relationships, peer pressure

DISTRIBUTION: Concord Video & Film Council

33. Hampstead Child Therapy Clinic

Video
Film
Hire & Sale

TOPICS: nursery school for the blind, growing up without sight

DISTRIBUTION: Concord Video & Film Council

34. Health Education Authority

Video
Film
Hire & Sale

TOPICS: sexual and personal relationships, child development, family relationships, smoking, parenting

DISTRIBUTION: Concord Video & Film Council and CFL

35. Help the Aged

Video
Tape/Slide
Hire

TOPICS: using Reminiscence Pack (by Faith Gibson)

DISTRIBUTION: Help the Aged

36. MENCAP (Royal Society for Mentally Handicapped Children & Adults)

Video
Hire & Sale

TOPICS: language simulation, mental handicap, leisure and holidays, case histories, marriage, training, institutions versus family care, drama therapy, parental stress, integration into society

DISTRIBUTION: Concord Video & Film Council

37. National Autistic Society

Video
Tape/Slide
Hire

TOPICS: introductory and training films on autistic children and adults

DISTRIBUTION: The National Autistic Society

38. NSPCC

Film
Hire

TOPICS: battered babies and child abuse

DISTRIBUTION: NSPCC (The National Society for the Prevention of Cruelty to Children)

39. **RNID**   TOPICS: tinnitus, problems of hearing impairment

Film   DISTRIBUTION: RNID (The Royal National Institute for the Deaf)
Hire

40. **Samaritans**   TOPICS: dealing with crises

Video   DISTRIBUTION: Concord Video & Film Council
Hire & Sale

41. **SENSE**   TOPICS: working with deaf/blind children; development of
                    motor skills, communication and touch in young deaf/blind
                    children; communication with deaf/blind and hearing peo-
                    ple; the work of SENSE

                    DISTRIBUTION: SENSE (The National Deaf, Blind and Rubella
Video   Association)
Hire

42. **Spastics**   TOPICS: cerebral palsy, the need for improved maternity ser-
Society   vices to reduce incidence of disability, preparation for parent-
                    hood

Video   DISTRIBUTION: Concord Video & Film Council
Film
Hire & Sale

SELECTED AUDIOVISUAL MATERIALS

This section contains a selection of materials collected from
catalogues used in compiling this chapter which will be of
interest to most psychology teachers. Many have been selected because they have been made by teachers to demonstrate
various aspects of their subject or have been widely used in
courses for a number of years. Each entry gives details of the
title, distributor, running times and a brief description of the
programme.

➤ *Human Social Development* (1984)

Video   Resource material with teachers' notes intended for use in a
Sale   psychology practical. The aim of the practical is to use a cate-
                    gory system and develop and use a sign system appropriate
                    for recording social participation in a group of nursery school
                    children and to calculate their relative merits.

                    DISTRIBUTION: London Guild Hall University: Media Services
                    Dept

➤ *Children's Development: Six Weeks to Four Years* (1987)

Video
Sale

The five parts in this series show the average developmental progress of specific children. Fine and gross motor development, vision and hearing tests and the development of speech and language are illustrated. The equipment used comes from the Stycar Assessment Systems.

Part 1: Six weeks (30 mins)
Part 2: Six months (30 mins)
Part 3: One year (38 mins)
Part 4: Two-and-a-half years (44 mins)
Part 5: Four years (42 mins)

DISTRIBUTION: Graves Medical Audio-Visual Library

➤ *Young Children in Brief Separation* (1968–1976)

Video
Film
Hire & Sale

Illustrates emotional and social development in very young children, and how reactions to separation from the mother are influenced by the quality of substitute care.

John, aged 17 months, for 9 days in residential nursery (43 mins)
Jane, aged 17 months, in foster care for 10 days (37 mins)
Lucy, aged 21 months, in foster care for 19 days (31 mins)
Thomas, aged 2 years 4 months, in foster care for 10 days (39 mins)
Kate, aged 2 years 5 months, in foster care for 27 days (23 mins)

An illustrated teaching guide is supplied when any of these films or videos are rented or bought.

DISTRIBUTION: Concord Video & Film Council

➤ *How Children Think* (1986)

Tape/Slide
Hire & Sale

Adults often find it hard to remember what it was like to be a child. Based on Piaget's analysis, this programme describes important conceptual developmental milestones in a way which should help adults to understand children better. It is particularly useful for anyone caring for sick children. Anatomy, physiology, neurological control mechanisms, investigative techniques and equipment are covered (80 slides; pulsed 1000 Hz; 27 mins).

DISTRIBUTION: Graves Medical Audio-Visual Library

➤ *Children Growing Up* (1970)

Video
Hire

Five films in the BBC Children Growing Up series which clearly explain aspects of child development in the first five years or so of life.

All in the Game (25 mins)
Making Sense (25 mins)
Mother and Child (25 mins)
One Step at a Time (25 mins)
Power of Speech (25 mins)

DISTRIBUTION: The Scottish Central Film and Video Library (only available in Scotland)

➤ *Rock a Bye Baby*

Film Hire

Good photography of classic experiments on mothering in human and other mammals up to 1970. Includes Harlow's experiments on monkeys with substitute mothers and Prescot's experiments with monkeys raised in isolation.

DISTRIBUTION: The Scottish Central Film and Video Library (only available in Scotland)

➤ *Learning to Talk: From Birth to Three*

Audio

Dr Louise Higgins has recorded her daughter's language development from birth to the age of three. This was done at home (Piaget style) from cries and laughter to the first words and complete sentences. The commentary is provided by Dr Higgins, a psychology teacher, and places the child's language development in the context of current theories of language acquisition (20 minutes with booklet).

DISTRIBUTION: BPS Books (The British Psychological Society)

➤ *Teaching Programmes in Cognitive Neuropsychology* (1992)

Video Sale

This series of five videos offers those with interests in cognitive neuropsychology an opportunity to observe for themselves the performance of individuals with particular cognitive disorders. The case studies illustrated have been selected from three specific topics of theoretical interest: reading, visual object recognition and visual attention.

Reading for Meaning: A Case Study of Deep Dyslexia (30 mins)
Words and Sentences: A Case Study of Phonological Dyslexia (33 mins)
Peripheral Agnosia: Early Disorders of Visual Object Recognition (38 mins)
Central Agnosia: The Loss of Knowledge about Objects (26 mins)
Attentional Dysfunctions: Problems in Orienting (23 mins)

DISTRIBUTION: Lawrence Erlbaum Associates

➤ *Introduction to Psychology* (1991)

Video Sale

Twelve videotapes that cover a wide range of topics. They show how to evaluate the models, theories and techniques described and provide basic skills for carrying out psychological research.

Two Research Styles (24 mins)
Child's Play (24 mins)
The Psychology of Addiction (24 mins)

Personnel Selection (24 mins)
Eye Witness Memory (24 mins)
The Clinical Psychologist (24 mins)
Autism (24 mins)
Understanding Violence (24 mins)

DISTRIBUTION: Open University Educational Enterprises Ltd

➤ *With People in Mind* (1992)

*Video
Sale*

This video describes the science of psychology and shows some of its applications. The production was filmed on location and focuses on students of psychology as well as teachers and practising psychologists.

DISTRIBUTION: The British Psychological Society

➤ *Computing for Beginners* (1992)

*Video
Sale*

A series of teaching videos with accompanying booklets and discs which allow groups of students or individuals to work at their own pace.
1. MS-DOS
2. WINDOWS
3. WORDS 5
4. dBASE IV

DISTRIBUTION: University of Sheffield

➤ *Software Learning Videos* (1993)

*Video
Sale*

A range of teaching videos of leading software titles for individual or group instruction. Each video lasts three hours. Latest titles include WordPerfect 5.1, Excel 4.0, Windows 3.1, Lotus 1-2-3, DOS 2.4 and 3.1, Harvard Graphics 3.0 DOS, Superbase 2.0 and Pagemaker 4.0.

DISTRIBUTION: Softvision Ltd

SUBJECT INDEX

The numbers given below are the entry numbers of the various distributors, libraries, societies and associations that appear in the Films and Videos section of this chapter, rather than page numbers.

health care 19
illness 5, 12, 15
mother – child interaction 7, 15, 20

nervous system 4, 10, 12, 20, 26
neurology 17
neuropsychiatry 23
neuropsychology 14

obesity 2
occupational
    psychology 12
    therapy *see* therapy

paediatrics 6
parenting 6, 8, 12, 34
peer groups 32
perception
    and communication 4, 7, 15, 20, 22
personal
    conflict 8
    construct therapy 8
personality 8, 15, 16, 22
philosophy 3
phobias 1, 12, 17, 22
physical
    handicap 2, 5, 8, 9, 15, 17
    violence *see* violence
physiology 7, 20
Piaget 16
play 16
police and judicial issues
    see also crime
politics 16
poverty 16
prejudice 8, 15
pre-school child *see* child
problem-solving
    children 22
prostitution 15
psychiatric
    centres 10
    hospitals 19
psychiatry 12, 17, 21
    see also neuropsychiatry
psycholinguistics 22
psychology 3, 7, 12, 16, 26
    see also abnormal psychology
    see also occupational psychology
    see also social psychology
psychosexual problems *see* therapy
psychosomaticism 12
psychotherapy 21, 24, 28

rape 5, 12, 15,
rehabilitation 6, 7, 10, 12
relationships 7, 15, 32, 34
    see also family
relaxation 12, 24
    and biofeedback 1, 23
    see also stress
religion 2
remedial assessment 13
residential
    care 12, 31
    communities 31, 35
    see also care
retirement 8

schizophrenia 12, 24
    see also care
self-
    image 8
    respect 8
sex education 7
sexual behaviour 15, 17
shock 12
shoplifting 8
sign language 41
sleep 1, 4, 12
    see also dreams
smoking *see* addiction
social
    behaviour *see* behaviour
    control 15
    issues 2, 16
    problems 2, 7, 12, 16, 17, 20, 26, 40
    psychology 15
    science 16
    workers 16
sociology 7, 16, 20
spasticity 42
speech and language disorders 12, 17
statistics 16
stress 8, 9, 10, 12, 16, 17, 19, 23, 26, 36
    see also relaxation
strokes 12
study skills 1, 13
stuttering 24
suicide 11, 12

terminal care 12
    see also death
therapy 20
    drama 36
    family 24

occupational 8, 12
psychosexual 23
see also psychotherapy
thought
children 22
tranquillizers 12
see also addiction

victims 7
violence 8, 12, 16, 17
vision 12
visual illusion 4

welfare 11
animal *see* animal
child *see* child
see also health
wildlife 2, 7, 10, 17, 20
women's liberation 11

young people 6, 7

zoology 17

Addresses

Aleph One Ltd
The Old Court House
High Street
Bottisham
Cambridge CB5 9BA
tel. (0223) 811679

British Agencies for Adoption and
  Fostering
11 Southwark Street
London SE1 1RQ
tel. (071) 4078800

British Association for Counselling
37a Sheep Street
Rugby
Warwickshire CV21 3BX
tel. (0788) 78328

British Broadcasting Corporation
  TV Enterprises
Film and Video Sales
Woodlands
80 Wood Lane
London W12 0TT
fax (081) 5762867

British Epilepsy Association
Anstey House
40 Hanover Square
Leeds LS3 1BE
tel. (0532) 439393

British Film Institute
Film and Video Library
21 Stephen Street
London W1P 1PL
tel. (071) 2551444

British Universities Film and
  Video Council
55 Greek Street
London W1V 5LR
tel. (071) 7343687

Brook Production
21–24 Bruges Place
Randolph Street
London NW1 0TF
tel. (071) 4826111

BSIP Europrofile
Hill House
96 Wimbledon Hill
London SW19 7PB
tel. (081) 9468644

Central Independent Television
  Video Resource Unit
Broad Street
Birmingham B1 2JP
tel. (021) 6439898

CFL Vision
PO Box 35
Wetherby
Yorkshire LS23 7EX
tel. (0937) 541010

Concord Video & Films Ltd
201 Felixstowe Road
Ipswich
Suffolk IP3 9BJ
tel. (0473) 715754/726012

Disabled Living Foundation
380–384 Harrow Road
London W9 2HU
tel. (071) 289 6111

Dr. Barnardo's Film Library
Tanners Lane
Barkingside
Ilford
Essex 1G6 1QG
tel. (081) 550 8822

Educational Media Film & Video Ltd
235 Imperial Drive
Rayners Lane
Harrow
Middlesex HA2 7HE
tel. (081) 8681908/1915

Educational Recording Agency Ltd
33–34 Alfred Place
London WC1 7DP
tel. (071) 436 4883

Edward Patterson Association Ltd
Treetops
Cannongate Road
Hythe
Kent CT21 5PT
tel. (0303) 264195

The Family Association
27–35 Mortimer Street
London N16 8TB
tel. (071) 6310555

Focal Point Audio-Visual Ltd
251 Copnor Road
Portsmouth
Hants PO3 5EE
tel. (0705) 665249

Glenbuck Films Ltd
Glenbuck House
Surbiton
Surrey KT6 6BY
tel. (081) 3990022

Graves Medical Audio-Visual
Library
c/o Concord Video & Film Council

Hampstead Child Therapy Clinic
21 Maresfield Gardens
London NW3
tel. (071) 7945641

Health Education Authority
Hamilton House
Mabledon Place
London WC1H 9TX
tel. (071) 6310930

Help the Aged
St James Walk
London EC1
tel. (071) 2530253

Hertfordshire School Library Service
New Barnfield
Travellers Lane
Hatfield
AL10 8XG
tel. (0707) 281630
fax (0707) 28161

Lawrence Erlbaum Associates
Afterhurst Mail Order Department
27 Church Road
Hove
East Sussex BN3 2FA
tel. (0273) 748427

London Guild Hall University Media
Services
Calcutta House Precinct
Old Castle Street
London E1 7NT
tel. (071) 3201000

Mental Health Film Council
380–384 Harrow Road
London W9 2HU
tel. (071) 286 2346

National Autistic Society
276 Willesden Lane
London NW2 5RB
tel. (081) 451 1114

National Deaf, Blind and Rubella
Association (SENSE)
311 Grays Inn Road
London WC1X 8PT
tel. (071) 278 1005

National Film Board of Canada
1 Grosvenor Square
London W1X 0AB
tel. (071) 258 6600

National Society for the Prevention
of Cruelty to Children
67 Saffron Hill
London EC1 8RS
tel. (071) 242 1626

Open University Educational
Enterprises Ltd
12 Cofferidge Close
Stony Stratford
Milton Keynes MK11 1BY
tel. (0908) 261662

Oxford Educational Resources Ltd
PO Box 106
Kidlington
Oxford OX5 1HJ
tel. (0865) 842552

Philip Harris Biological Ltd
Oldmixen
Western-Super-Mare
Avon BS24 9BT
tel. (0934) 413063

Psychology News Ltd
17a Great Ormond Street
London WC1 3RA
tel. (071) 8313385

Royal National Institute for the Deaf
105 Gower Street
London WC1 6AH
tel. (071) 3878033

Royal Society for Mentally
  Handicapped Children and Adults
  (MENCAP)
Mencap Centre
123 Golden Lane
London EC1Y 0RT
tel. (071) 454 0454

Samaritans
17 Uxbridge Road
Slough
SL1 1SN
tel. (0753) 32713

Scottish Central Film & Video Library
Dowanhill
74 Victoria Crescent Road
Glasgow G12 NJN
tel. 041 334 9314

Sheffield University Television
Sheffield S10 2TN
tel. (0742) 768555

Softvision Ltd
Stanton Road
Southampton
SO9 1BH
tel. (0703) 701470

Spastics Society
12 Park Crescent
London W1
(071) 6365020

Tavistock Publications
11 New Fetter Lane
London EC4P 4EE
tel. (071) 9609704

University of Aberdeen
Dept of Medical Illustration
University Medical Building
Forest Hill
Aberdeen AB9 2ZD
(0224) 272000

University of Birmingham
Television and Film Unit
PO Box 363
Birmingham B15 2TT
tel. (021) 4143344

University of Manchester
Dept of Psychiatry
West Didsbury
Manchester M20 8LR
tel. (061) 4474359

University of Newcastle upon Tyne
Audio-Visual Centre
The Medical School
Framlington Place
Newcastle upon Tyne NE2 4HH
tel. (091) 2226000

Viewtech Audiovisual Media
161 Winchester Road
Brislington
Bristol BS4 3NJ
tel. (0272) 773422

PSYCHOLOGY AND CINEMA

Robert Burden

❑ *genres: westerns, science fiction* • auteur *theory: Truffaut, Hitchcock, Roeg, Bergman* • *specific themes: psychology and psychiatry, adolescence, disability, women and film* • *filmography*

The purpose of this chapter is to illustrate how the use of feature films and, beyond this, the study of cinema itself can become at least a useful adjunct, at best a central aspect of the teaching of psychology. Such an approach could form part of the earliest introduction to psychology as an academic discipline or equally well offer an attractive and worthwhile final year option on any undergraduate course. Space limitations will not allow an in-depth exploration of these two possibilities, but an attempt will be made to provide information and ideas which may help to transfer each into meaningful reality.

I begin with a statement of belief – two statements, in fact, about the nature of psychology and the nature of cinema. I start from the premise that psychology is essentially an attempt to understand why people think and feel and act in the way that they do and how this affects them and others. The art of cinema in its broadest sense is bringing this quest to life on celluloid so that it can be shared by a comparatively large group of people at any one time in a darkened auditorium. I believe this latter statement to be true even when the films under consideration are fictionalized and fantastical. Films such as *Pinocchio* and *Frankenstein* present us with as 'true' a vision of the human condition as do documentaries or other films with apparently more serious intent.

The advantage that cinema has over all other art forms is its comprehensiveness. No other art form can make possible the combination of sight and sound images, can transcend the boundaries of time and space, touch the emotions or stimulate the intellect as can a film.

It has been argued that this very comprehensiveness is also the cinema's weakness, since at its worst it represents no one person's reality, whilst at its best it leaves little to the imagination. Whilst having some sympathy for the former point – there have been an awful lot of bad films produced – I would take issue with the latter. The best films stimulate the imagination and provoke discussion in a manner that is readily accessible to all those involved as an audience.

It is difficult to find words to describe this experience appropriately as it is not one of the passive spectator, as is sometimes assumed, but is truly interactive as far as the mind and senses are concerned, though not in the sense that the images can themselves be shaped by audience response. In seeking to make sense of and respond to those images, however, the audience itself becomes involved in a complex set of psychological processes. It is the nature of these processes, as well as those involved in making and analysing films as such, that has been the concern of many so-called cinema theorists.

In his *Introduction to The Major Film Theories*, Andrew (1976) helps us to see how early film pioneers were influenced by ideas from Gestalt psychology, particularly the notion that the mind provides meaning not only to our understanding of reality but even to its physical characteristics. The work of the great Soviet film-maker, Sergei Eisenstein, can be seen to reflect the ideas of both Pavlov and Piaget in his dialectical thinking about film montage. Later theorists encompass the phenomenological aspects of filmmaking and attempt to develop ways describing the processes of signification in the cinema. This latter enterprise has developed into the science of semiotics.

At the same time, others, most notably represented by Parker Tyler in his influential book *Magic and Myth of the Movies* (1971), began to explore the mythical and dreamlike quality of films, to relate these to both the individual and collective unconscious and to provide direct psychoanalytic interpretations in their critical writings. Somewhat surprisingly, however, it has not been until comparatively recently that psychoanalytical approaches to cinema have been explored in any great depth, despite the powerful influence of the former on literary criticism over many years (Kaplan, 1990).

It can be seen from even this brief introduction to some of the central issues relating psychology to cinema that it would be perfectly possible, indeed desirable under certain circumstances, to proceed from a study of cinema itself to considering its various psychological manifestations. However, since it is likely that most readers will find rather more straightforward approaches initially preferable, I shall confine myself from hereon to describing ways in which films can be used to illustrate aspects of psychology.

Three potentially illuminating approaches come immediately to mind. I shall present them in order of decreasing complexity and will devote most of my space to the third as this would seem to be the most useful starting point for the newcomer to this field. These approaches can be conveniently summarized under the headings of genre, *auteur* theory and themes.

GENRES

Simply expressed, a genre is a particular category of films, such as westerns, science fiction, comedy, horror or gangster movies. There is often a centrally accepted format against which new additions to the genre are judged, and it is interesting to note how regular film magazine polls on 'The Ten Best Westerns/Musicals, etc. Ever' tend to generate responses directly related to the expression of this 'classic' form.

Westerns

Westerns offer an excellent opportunity to make an in-depth psychological exploration of a genre because of their particularly powerful emphasis upon metaphor and myth and because of the endless playing out of universal themes of existential conflict. Just about the last thing to be represented in most westerns is the old West as it really was. This can be clearly seen in a film like *Shane*, where the enactment of the universal myths of good and evil takes place against the back-cloth theme of the inevitability of change.

This theme of change and its consequences at both a personal and social level is one that runs through the work of the director, John Ford, who has used the West, in particular, to provide a metaphorical context. It is interesting to track this director's employment of the actor John Wayne through films like *Stagecoach, Fort Apache, She Wore A Yellow Ribbon, The Searchers* and, in the opinion of many, one of his finest films, *The Man Who Shot Liberty Valance*. In all of these films, Wayne's character is portrayed as one faced with critical decisions which will affect his future in a changing world, but which will also affect in some way the future of that world. The depth of psychological understanding revealed by Ford in his later films contrasts sharply with the more simplistic sociological approach of the earlier films.

Other directors of westerns have also taken up the theme of personal and social change, most notably Howard Hawks in *Red River*, Sam Peckinpah in *Ride the High Country* and Clint Eastwood in *The Outlaw Josey Wales* and *Unforgiven*.

In the developing work of each of these directors and, in particular, that of Anthony Mann we can also see the genre used as a vehicle for expressing implicit psychological theories about an individual's search for meaning in life. 'A man's gotta do what a man's gotta do ...' is not just a hoary old western cliché but an expression of just this point.

Although I know of no evidence that Mann ever read Jung's work or undertook Jungian analysis, his films are full of Jungian archetypes and symbolism. The hero in such films as *The Man From Laramie, The Bend in The River* and *The Far Country* is always faced with a series of choices, the outcome of which will lead him closer to an integration of the self or towards ultimate despair. The hero, always played by James Stewart at a finely-balanced emotional knife-edge, is usually confronted by a protagonist who represents his Jungian 'shadow'– the dark side of his personality about whom he feels a great ambivalence, both attraction and repulsion. In order to achieve integration the hero must inevitably recognize his ambivalence and face up to the shadow within himself as well as his symbolic enemy. Mann's villains are at least as interesting as his heroes in their representation of men for whom the balance between 'animus' and 'anima' has never been achieved.

There are westerns which are open to Freudian interpretation (*The Last Sunset, Johnny Guitar, The Left-Handed Gun*), and those representing themes of racial prejudice (*Tell Them Willy Boy Is Here, Cheyene Autumn*) and genocide (*Soldier Blue*), but it is perhaps the exploration of myth and personal responsibility to which this genre lends itself best. At the same time, the western is essentially a masculine genre which would nevertheless repay an in-depth analysis of the putative role of women. In fact, in analysing westerns from a feminist perspective, it becomes possible not only to determine something significant about a director such as Ford's view of women, but also to re-evaluate the significance of such films as *Destry Rides Again* and *Rancho Notorious*.

Laura Mulvey (1990) offers an interesting feminist perspective on the changing role of the heroine in westerns as representative of the changing function of 'woman' from passive to active participant. The overt sexuality of the heroine in King Vidor's *Duel in the Sun* is seen as a significant milestone in this respect, as also is the focus placed upon the importance of the heroine's choice between the different options offered by the John Wayne and James Stewart characters in *The Man Who Shot Liberty Valance*.

Science Fiction There are those who find science fiction films just as rewarding in their reworking of universal themes. The eminent critic and theorist, Raymond Durgnat (1976), makes a strong case for this even with regard to such apparently mundane science fiction epics as *This Island Earth*. One science fiction film which does have interesting psychological undertones is *The Forbidden Planet*. At one level this film can be seen as a fascinating reworking of *The Tempest*, but what adds to it psychologically is the director's use of Freudian psychology to make the Caliban figure a form of psychic energy directly emanating from the incestuous feelings of the highly intelligent Prospero-like central character for his daughter.

One can readily see how science fiction touches upon our interest in and fear of the unknown. The director, John Carpenter, is particularly adept at conveying this in such films as *Halloween, The Thing, The Fog* and even *Assault on Precinct 13*, which, though set in the South Bronx, could just as easily be a western or set on another planet. Most of Carpenter's films dwell upon our perception of the unknown as an evil force, but one of his very best, *Starman*, takes a much gentler approach to the problems faced by a visitor to an alien world and re-introduces the issue of prejudice in a novel manner.

Other science fiction films worthy of consideration are the *Aliens* trilogy which all show the development of the strong female lead character in a universe otherwise populated by weak and inadequate males. In an historical sequence dealing with essentially the same theme (some have suggested an analogy to AIDS), each of the *Aliens* films stands in its own right and offers rich scope for psychological analysis.

Perhaps the greatest of all paranoia movies, Don Siegel's *Invasion of the Body Snatchers*, is usually considered to be a landmark allegorical statement against the 'un-American' US hearings led by the notorious senator Joe McCarthy. What is particularly interesting in retrospect is that the film can be interpreted just as easily as an indictment of communism as of McCarthyism. It would be worthwhile comparing the original black and white, low budget version of *The Body Snatchers* (first distributed as a 'B' movie) with the not uninteresting remake by Philip Kaufman and a more gruesomely explicit version on the same theme, *They Live*, by John Carpenter.

AUTEUR THEORY

A somewhat different approach which nevertheless overlaps in part with the study of film genres is one which take up the ideas of so-called *auteur* theory. This set of ideas (it hasn't really the status of a theory), emerged from the writings of a group of young French film critics writing after the Second World War in a journal called *Cahiers du Cinéma*. Prominent amongst this group were people like François Truffaut and Jean Luc Godard who were to go on to become famous as film-makers in their own right.

Basically, *auteur* theory suggests that it is worth examining the films of a particular director (just as it is the authors of literary works) as the same themes will continue to be worked through again and again, thereby giving us access to that director's particular view of the world and his or her attempts to make sense of it. Thus films become a kind of projective technique, the responses to which are open to interpretation by the psychologist-critic, who seeks both individual and universal insights within the work of 'important' film-makers.

It follows, therefore, that just as writers like Dostoyevsky, Proust, Hardy or P.G. Wodehouse can illustrate and help to illuminate some aspect of the human condition, so can certain directors – provided of course that they can make the kind of films they want to make. This proviso is an important one because, in the 'golden' days of Hollywood at least, it was rare for a director ever to have full control over any film he (until recently it was a predominantly male profession) completed.

If we take a moment to make a brief comparison between the work of two great Hollywood directors, John Huston and Howard Hawks, an important aspect of *auteur* theory may become clearer. Huston was essentially only ever interested in making films of other people's stories. For him the art of the film-maker was finding ways of bringing the essence of such novels as *Moby Dick, Moulin Rouge* or *The Treasure of Sierra Madre* to the screen. In attempting to do this he experimented with various visual techniques, colour and sound, but never imposed his interpretation upon the stories. Thus one may enjoy a John Huston film or be profoundly moved by it but this will depend almost entirely upon his success in capturing the essence of the original book.

Howard Hawks, on the other hand, made essentially the same film again and again for years, almost every time centering upon the nature of friendship, trust and loyalty between males. Every Howard Hawks film says something about Howard Hawks' view of the world. If male bonding is a theme which you as a psychologist find particularly interesting, then the films of Howard Hawks provide some interesting and useful insights.

In the section which follows, the work of four directors will be considered from the viewpoint of *auteur* theory. Each has a unique view of humanity which finds full expression in his films, a view which any psychologist seeking to understand why people think and feel and act in the way that they do will find enlightening. Although the four have been chosen to represent a broad cross-section of rich and complex viewpoints, they by no means stand alone in this regard and any one could just as easily have been replaced by Godard, Wilder, Fellini, Bũnuel, or a dozen others. What they do have in common is that the work of each is largely his own, relatively untampered with by others on the cutting room floor.

This final point is worth reiterating. The interested reader is referred to Peter Wollen's *Signs and Meaning in the Cinema* (1972) for a fuller description of *auteur* theory. Films are *never* the work of just one person but an amalgam of many people's efforts over a long period of time. It has been argued that the screen writer's conception is just as important as that of the director, and often it is not within the latter's power to select the actors. Moreover, there are some directors who claim never to have had one of their films distributed in the form in which it was conceived and completed. It was the proud boast of the Hollywood mogul Daryl F. Zannuck that any film appearing under his name had been personally edited to fit with *his* conception of the world, no matter who the director was.

Such information may be of considerable interest but little practical value to the psychology teacher. In seeking to use the work of specific directors to illustrate some aspects of psychology, it is not suggested that all or even many of their films are considered in detail. It would be enough in the first instance to show two or three definitive works (marked with an asterisk in the list at the end of this chapter of the directors' main films) and set the students the task of finding common themes and messages signified in ways which are unique to that particular director's use of cinematic language in its broadest sense. At the same time, a comparison of the work of any two *auteurs* such as Truffaut and Loach, Roeg and Bergman, would help to bring out the distinctive nature not only of *auteur* theory but of the meaning that each individual brings to the world.

François Truffaut

Truffaut was one of the earliest adherents to the notion of director as *auteur* in his early work as a film critic and has published a particularly interesting study of the films of Alfred Hitchcock based on a series of interviews with Hitchcock. The greater part of his own early work was a series of semi-autobiographical films covering various stages of life. His first full-length feature film, *Les Quatres Cents Coups (The 400 Blows)*, remains not only a classic of the cinema but a beautiful illustration of how an essentially nice boy can find himself caught up in life events that propel him towards despair and delinquency. And yet, Truffaut was essentially an optimist, a lover of life, who conveyed in several of his subsequent films with the same actor (Jean-Paul Léaud), who played the boy in *The 400 Blows*, the difficulties and joys of growing up, coming to terms with warring parents, finding one's first job, falling in and out of love and getting married.

Interestingly, in *L'Enfant Sauvage (The Wild Child)*, a film apparently quite independent of his autobiographical work, Truffaut depicts the attempts of the French psychologist and educator, Itard, to socialize the so-called 'Wild Boy of Aveyron'. Although in some ways Truffaut's most pessimistic film in that Itard comes to see his experiment as largely a failure, *The Wild Child* is particularly fascinating in depicting with great integrity an early form of behaviour modification. This is an important point: there have been plenty of poor or exploitative films with psychology or (more usually) psychiatry as a central theme, but very few that succeed on all fronts. *The Wild Child* is one such film.

In examining the themes that keep recurring throughout Truffaut's films and the way in which he deals with them, we come to realize that his optimistic view of life is tempered by his awareness of people's limitations. In the final analysis he is essentially a fatalist who believes that we should come to accept ourselves as we are and make the most of whatever each day brings. We may not be able to play a significant part in changing the world, but each individual has a personal responsibility to be true to him or herself and play out his or her own part, however small. This theme is perhaps most explicitly stated in his adaptation of Ray Bradbury's *Fahrenheit 451*.

**Alfred
Hitchcock**

One director to whom the description of *auteur* has been applied by Truffaut and others is Alfred Hitchcock. Although he constantly denied that his films had any underlying meaning, Hitchcock is nevertheless a classic example of the director-as-psychologist in the way in which he uses the medium of film to manipulate his audience, often with stunning effect. In examining his most explicitly 'psychological' films we cannot fail to be impressed by the way in which he uses the camera, colour and sound to make a psychological point or produce a required effect. In his most famous early Hollywood film, *Spellbound*, Hitchcock employed Salvador Dali to produce the symbolical dream sequence. For many years this essentially simplistic story set in a sanatorium with 'good' and 'bad' psychoanalysts provided the classic model of psychology for the film-going public. One of the most important features of this film was its commercial success and the consequent establishment of a particular image of psychology in the public consciousness. For all its faults, *Spellbound* is never less than fascinating and treats its audience like its heroine, as intelligent participants in the central mystery.

In two later films, *Psycho* and *Vertigo*, Hitchcock used the camera to good effect in the role of the observer/victim and in the former film manages by means of Bernard Hermann's excellent musical score to convey and produce a variety of emotions. In the notorious shower sequence, it is the use of sound which heightens the shock and thereby removes the need to present any particularly gruesome visual image. In one of his later films, *Marnie*, ostensibly the story of a kleptomaniac who preferred horses to men, Hitchcock also explores the use of colour to excellent effect to express emotions.

In one of the most convincingly accessible books on film theory, *The World in a Frame: What we see in Films* (1984), Leo Braudy makes the distinction between 'open' and 'closed' films. Basically, open films teach us about the world, closed films teach us about ourselves. For Braudy, Hitchcock is a prime example of the closed film-maker because of the way in which he sees the world as a place upon which we impose meaning. The audience of a closed film is lured into the world of the characters and becomes an accomplice, even when not identifying directly with the characters. We empathize with Janet Leigh stealing her employer's money in *Psycho* or with James Stewart's voyeurism in *Rear Window* even though we would be unlikely to condone either action.

For Hitchcock there is a close link, a juxtaposition between good and evil that runs right through all his films and often leads to the death of innocent bystanders. The central character is often an apparently 'cool' blonde woman who may be a victim, as in *Psycho*, *Vertigo* and *The Birds*, often for reasons of repressed sexuality, or the one sane character in an otherwise apparently insane world. In Hitchcock films nothing can be taken for granted; again and again we are shown that even the most innocuous objects can be invested with malevolence. The world, says Hitchcock, is what we make it and beneath the most innocent personal or social exterior lies a very different world as seen, for example, in *Rear Window*. In many respects he can be seen as the most psychological of all film-makers, not because of his explicit psychological and psychiatric references in films like *Spellbound*, *Psycho* and *Marnie*, but because the wellspring of his films is rich with Freudian, Jungian, and other psychological connotations.

Again, a consideration of Hitchcock's view of women would repay closer analysis. In his unauthorized and highly controversial biography of Hitchcock, Spoto (1983) suggests that he was a misogynist who was basically terrified of sex and who treated most of his leading female stars abominably. If we bear this viewpoint in mind whilst watching a Hitchcock film, it is easy to identify the central female as victim or, more potently, as a powerful force setting off a chain of malevolent events.

Nicholas Roeg Nicholas Roeg is another film-maker whose films are rich in psychological references, themes and underpinnings. His first film, *Performance*, was something of a *cause célèbre* largely because of its exploration of the association between human sexuality and violence. This is a theme to which he has returned again and again, as in *Walkabout*, where awakening awareness of her sexuality by an adolescent girl in the Australian outback, causes the tragic death of an Aboriginal boy; *Bad Timing*, where the protagonist is a disturbed psychoanalyst who makes love under a portrait of Freud; and *Track 29*, where the oedipal theme is explored. These and other Roeg films, like *The Man Who Fell To Earth* and *Don't Look Now*, are complex, often difficult, but usually very rewarding in their exploration of fantasy, emotions and other aspects of the human condition.

Ingmar Bergman Although *auteur* theory arose from an interest in, and has mainly been applied to, Hollywood film-makers, it is in many ways more applicable to Europeans such as Bergman, Bůnuel, Visconti, Resnais and others from as far afield as Japan, India and Australia, partly because they have tended to have far more control over all aspects of film production. It would be a great mistake to concentrate any psychological analysis of films and film-makers entirely upon the USA, despite the greater availability and more ready distribution of films from that country. However, space permits the examination of just one more director, which in this instance will be Ingmar Bergman, in some people's minds the greatest of modern film-makers. Bergman is a true psychologist who focuses explicitly upon the human condition and has no hesitation in using his own view of life as the central theme of his work.

Many of Bergman's early films have religion as a central theme, but this is explored in terms of the meaning that it has for the central characters, as in *The Seventh Seal*. Symbolic meaning is invested in otherwise ordinary objects and events. Braudy (1984) sees Bergman and Hitchcock as alike in that both perceive the world to be an array of otherwise disparate or even chaotic things on which meaning has to be imposed through fantasy, allegory, ritual, dream, paranoia or religion.

In his 'middle' period Bergman moves more to an exploration of human relationships, particularly with respect to breakdown. Often there are two central characters as in *The Silence, Through A Glass Darkly* and *Scenes From a Marriage*, who fail to communicate. At its extreme form, in *Persona*, we are unsure if the two characters are really one, as the theme of schizophrenia, introduced in *Through A Glass Darkly*, is fully played out.

SPECIFIC THEMES

It has to be said that seeking connections between psychology and cinema through an exploration of genre or the work of *auteurs* requires an interest in and knowledge of films that probably goes beyond the immediate needs of most psychology teachers and lecturers. The thematic approach is a useful starting point from which a deeper study of both *auteur* theory and genre could easily emerge. Here films are mainly used as illustrations rather than explorations, although even this statement need not necessarily apply. The greatest film-makers provide few answers to the questions that their films raise. In fact, the great Soviet director, Tarkovsky, has been quoted as saying that even the film-maker should be unaware of what his or her films are about. Thus, the use of one of his films, for example, *The Awakening*, in a series selected to illustrate various views of childhood can certainly be seen as a search for meaning which is never made evident, because the director sees confusion of images as both part of the creative film-making process and of life itself.

Nevertheless, I shall now recommend several films which I consider can be usefully used to illustrate various aspects of each of four selected themes. Inevitably, there is a degree of bias in the choice of both the themes and the individual films which probably reveals as much about the author as it does about the films.

Psychology and Psychiatry   Despite the close links between psychology and the cinema discussed earlier and the obvious fascination that psychology and psychiatry have had for film-makers throughout the history of the cinema, comparatively few films have taken psychology itself as a major theme and done the topic justice. I would argue that possibly the best film to have done so is one which has received very little recognition – *Mon Oncle d'Amerique*, by the French director Alain Resnais. Here Resnais observes and seeks to explain the actions of his characters by direct reference to behaviourist theories and by intercutting scenes of rats in stress boxes to real-life situations. It is a film not to be missed.

As a supreme storyteller, John Huston presents his film *Freud: The Secret Passion* in a straightforward manner that captures the interest and provides an uncomplicated introduction to some of the great man's ideas. The central casting of Montgomery Clift as Freud provides a more substantial portrayal than might have been expected, but one suspects that he portrays the founder of psychoanalysis in a less arrogant and more sympathetic light than may have been the case.

Bergman's *Persona* and Loach's *Family Life*, a film which illustrates the political and sociological implications of the Laingian view of mental illness, should also be on the list along with another film about which critics are very divided, Robert Altman's *Images*. In this story of a schizophrenic woman, Altman depicts the main character as attempting to deal with her delusions by willpower and by concealment. As the film unfolds, the audience itself is drawn into the girl's world by not being informed where reality ends and delusions begin. The director uses the visual images on the screen to depict confusion and 'splitting' in a very real sense, whilst the girl seeks to take control of what she sees by her use of language and reference to myth. This film has been dismissed by some as mannered and indecipherable. It can also be seen as one of the few honest attempts by a film-maker to enable the audience to enter the world of someone mentally disturbed by making full use of the range of techniques open to him.

Two other films worth considering for their depictions of psychiatrists/psychotherapists are *Equus* and *Ordinary People*. The latter has been criticized by some for what they see as an inaccurate or sanitized view of the therapeutic encounter. I find this quite surprising and have to express my own prejudice in finding both the unhappy boy and his therapist totally believable. What's more, *Ordinary People* in its own way makes as valid a set of points about families, communication, relationships and coming to terms with grief as many more vaunted art movies.

One particularly interesting aspect of films about psychologists and psychiatrists has been the way in which they have been depicted historically, by Hollywood in particular: at times with affection (Fred Astaire in *Carefree*), more often with a sense of awe (Claude Rains in *Now Voyager*), or even as just plain crazy (Michael Caine in *Dressed to Kill*). The interested reader can find a fuller filmography on this theme in Burden (1979, 1980). There is a wide variety of portrayals of women as psychologists/psychiatrists from the repressed Ingrid Bergman in Hitchcock's *Spellbound* through to the obsessional neurotic in David Mamet's *House of Games* to an erotic killer in *Basic Instinct*.

Adolescence   There are literally hundreds of films devoted to aspects of child development, most particularly adolescence. I have found it quite possible to teach several courses on understanding adolescents through film whilst rarely showing the same film twice. The following titles are examples of a rich vein to be tapped.

In some ways Elia Kazan's *Splendour In The Grass* has never been bettered as an example of the agony and ecstasy of adolescence and its effects on a highly strung girl, played superbly by Natalie Wood in an early role, as is also her boyfriend by a young Warren Beatty. Two things stand out as being of vital importance in making successful films about adolescence, both of which are well illustrated in this film. One is the director's ability to empathize with young people in a non-exploitative way; the other is the actors' ability to be themselves rather than to act a part. This is perhaps what has helped generations of adolescents to identify with James Dean in another excellent Kazan film, *East of Eden* and, more famously, in Nicholas Ray's *Rebel Without a Cause*. With Dean such issues as the generation gap, individuation, peer-group identity and so on are well to the fore and one might be forgiven for drawing the conclusion that adolescence really is a time of storm and stress. Similar issues are dealt with in a less dramatic way in Peter Bogdanovich's *The Last Picture Show* and John Sayles' *Baby It's You*. Joseph Losey's *The Go Between* deals delicately with pre-adolescent incomprehension of adult relationships and the corruption of innocence, whilst *The Member of the Wedding* is a beautifully underplayed version of Carson McCullers' novel about the gradual changes in a young girl at the time of puberty.

When considering adolescence as a theme, however, the teacher must be wary of presenting an angst-ridden version of what research has clearly demonstrated to be a much more relaxed and enjoyable experience for most young people. Fortunately, there are also excellent films about the joyful side of youth, an excellent example being Peter Yates' *Breaking Away*. As his later films show, George Lucas has never lost his ability to identify with adolescents, so it is hardly surprising that many people, myself included, still consider that his *American Graffiti* is a key film in capturing much of the essence of the American adolescent experience.

The Australian cinema has been particularly adept in depicting the joys and difficulties of adolescence. The history of feminist cinema will be indebted to *The Getting of Wisdom* and *My Brilliant Career* as landmark films depicting strong-minded young heroines. *The Year My Voice Broke* and its companion piece *Flirting* are worthwhile depictions of coming of age traumas, particularly the latter's illustration of an inter-racial love affair.

Disability   The theme of disability has been introduced into films traditionally, and most straightforwardly, by focusing explicitly on the disability itself and depicting its effects upon the lives of the sufferers and those of their families and others associated with them. Classic examples of this approach are seen in *The*

Best Years of Our Lives, The Miracle Worker, Mandy and *Children of a Lesser God.*

Such films face the problem of presenting disability in a way that is 'true-to-life' whilst at the same time capturing the audience's imagination. Some disabilities clearly lend themselves better to this than others. Thus, the worthy *Stanley and Iris* could make little of interest out of the theme of learning disability, as compared with, say, *My Left Foot*, where triumph over physical adversity was all too plain to see. Often, it is only when the disability is presented as an integral part of a strong storyline, as in *Of Mice and Men* or *Rain Man* that we can retain our interest and increase our awareness about the disability itself. One exception to this rule, is the virtually unknown semi-documentary *Best Boy*, covering three years in the life of Philly, an adult with a severe learning disability, cared for by his elderly parents who refer to him as their 'best boy'. In focusing on Philly's efforts to learn to live independently, this film provides a form of cinéma vérité which is both moving and enlightening.

Sometimes the power of cinema as a medium of fantasy can detract from the awful grinding reality of disability. Whereas *Rain Man* presents a fascinating introduction to autism and its effects upon the self and others, it can also be seen as a sanitized view of the condition. Moreover, for dramatic effect, it also presents the highly contentious explanation that the roots of autism may lie in early childhood experience. Similarly, Peter Bogdanovich's *Mask* tells to excellent dramatic effect the apparently true story of a highly intelligent boy suffering from lionitis who has to endure the reactions of others to his features daily. However, our understanding of the condition is not helped by an overblown performance by Cher as his 'biker' mother or by the director's device of introducing a love affair with a beautiful blind girl (who, of course, loves him for his nature, not his looks).

It is fascinating to compare *Mask* with David Lynch's *Elephant Man*, in which John Hurt manages to convey a whole range of emotions and capture our full sympathy for the hideously deformed John Merrick with only the use of his voice and eyes. Here we have a classic example of the alternative approach to disability on film. *Elephant Man*, like *My Left Foot*, emphasizes the psychological turmoil and trauma faced by those living with a disability. Although Daniel Day Lewis gave an outstanding performance in the latter film, which deservedly won him an Oscar, the question can rightly be raised here as to why an actor with cerebral palsy wasn't chosen for the role and whether such an actor might even have played it differently. Again, the 'laws' of Hollywood insisted upon an 'upbeat' ending to this film, neglecting any mention of Christy Brown's sad death from alcoholism.

Hollywood's long-standing fascination with disability is revealed by the fact that Cliff Robertson was also awarded an Oscar for his performance in the title role of *Charly*, a young man with a severe learning disability who becomes a genius as a result of a psychological experiment, the effects of which then begin to wear off. This is a difficult theme which is less successfully handled in the film than in the novel, *Flowers For Algernon*, on which it is based, but the two taken in conjunction make an excellent focus for psychological study.

Disabilities resulting from accidents, as in the recent commercially unsuccessful but critically highly rated, *The Waterdance*, or from war injuries have provided rich material for some excellent psychological studies. Basically, the major theme in such films is learning to live with an imposed disability and how the victim(s) comes to terms with social, emotional and existential issues arising from it. With this in mind, a comparison of such films as *The Men*, *Coming Home*, *Cutter's Way* and *Born on the Fourth of July* would provoke considerable thought and fascinating discussion.

Women and Film

Reference has been made throughout this chapter to the way in which women have been depicted in films by various directors and in different genres. This is a theme which warrants far more in-depth analysis than can be provided here. Indeed, several books have been devoted to it in recent years (Kaplan, 1983; Mellen, 1974; *Screen*, 1992). Kaplan provides illustrative examples of thought-provoking films which can be used as starting points for exploring this theme. Mellen, on the other hand, takes the topic of female sexuality and examines how this has been conveyed within an historical context and by different directors and films. The *Screen* book of readings takes up the theme of sexuality and provides a number of Freudian and Lacanian perspectives on this.

My own starting point with respect to this theme is at a somewhat more basic level. Firstly, there can be no doubt that directors differ considerably in their use of actresses and conceptions of appropriate roles for women. There are those such as George Cukor and Victor Flemming who were renowned as 'women's' directors, thereby bringing out strong performances from the central characters in such films as *Gone With the Wind* and *Little Women*. Others, such as Elia Kazan, Robert Altman and Ridley Scott convey in films like *Wild River*, *McCabe and Mrs Miller*, and *Thelma and Louise* an empathy with women by presenting them as complex individuals as opposed to sexual stereotypes. Two other male directors whose work is well worth examining with regard to their presentation of women are Luis Buñuel (see especially *Tristana*, *Viridiana*, *Belle de Jour* and *That Obscure Object of Desire*), and Eric Rohmer (see especially *Claire's Knee*, *My Night with Maude* and *Chloe in the Afternoon*). Of particular interest also is the way in which the writer-producer-director team of Ruth Prawer Jhabvala, Ishmael Merchant and James Ivory have centralized strong women characters in their adaptations of the E.M. Forster novels *A Room with a View* and *Howards End*.

A further fascinating aspect of the role of the director with regard to this theme is reflected in the emergence of women directors from the early, somewhat inhibited efforts of Susan Sontag, Elaine May and Agnes Varda through to the more aggressive style of Jill Tewksbury's *Old Boyfriends* and Susan Seidelman's *Desperately Seeking Susan*.

A variation on this theme is provided by a consideration of the role played by female stars within the Hollywood system in particular. The careers of Mary Pickford, Louise Brooks, Mae West, Gloria Swanson, Jean Harlow, Marilyn Monroe, Bette Davis, Katherine Hepburn and others can be seen as representing a series of conflicts between private and public personae caught up in the hypocrisy of the Hollywood myth. The careers of some, like Davis and Hepburn, have suffered from confronting this hypocrisy, whilst others, like Monroe have suffered more tragically. Nevertheless, there can be no doubt that many leading female figures within the star system have been able to use their status to influence the way in which changing views of women are presented.

CONCLUDING REMARKS

Three potentially fruitful areas for exploration have been offered within which a close association between psychology and cinema can be found. Those interested in *auteur* theory will gain further useful insights from interesting biographies and autobiographies of Hitchcock, Truffaut, Kazan, Houston and others. The study of genres has also been explored in several good books. The thematic approach is virtually limitless in its scope. Central themes within social, educational and clinical psychology in particular, such as prejudice, gender, sexuality, propaganda, alcoholism, drug abuse and others, have received considerable cinema coverage. This chapter has merely scratched the surface of a relatively untapped fund of potential resources.

The references and filmography which follow should provide a reasonable starting point and information base for further action. Film titles are given in chronological order for directors but in alphabetical order for themes. Country of origin, length and date of distribution are also given. An asterisk preceding a film title indicates a good and accessible introduction to a director's work. Good viewing!

REFERENCES

ANDREW, J.D. (1976) *Introduction to the Major Film Theories.* Oxford: Oxford University Press.

BRAUDY, L. (1984) *The World in a Frame: What we see in Films.* Chicago: University of Chicago Press.

BURDEN, R.L. (1979) Celluloid psychiatry: Who shall we get to play the shrink? *Bulletin of The British Psychological Society, 32,* 315–316.

BURDEN, R.L. (1980) Psychology: the movie. *Bulletin of The British Psychological Society, 33,* 309–311.

DURGNAT, R. (1976) *Durgnat on Film.* London: Faber.

HUSTON, J. (1980) *An Open Book.* London: Butler & Tanner.

KAPLAN, E.A. (1983) *Women and Film: Both Sides of the Camera.* London: Methuen.

KAPLAN, E.A. (Ed.) (1990) *Psychoanalysis and Cinema.* London: Routledge.

KITSES, J. (1969) *Horizons West.* London: Thames & Hudson.

MELLEN, J. (1974) *Women and their Sexuality in the New Film.* London: Davis-Poynter.

MULVEY, L. (1990) Afterthoughts on 'Visual Pleasure and Narrative Cinema' inspired by Duel in the Sun. In E.A. Kaplan *Psychoanalysis and Cinema.* London: Routledge.

SCREEN (1992) *The Sexual Subject: A Screen Reader in Sexuality.* London: Routledge.

SPOTO, D. (1983) *The Dark Side of Genius: The Life of Alfred Hitchcock.* London: Muller.

TRUFFAUT, F. (1978) *Hitchcock.* London: Grenada.

TYLER, P. (1971) *Magic and Myth of the Movies.* London: Secker & Warburg.

WOLLEN, P. (1972) *Signs and Meaning in the Cinema.* London: Secker & Warburg.

FILMOGRAPHY: genres

Film title	Date	Director	Country of Production	Running time in minutes
WESTERNS				
The Bend in the River	1952	Anthony Mann	USA	91
Cheyenne Autumn	1964	John Ford	USA	160
Destry Rides Again	1939	George Marshall	USA	94
Dual in the Sun	1946	King Vidor	USA	138
The Far Country	1955	Anthony Mann	USA	97
Fort Apache	1948	John Ford	USA	127
Johnny Guitar	1954	Nicholas Ray	USA	110
The Last Sunset	1961	Robert Aldrich	USA	112
The Left-Handed Gun	1958	Arthur Penn	USA	102
The Man from Laramie	1955	Anthony Mann	USA	104
The Man who Shot Liberty Valance	1962	John Ford	USA	122
My Darling Clementine	1946	John Ford	USA	98
The Outlaw Josey Wales	1976	Clint Eastwood	USA	118
Rancho Notorious	1952	Fritz Lang	USA	89
Red River	1948	Howard Hawks	USA	125
Ride the High Country	1962	Sam Peckinpah	USA	94
The Searchers	1956	John Ford	USA	119
Shane	1953	George Stevens	USA	118
She Wore a Yellow Ribbon	1949	John Ford	USA	103
Soldier Blue	1970	Ralph Nielson	USA	112
Stagecoach	1939	John Ford	USA	90
Tell Them Willy Boy is Here	1989	Abraham Polonsky	USA	96
Unforgiven	1992	Clint Eastwood	USA	98
SCIENCE FICTION				
Alien	1979	Ridley Scott	USA	124
Aliens	1986	James Cameron	USA	110
Alien 3	1992	David Fincher	USA	114
Assault on Precinct 13	1976	John Carpenter	USA	91
The Day the Earth Stood Still	1951	Robert Wise	USA	92
The Fog	1980	John Carpenter	USA	91
The Forbidden Planet	1956	Fred M. Wilcox	USA	98
Halloween	1978	John Carpenter	USA	90
The Invasion of the Body Snatchers	1956	Don Siegel	USA	80
The Invasion of the Body Snatchers	1978	Philip Kaufman	USA	114
Starman	1986	John Carpenter	USA	93
They Live	1989	John Carpenter	USA	100
The Thing	1985	John Carpenter	USA	93
This Island Earth	1955	Joseph Newman	USA	87

FILMOGRAPHY: directors

Film title	Date	Running time in minutes
INGMAR BERGMAN (Sweden)		
*The Seventh Seal	1957	105
Wild Strawberries	1958	90
Through a Glass Darkly	1963	95
The Silence	1964	105
*Persona	1966	81
Hour of the Wolf	1968	90
A Passion	1970	93
Cries and Whispers	1972	91
Scenes from a Marriage	1973	168
*Fanny and Alexander	1983	197
ALFRED HITCHCOCK (USA)		
*Spellbound	1945	111
Strangers on a Train	1951	101
*Rear Window	1954	112
The Wrong Man	1957	105
*Vertigo	1958	128
*Psycho	1960	108
The Birds	1963	120
Marnie	1964	130
ANTHONY MANN (USA)		
Winchester '73	1950	92
*Where the River Bends	1952	91
The Naked Spur	1952	91
*The Far Country	1954	96
*The Man from Laramie	1955	101
Man of the West	1958	95
FRANÇOIS TRUFFAUT (France)		
Les Mistons (The Mischief Makers)	1957	23
*Les Quatre Cents Coups (The 400 Blows)	1959	93
Love at Twenty (first section)	1962	29
Fahrenheit 451	1966	(UK) 111
Baisers Volés (Stolen Kisses)	1968	90
*Domicile Conjugal (Bed and Board)	1970	100
*L'Enfant Sauvage (The Wild Child)	1970	83
L'Amour en Fuite (Love on the Run)	1979	94
NICHOLAS ROEG (UK)		
*Performance	1972	106
*Walkabout	1972	95
Don't Look Now	1973	110
The Man who Fell To Earth	1976	140
*Bad Timing	1979	(USA) 109
Eureka	1983	(USA) 97
Track 29	1988	(USA) 110

FILMOGRAPHY: specific themes

Film title	Date	Director	Country of Production	Running time in minutes
PSYCHOLOGY AND PSYCHIATRY				
Bad Timing	1979	Nicholas Roeg	USA	109
Basic Instinct	1992	Paul Verhoeven	USA	120
Carefree	1938	Mark Sandrich	USA	83
Dressed to Kill	1980	Brian De Palma	USA	105
Equus	1976	Sidney Lumet	USA	137
Face To Face	1975	Ingmar Bergman	Sweden	183
Family Life	1972	Ken Loach	UK	108
Freud: The Secret Passion	1962	John Huston	USA	139
House of Games	1988	David Mamet	USA	100
High Anxiety	1977	Mel Brooks	USA	94
Images	1972	Robert Altman	USA	101
I Never Promised You a Rose Garden	1975	Anthony Page	USA	92
L'Enfant Sauvage	1970	François Truffaut	France	84
Marnie	1964	Alfred Hitchcock	USA	130
My American Uncle	1980	Alan Resnais	France	110
Now Voyager	1942	Irving Rapper	USA	117
Ordinary People	1980	Robert Redford	USA	124
Persona	1966	Ingmar Bergman	Sweden	81
Spellbound	1945	Alfred Hitchcock	USA	111
Through a Glass Darkly	1973	Ingmar Bergman	Sweden	95
Zelig	1987	Woody Allen	USA	93
CHILD DEVELOPMENT: ADOLESCENCE				
American Graffiti	1973	George Lucas	USA	110
Aparajito (The Unvanquished)	1958	Satyajit Ray	India	113
Baby It's You	1986	John Sayles	USA	104
The Breakfast Club	1986	John Hughes	USA	97
Breaking Away	1979	Peter Yates	USA	99
East of Eden	1955	Elia Kazan	USA	115
Flirting	1991	John Duigan	Australia	99
The Four Hundred Blows	1959	François Truffaut	France	93
The Getting of Wisdom	1980	Bruce Beresford	Australia	103
The Go Between	1971	Joseph Losey	UK	116
Gregory's Girl	1985	Bill Forsyth	UK	91
Kes	1970	Ken Loach	UK	110
The Member of the Wedding	1953	Fred Zinnemann	USA	91
The Last Picture Show	1971	Peter Bogdanovich	USA	118
Le Souffle au Coeur	1971	Louis Malle	France	110
My Brilliant Career	1979	Gillian Armstrong	Australia	110
Rebel Without a Cause	1955	Nicholas Ray	USA	111
Sixteen Candles	1984	John Hughes	USA	96
Splendour in the Grass	1961	Elia Kazan	USA	124
The Year My Voice Broke	1989	John Duigan	Australia	105

FILMOGRAPHY: specific themes *cont.*

Film title	Date	Director	Country of Production	Running time in minutes
DISABILITY				
A Day in the Death of Joe Egg	1972	Peter Medak	UK	106
Best Boy	1979	Ira Wohl	USA	104
The Best Years of Our Lives	1946	William Wyler	USA	172
Birdy	1986	Alan Parker	USA	120
Born On the Fourth of July	1989	Oliver Stone	USA	144
Charly	1968	Ralph Nelson	USA	103
Children of a Lesser God	1987	Randa Haines	USA	115
Coming Home	1978	Hal Ashby	USA	128
Cutter's Way	1981	Ivan Passer	USA	109
The Elephant Man	1980	David Lynch	UK	123
The Heart is a Lonely Hunter	1968	Robert Ellis Miller	USA	125
Mandy	1953	Alexander Mackendrick	UK	93
Mask	1986	Peter Bogdanovich	USA	120
The Men	1950	Fred Zinnemann	USA	85
The Miracle Worker	1962	Arthur Penn	USA	107
My Left Foot	1989	John Sheridan	UK	98
Of Mice and Men	1939	Lewis Milestone	USA	107
The Raging Moon	1971	Bryan Forbes	UK	111
Rain Man	1989	Barry Levinson	USA	124
Stanley and Iris	1990	Martin Ritt	USA	105
The Waterdance	1991	Neal Jimenez	USA	107
Whose Life Is It Anyway	1981	John Badham	USA	110
WOMEN AND FILM				
Belle de Jour	1967	Luis Buñuel	France	114
Claire's Knee	1970	Eric Rohmer	France	97
Chloe in the Afternoon	1972	Eric Rohmer	France	93
Desperately Seeking Susan	1984	Susan Seidelman	USA	102
Gone With the Wind	1939	Victor Fleming	USA	219
Howards End	1992	James Ivory	UK	128
Little Women	1933	George Cukor	USA	120
McCabe and Mrs Miller	1971	Rober Altman	USA	207
My Night with Maude	1969	Eric Rohmer	France	94
Old Boyfriends	1986	Jill Tewksbury	USA	98
A Room with a View	1986	James Ivory	UK	114
That Obscure Object of Desire	1977	Luis Buñuel	Spain	112
Thelma and Louise	1991	Ridley Scott	USA	102
Tristana	1970	Luis Buñuel	Spain	105
Viridiana	1961	Luis Buñuel	Spain	108
Wild River	1960	Elia Kazan	USA	115

LITERARY RESOURCES

John Radford and Deana Smith

❏ *novels and literary extracts* • *biography, autobiography and firsthand accounts* • *popular press* • *science fiction* • *religious literature*

*U*nder this title can be collated several sorts of writing which do not have a primarily psychological purpose, but which can be, and have been, used in teaching the subject.

Psychology and literature have quite a complex relationship, discussed, for example, by Sederberg and Sederberg (1975), by Weatherell, Potter and Stringer (1983) and Potter, Stringer and Weatherell (1984), and by Lester (1987). Richards (in Radford and Smith, 1991) considers literature as a method of psychological research, as a source of data and theories, and as a psychological instrument. His views overlap with those of Weatherell *et al.* who suggest four sorts of interaction:

1. Literature 'as an independent variable ... exercising a causal influence ... on readers' personalities and attitudes'. For example, Gerrig and Prentice (1991) discuss the extent to which fiction is incorporated into real-world knowledge, while Appleyard (1990) gives an account of the whole process of becoming a reader (of fiction), from childhood to adulthood.
2. Literature as a dependent variable, involving work 'on the psychological conditions which determine the make-up of a text'.
3. Psychology used to illuminate literature. Most work here is probably in the psychoanalytic tradition, and much of this currently appears in the journal *Psychology and Literature*.
4. Literature used to illuminate psychology. This is probably the main aspect likely to be used in teaching, but the others can also be relevant.

Perhaps one might add a fifth sort of interaction, in which psychology has been one of the sources of literature, or vice versa. Thus Williams and Waddell (1991) discuss the literary origins of the psychoanalytic model of the mind; and there is a long literary tradition of presenting human personality in terms of what would now be called 'types' and 'traits', which contributed to the development of personality theory (Kirby and Radford, 1976). Examples of the reverse relationship abound in science fiction (see below).

Wetherell *et al.* (1983) argue against treating literature as a resource for teaching psychology, as suggested by Rose and Radford (1981), on the grounds that psychology and literature should both be regarded 'as forms of making sense of people's actions, identities, and social lives'. The present writers feel, however, that such a view ought to make literature even more useful to teachers of psychology.

Rose and Radford (1981) suggested four ways in which literature might be of use in teaching psychology. First the inclusion of illustrative 'non-psychological' literature in the reading list may help to sustain, or arouse, interest. Psychology may be linked to things already of interest, or at least familiar, to students. For example Napoletano (1988) reports using popular song lyrics in teaching the psychology of adolescence.

Second, the world of literature can provide a 'social laboratory' in terms of which to examine the tenets of academic psychology. It can 'provide a kind of systematic experiencing of a social world – albeit an imaginary one – with all the parts interacting in a credible fashion' (Sederberg and Sederberg, 1975). For examples of this, see articles by Bayne and by Green (both in Radford and Smith, 1991).

A third sort of application is in counterbalancing the fragmentation involved in the scientific approach. Necessarily, objective psychology often involves studying aspects of behaviour as though they were isolated from others. Subjective literary description, on the other hand, readily accepts complexity and ambiguity, and can help to redress the balance in favour of the 'whole person'.

Fourthly, literature (like other arts, and other disciplines, of course) can broaden the student's experience, at least vicariously, by introducing him or her to situations, states, and human types which would not normally be encountered. These could include extremes of behaviour such as mental disorders, disablement, disease and bereavement (for example, Nixon and Wear, 1991); or other cultures and historical periods. This is the function which Sederberg and Sederberg (1975) have designated 'transmitting the non-transmissible'. However, Bratus (1986) points to limitations in the use of fictional literature to describe psychological phenomena such as personality traits. These include bias on the part of the author in the selection of character traits that give particular meaning to the plot, and the different aims of literature and psychology in their examination of behaviour. And, of course, authors, like psychologists, vary widely in their skill in grasping and presenting human personality. A fictional account may quite simply be wrong (portrayals of psychiatric disorders are often garbled, and the film *Little Man Tate*, for example, gives a most misleading picture of a child prodigy); but then the psychology student ought to see why.

Again perhaps a fifth application can be distinguished, though it overlaps with the first four: the use of literary and similar sources simply to supply some convenient examples of a particular phenomenon or problem. Some recent examples of what has, in fact, become quite a popular teaching tool, are: Adler and Clark (1991) on adolescence; Cole, Van Tassel and Kastenbaum (1992) on ageing; Kautzmann (1992) on caregiving; Knapp (1991) on giftedness; Lester (1991) on suicide; Sno, Linszen and de Jonghe (1992) on *deja vu* experiences.

A further discussion is offered by Radford and Smith (1991). We turn here, however, to examples of relevant material, under the following headings:

- novels and literary extracts
- biographies, autobiographies and firsthand accounts
- popular press
- science fiction
- religious literature

We do not attempt to be either comprehensive or systematically evaluative.

NOVELS AND LITERARY EXTRACTS

The first collection of literary extracts intended to illustrate various psychological principles appears to be that of Schroeder *et al.* (1943). Since then a number of publications have appeared in which the selection has been made to illustrate some particular aspect of psychology: abnormal personality (Stone and Stone, 1966); social psychology (Fernandez, 1972); child development (Landau *et al.*, 1972); adolescence (Burden, 1974); human development and gerontology (Wolf, 1987). Some of these include explicit discussion of relevant psychological material (for example, Landau *et al.*), while others leave this mainly to be inferred by the reader (for example, Fernandez).

Chrisler (1990) advocates the use of main characters of novels or biographies about mental illness as case studies. Students are asked to describe the character's symptoms and diagnosis, suggest a treatment plan and identify theories of mental illness that best explain the symptoms.

Using a slightly different approach, Kellogg (1980) advocates the use of extracts from Sherlock Holmes stories to illustrate factors influencing human learning and problem solving. Radford (1988) paralleled Holmes's investigations and explanations of behaviour with those developing simultaneously within psychology, particularly psychoanalysis, and (1990) attempted to assess Holmes's admittedly remarkable intelligence in terms of modern theory. Several other writers have also compared Sherlock Holmes with Freud, the most recent being Marcus (1984) and Shepherd (1985). Sherlock Holmes stories have also been used as an independent variable in an empirical study: Mazziotta, Phelps and Kuhl (1982) demonstrated that the area of activation in the left hemisphere was larger than that in the right when subjects listened to the stories. Sebeok and Umiker-Sebeok (1979) argued that Holmes's methods of detection were very similar to the process of 'abduction' of C.S. Pierce: correct decision-making in situations of incomplete information, which has resonances with current work in this area.

Additional sources of literary material of this type are the various published lists of 'psychological thrillers' (McCollom, 1971, 1973, 1975; Le Unes, 1974; Benel, 1975; Swain, 1977). A 'psychological thriller' is a book of demonstrated popularity which is more readable, 'softer' and 'lower key' (Le Unes, 1974) than a psychology text, but which is relevant to some aspect of a psychology course. The lists cited above include some psychology books as well as titles from non-psychological literature. Perhaps worthy of a special mention are those novels which more or less explicitly turn on some aspect of psychology and thus have a case for inclusion in the science fiction section. The best known are probably Huxley's *Brave New World*, Orwell's *1984*, and Skinner's *Walden Two*. Foster (1988) explores a particular psychological theme over several centuries of writing in *Sex Variant Women in Literature*.

BIOGRAPHY, AUTOBIOGRAPHY AND FIRSTHAND ACCOUNTS

So far we have been concerned with the use of fiction in teaching psychology. Equally valuable, however, are some types of non-fiction. White (1952, 1974) has reported using biographical material in the teaching of personality, and Levin (1979) adopts a biographical approach in a general introduction to psychology. In this latter case biographical details of 15 famous people are used as a way to introduce and illustrate the basics of psychology.

Although it goes somewhat beyond the normal definition of literature, students' own autobiographical details have also been used as illustrative material (White, 1952, 1974; Hettich, 1976; Polyson, 1985; Wolf, 1987). Junn (1989) describes an exercise in which students wrote semi-autobiographical letters to both an actual or future child and to a parent as an aid to understanding and applying developmental theory.

Howe (1982) discusses the use of biographical evidence in psychological research – in particular, in understanding the development of outstanding individuals. Many autobiographies by individuals brought up in very different cultures or subcultures give insights no alien anthropologist can (one classic example is *Beyond a Boundary* by C.L.R. James). Graham Richards, when at the Polytechnic of East London, included in a course on personality a requirement for students to read at least two biographies. He offered a list of about 100 persons, 'as mixed a bag as I could find, though deliberately low on royalty, with biographies of them that should be available from public libraries fairly easily. One could adopt a number of tacks, for example it would be possible to look at several different biographies of the same person, to look at families such as the Brontës, Huxleys, Wildes, to look at several people in the same category (women novelists, generals, scientists), or simply pick a couple of figures who particularly interest you'. The aims were: to give students a view of a personality other than their own; to consider the applicability of psychological theories to an individual life; and to raise methodological issues (personal communication). For discussions of autobiographical memory in general see Rubin (1986).

There are also, of course, numerous biographies and autobiographies of eminent contributors to psychology, which can add interest and insight, and some of which certainly rank as literature, for example, Hearnshaw's (1979) life of Burt and Jones' (1953) of Freud. Numerous shorter accounts appear in the *History of Psychology in Autobiography* (ed. Gardner Lindzey), and some in more general works such as the *Encyclopaedia Brittanica*, the *Dictionary of National Biography*, and the *Dictionary of Scientific Biography*. Other general works on the history of psychology also give biographical sketches of psychologists, for example, Hearnshaw (1987). Among subjects treated at book length are:

Bain (Bain, 1904)
Bartlett (Crampton, 1978)
Ruth Benedict (Modell, 1984)
Cyril Burt (Hearnshaw, 1979)
Charcot (Owen, 1971)
Dilthey (Rickman, 1979)
Havelock Ellis (Ellis, 1940; Grosskurth, 1980)
Eysenck (Gibson, 1981; Eysenck, 1990)
Ferenczi (Dupont, 1989)
Anna Freud (Peters, 1985; Young-Bruehl, 1988)
Sigmund Freud (Freud, 1935; Jones, 1953; Clark, 1982; Sulloway, 1979; Sachs, 1945)
Galton (Pearson, 1914; Forrest, 1974)
Gibson (Reed, 1989)
Horney (Rubins, 1978; Quinn, 1988)
Ernest Jones (Brome, 1982)
James (Bird, 1986; Myers, 1986)
Jung (Brome, 1978; Wehr, 1985 trans. 1987)
Klein (Grosskurth, 1986; Wright, 1988)
Laing (Laing, 1986)

Lewin (Marrow, 1968)
Lorenz (Nisbett, 1976)
Luria (Luria, 1979)
Maslow (Hoffman, 1988)
Margaret Mead (Mead, 1973; Howard, 1984)
Mesmer (Buranelli, 1975)
Pavlov (Babkin, 1949)
Wilhelm Reich (Reich, 1969; Sharaf, 1983; Reich, 1988)
Rogers (Kirschenbaum, 1979)
S.B. Sarason (Sarason, 1988)
B.F. Skinner (Skinner, 1975; 1985)
Terman (Seagoe, 1975)
Thorndike (Clifford, 1984)
Vygotsky (Wertsch, 1985)
Watson (Cohen, 1979)

For brief biographies of several psychologists see also Cohen (1977), Hearnshaw (1987) and Schellenburg (1978). There are several relevant volumes in the Fontana/Collins series 'Modern Masters' including Chomsky, Fanon, Freud, Jung, Levi-Strauss, Laing, Marcuse, Popper, Piaget, Reich, Merleau-Ponty, and Sherrington. Published letters of such individuals might also provide a source of useful insights: Goodwin (1991), for example, describes the use of psychologists' letters to their contemporaries in teaching about the introspective method within experimental psychology.

Other non-fictional works which are of use in psychology courses come under the heading of 'first-hand accounts'. These are subjective accounts by individuals or their close relatives of their experiences in coping with a variety of real-life situations or events. They include accounts of coping with physical and mental diseases and disabilities, death and bereavement, delinquency, and working with children generally. The reader will find an introduction to this literature in a series of annotated bibliographies (Rippere, 1976, 1977, 1978, 1979a,b, 1980; Pearson, 1977, 1980) which between them cover well over 200 separate titles. More recent accounts of coping with mental illness include Sutherland (1987), Wigoder (1987) and Read (1989). Chadwick (1992) includes an account of his own experience of psychosis in his academic text on this subject.

Firsthand accounts certainly add interest to a course. However, much more importantly, they provide a perspective on real-life situations which no amount of objective measurement can possibly provide and which in many instances is very much more relevant to the objectives of the course than a scientific survey. Much of the firsthand account literature is perhaps primarily of value in teaching psychology in the context of the medical and paramedical professions. However, it is a rich source of reference material which merits inspection by teachers of psychology in other contexts also.

Finally, in the category of biography – though not strictly

literature – mention may be made of case studies. The case study method, in which a real-life situation or event is used to focus attention upon and illustrate certain concepts and areas of information, has of course been extensively used in applied psychology. However, its wider use in psychology teaching has been urged by Vande Kemp (1980). (See also Bertaux, 1983, and Wrightsman, 1981.) Some case studies have been presented in a rather more literary form, for example Ellis and Pitt-Aikens (1988), respectively a popular novelist and a psychiatrist, based their book on a case study by the latter author. A follow-up to this work has been published (Pitt-Aikens and Ellis, 1990) in which the authors develop a theory of delinquency and provide a number of short case studies. Also in this sub-category might be included the collections of neurological case studies by Sacks (1984, 1985), which provide interesting illustrations of a variety of neuropsychological deficits or dysfunctions.

POPULAR PRESS

Many non-psychological newspapers and periodicals carry material of psychological interest on occasion, especially reports of major conferences, the most consistent general source in this country being probably *The Sunday Times*, closely followed by other quality newspapers. Most of these have a weekly section on general health matters which often include articles on mental health, psychological adjustment to physical illness, or child developmental problems. General and women's magazines also often carry psychological features. Agony aunts and uncles can provide interesting insights: the monthly magazine 'New Woman' includes a professional psychologist on its 'problem page' panel. This magazine also includes at least a short report in each issue referring to recently published psychological research thought to be of interest to its readership.

SCIENCE FICTION

Science fiction is often considered a branch of literature, but in the present writers' view is better regarded as a group of concepts which can be, and have been, expressed in any medium; the printed word, but also film, TV, visual art, music and so on. There have been a few attempts to classify the concepts, the most systematic probably being that of Croghan (1981). The written form is perhaps the most easily accessible for teaching purposes and there are some theoretical grounds for giving it primacy. However, science fiction is perhaps unique in combining popular entertainment with genuinely important themes; there is scarcely an episode of *Star Trek* (especially the second series, *The Next Generation*) that does not present such themes. It is odd that science fiction continues to be critically undervalued; as Kingsley Amis has put it: 'SF's no good', they bellow till we're deaf / 'But this looks good' – 'Well then, it's not SF'.

The numerous definitions of science fiction nearly all depend on finite sets of criteria, often only one. In fact science fiction is multi-componential and some of the features frequently found can be of particular interest to psychologists (Saeger, 1977, 1979; Radford, 1985). McMahon (1989), from a psychoanalytic viewpoint, suggests three roles for science fiction: one in mediating adaptation to change through exploration of possible futures and parallel worlds; one in the discovery of poetic or philosophical meanings in technological change; and lastly simply as entertainment. Blish (1987), one of the most insightful writers on the subject, also lists three functions: the first is that 'it confronts the theories and data of modern science with the questions of modern philosophy, to create "thought experiments" like that of Einstein's free falling elevator which may in themselves advance science'; the second is that it adds to our knowledge of reality by evoking emotions – especially those associated with scientific discovery such as wonder, excitement, desire to understand; and the third is that it creates myths. All of these various functions and no doubt others are replete with psychological interest. Radford (1985) has isolated four areas which are of particular interest to psychologists.

First is the use of psychological science as the basis, or as a background, of a work. This is often explicit, employing an actual reported finding or theory and/or some supposed extension of it. Sometimes ideas which derive directly from psychology appear without acknowledgement, and of course one cannot say just how the author acquired and developed them. In these uses, science fiction raises the questions of what psychological knowledge is now, or could shortly be, available to us, and what the implications are.

Second, science fiction deals, again both explicitly and implicitly, with two questions that are fundamental to psychology in its widest aspect; what is science, and what is human? Science fiction addresses the question of what is human in a way somewhat analogous to that of myth, by contrast with non-human entities, specifically robots (artificial simulacra of the human) and aliens (sentient, intelligent, natural, but not human). The question of what is science is raised both by speculation as to what may be scientific knowledge in worlds other than our own, and by contrast with other systems of thought, non-logical and magical, for example.

Third, it may be suggested that science fiction is itself a psychological phenomenon worthy of study, both in its subcultural aspects and in its role in individual belief systems.

Fourth, science fiction characteristically reflects back to us the way we regard ourselves. This is particularly apposite for psychology, it may be suggested, in that it is itself a reflexive science, unique in that its exponents are themselves part of their own subject matter. In the distorting mirror of science fiction, the psychological scientist meets him or herself coming back.

Most of the publications on the use of science fiction in teaching psychology have concentrated on the first of these aspects, the most obvious, and on the written word. Several readers have been published of science fiction stories, pointing out the psychological lessons to be learned: for example, Jones and Roe (1974); Katz *et al.* (1974); Estrada and Estrada (1977); Melvin *et al.* (1977); Ridgway and Benjamin (1987). An unpublished reader by Radford and Kirby (1973) is available at the Science Fiction Foundation at the University of Liverpool, which has one of the major world collections of science fiction. Two other relevant collections are edited by Evans (1969, 1970).

Other publications not specifically devoted to psychology include some relevant material. *The Science of Science Fiction* (ed. Nicholls, 1982), includes sections on artificial intelligence, conditioning and brainwashing, psychotropic drugs, crime and punishment, telepathy and telekinesis, and feral children, and Wingrove (1984) discusses issues of psychological interest such as survival after brain death. Dunn and Erlich (1982) deal with artificial intelligence and the nature of what is human, while Panshin and Panshin (1989) consider science fiction and the quest for transcendence.

Some sources of science fiction material in general, from which appropriate selections can be made, include: Aldiss with Wingrove (1986 – history of science fiction); Barron (1987 – critical essays and source book of materials, including teaching materials and other source books); Clute and Nicholls (1993 – up-to-date encyclopaedia); Magill (1979 – 500 essay reviews plus 2500 bibliographical references); Pringle (1985 – short essays on one hundred novels); Spinrad (1990 – essays on various aspects of science fiction).

Finally, there are two earlier reviews of the science fiction approach to psychology by Saeger (1977, 1979).

RELIGIOUS LITERATURE

The psychology of religion is a distinct area of study that is outside our remit, but the texts, scriptures and other writings of various different religions are a further source of material that can be used to illustrate areas of psychological interest. These contain many life accounts of important religious figures which show the influence of early experience or emotional factors on their behaviours, beliefs or interpretations of events. Freeman (1984) provides a discussion of models of personal growth in the New Testament and compares them to the developmental models of Jung and Kohlberg.

Religious literature also provides guidelines for desirable behaviour either through explicit rules, such as the Ten Commandments or the Buddhist Precepts, or through the teachings and examples of individuals like Christ or the Buddha. A comparison of different religions might be used in a teaching context for a discussion of cross-cultural differences in social norms for behaviour, and in views of psychological adjustment. Balodhi and Keshavan (1986), for example, discuss the concept of the mentally healthy person reflected in the *Bhagavadgita* and the relevance of its teaching to current forms of psychotherapy. Approaches to the management or modification of certain emotions and behaviours are also documented in religious texts: Stafford (1986) analyses over 500 references to anger in the Bible which suggest that it is an acceptable emotion if handled in specific ways. In a review of early Buddhist literature, de Silva (1984) gives examples of techniques for the treatment of many disorders, including obesity and obsessional thoughts, which appear remarkably similar to behaviour therapies used by psychologists today. Of all major religions, perhaps Zen Buddhism has made the most direct attempt to control and modify human behaviour and experience (see Kraft, 1988).

Ostbye and Rochon (1993) discuss an early 'clinical trial' described in the Old Testament, of which many of the issues raised are relevant to the design of psychological studies. Flaws in the study design are discussed, such as confounding factors, subjectivity of outcome measures and the small sample size.

The central characters of many religious texts are often endowed with many human characteristics and therefore, like science fiction, this body of literature also reflects the qualities we perceive in ourselves. Even God is not immune to feelings of anger (Stafford, 1986), and Prue Green (personal communication) suggests the Bible as a non-psychological work of relevance to psychology by pointing out God's 'infantile grandiosity'. For a more extensive discussion, especially from a Buddhist point of view, see Valentine (in Radford and Smith, 1991).

REFERENCES

ADLER, E. and CLARK, R. (1991) Adolescence: A literary passage. *Adolescence, 26*, 757–768.

ALDISS, B.W. with WINGROVE, D. (1986) *Trillion Year Spree*. New York: Atheneum.

APPLEYARD, J.A. (1990) *Becoming a Reader: The Experience of Fiction From Childhood to Adulthood*. New York: Cambridge University Press.

BABKIN, B.P. (1949) *Pavlov, A Biography*. Chicago: University of Chicago Press.

BAIN, A. (1904) *Autobiography*. London: Longman.

BALODHI, J.P. and KESHAVAN, M.S. (1986) Bhagavadgita and psychotherapy. *NIMHANS Journal*, 4(2), 139–143.

BARRON, N. (Ed.) (1987) *Anatomy of Wonder: A Critical Guide to Science Fiction*, 3rd edn. New York: R.R. Bowker Co.

BENEL, R.A. (1975) Psychological thrillers: thrilling to whom? *Teaching of Psychology*, 2, 176.

BERTAUX, D. (Ed.) (1983) *Biography and Society: The Life History Approach in the Social Sciences*. London: Sage.

BIRD, G. (1986) *William James*. London: Routledge & Kegan Paul.

BLISH, J. (1987) *The Tale That Wags The God*. Chicago: Advent Publishers Ltd.

BRATUS, B.S. (1986) The place of fine literature in the development of a scientific psychology of personality. *Soviet Psychology*, 25(1), 91–103.

BROME, V. (1978) *Jung, Man and Myth*. London: Macmillan.

BROME, V. (1982) *Ernest Jones: Freud's Alter Ego*. London: Caliban Books.

BURANELLI, V. (1975) *The Wizard From Vienna: Franz Anton Mesmer*. New York: Coward, McCann & Geoghegan.

BURDEN, R. (1974) Adolescence through literature: a novel approach to an age-old problem. *Psychology Teaching*, 2, 251–258.

CHADWICK, P.K. (1992) *Borderline: A Psychological Study of Paranoia and Delusional Thinking*. London: Routledge.

CHRISLER, J.C. (1990) Novels as case-study materials for psychology students. *Teaching of Psychology*, 17, 55–57.

CLARK, R. (1982) *Freud*. London: Weidenfeld & Nicholson.

CLIFFORD, G.C. (1984) *Edward L. Thorndike: The Sane Positivist*. Middletown, Conn.: Wesleyan University Press (originally published as *The Sane Positivist: Edward L. Thorndike*, 1968).

CLUTE, J. and NICHOLLS, P. (1993) *The Encyclopaedia of Science Fiction*, 2nd edn. London: Granada.

COHEN, D. (1977) *Psychologists on Psychology*. London: Routledge & Kegan Paul.

COHEN, D. (1979) *J.B. Watson, The Founder of Behaviourism*. London: Routledge & Kegan Paul.

COLE, T.R., VAN TASSELL, D.D. and KASTENBAUM, R. (Eds) (1992) *Handbook of the Humanities and Aging*. New York: Springer Publishing Company.

CRAMPTON, C. (1978) *Sir Frederick Bartlett and the Cambridge School*. Unpublished PhD thesis, University of Edinburgh.

CROGHAN, A. (1981) *Science Fiction and the Universe of Knowledge – The Structure of an Aesthetic Form*. London: Coburgh.

DE SILVA, P. (1984) Buddhism and behaviour modification. *Behaviour Research and Therapy*, 22(6), 661–678.

DUNN, T.P. and ERLIC, R.D. (1982) *The Mechanical God: Machines in Science Fiction*. Westport, Conn: Greenwood Press.

DUPONT, J. (Ed.) (1989) *The Clinical Diary of Sandor Ferenczi*.

Cambridge, Mass.: Harvard University Press.

ELLIS, A.T. and PITT-AIKENS, T. (1988) *Secrets of Strangers.* Harmondsworth: Penguin.

ELLIS, H. (1940) *My Life.* London: Spearman.

ESTRADA, A. and ESTRADA, D. (Eds) (1977) *The Future of Being Human: Psychology Through Science Fiction.* New York: Harper & Row.

EVANS, C. (Ed.) (1969) *Mind at Bay.* London: Panther Books.

EVANS, C. (Ed.) (1970) *Mind in Chains.* London: Panther Books.

EYSENCK, H.J. (1990) *Rebel With a Cause: The Autobiography of Hans Eysenck.* London: W.H. Allen.

FERNANDEZ, R. (Ed.) (1972) *Social Psychology Through Literature.* New York: Wiley.

FORREST, D.W. (1974) *Francis Galton: The Life and Work of a Victorian Genius.* London: Elek.

FOSTER, J.H. (1988) *Sex Variant Women in Literature.* London: Naiad Press (originally published by Vintage Press, 1956).

FREEMAN, A. (1984) Styles of discipleship: Personal growth models in the New Testament. *Studies in Formative Spirituality, 5*(2), 171–188.

FREUD, S. (1935) *An Autobiographical Study.* London: Hogarth Press.

GERRIG, R.J. and PRENTICE, D.A. (1991) The representation of fictional information. *Psychological Science, 2*, 336–340.

GIBSON, H.B. (1981) *H.J. Eysenck.* London: P. Owen.

GOODWIN, C.J. (1991) Using psychologists' letters to teach about introspection. *Teaching of Psychology, 18*, 237–238.

GRANT, L. (1987) Psychology and literature: A survey of courses. *Teaching of Psychology, 14*(2), 86–88.

GROSSKURTH, P. (1980) *Havelock Ellis: Stranger in the World.* London: Allen Lane.

GROSSKURTH, P. (1986) *Melanie Klein: Her World and Her Work.* Sevenoaks: Hodder & Stoughton.

HEARNSHAW, L.S. (1979) *Cyril Burt, Psychologist.* Sevenoaks: Hodder & Stoughton.

HEARNSHAW, L.S. (1987) *The Shaping of Modern Psychology.* London: Routledge & Kegan Paul.

HETTICH, P. (1976) The journal, an autobiographical approach to learning. *Teaching of Psychology, 3*, 60–63.

HOFFMAN, E. (1988) *The Right to be Human: A Biography of Abraham Maslow.* Los Angeles: Jeremy B. Tarcher.

HOWARD, J. (1984) *Margaret Mead: A Life.* London: Harvill Press.

HOWE, M.J.A. (1982) Biographical evidence and the development of outstanding individuals. *American Psychologist, 37*, 1071–1081.

HUXLEY, A. (1932) *Brave New World.* London: Chatto & Windus.

JAMES, C.L.R. (1963) *Beyond a Boundary.* London: Stanley Paul (rev. edn, 1976).

JONES, E. (1953) *The Life and Work of Sigmund Freud.* New

York: Basic Books.

JONES, R. and ROE, R.L. (Eds) (1974) *Valence and Vision: A Reader in Psychology*. San Francisco, CA: Rinehart Press.

JUNN, E.N. (1989) "Dear Mom and Dad": Using personal letters to enhance students' understanding of developmental issues. *Teaching of Psychology, 16*, 135–139.

KATZ, H.A., GREENBERG, M.N. and WARRICK, P. (Eds) (1977) *Psychology Through Science Fiction*, 2nd edn. Chicago: Rand McNally.

KATZ, H.A., WARRICK, P. and GREENBERG, M.N. (1974) *Introduction to Psychology Through Science Fiction*. Chicago: Rand McNally.

KAUTZMANN, L.N. (1992) Using literature to educate students: Images of caregivers in poetry and prose. *Educational Gerontology, 18*, 17–26.

KELLOGG, R.L. (1980) Sherlock Holmes and the educational process. *Teaching of Psychology, 7*, 41–44.

KIRBY, R. and RADFORD, J. (1976) *Individual Differences*. London: Methuen.

KIRSCHENBAUM, H. (1979) *On Becoming Carl Rogers*. New York: Delacorte.

KNAPP, S. (1991) Profiles in giftedness: Fictional portraits of intelligent and gifted children. In R.M. Milgram (Ed.) *Counseling Gifted and Talented Children: A Guide for Teachers, Counselors and Parents*. Norwood, NJ: Ablex Publishing Company.

KRAFT, K. (1988) *Zen: Tradition and Transition*. London: Rider.

LAING, R.D. (1986) *Wisdom, Madness and Folly: The Making of a Psychiatrist*. London: Papermac.

LANDAU, E.D., Epstein, S.L. and Stone, A.P. (Eds) (1972) *Child Development Through Literature*. Englewood Cliffs, NJ: Prentice-Hall.

LESTER, D. (1987) Psychology and literature. *Psychology: A Quarterly Journal of Human Behaviour, 24*(1–2), 25–27.

LESTER, D. (1991) The study of suicidal lives. *Suicide and Life-Threatening Behavior, 21*, 164–173.

LE UNES, A. (1974) Psychology thrillers revisited. A tentative list of master thrillers. *American Psychologist, 29*, 211–213.

LEVIN, M.J. (1979) *Psychology. A Biographical Approach*. New York: McGraw-Hill.

LINDZEY, G. (Ed.) (1980) *A History of Psychology in Autobiography*. Oxford: W.H. Freeman.

LURIA, A.R. (1979) *The Making of Mind: A Personal Account of Soviet Psychology*. Cambridge, Mass: Harvard University Press.

McCOLLOM, I.N. (1971) Psychological thrillers: psychology books students read when given freedom of choice. *American Psychologist, 26*, 921–927.

McCOLLOM, I.N. (1973) Let's get them to read psychology books. *Newsletter of the American Psychological Association Division on the Teaching of Psychology*, December.

McCOLLOM, I.N. (1975) Readings readers recommend. *Teaching of Psychology, 2,* 42.

McMAHON, D.F. (1989) The psychological significance of science fiction. *Psychoanalytic Review, 76,* 282–295.

MAGILL, F.N. (Ed.) (1979) *Survey of Science Fiction Literature.* Five vols. Englewood Cliffs, NJ: Salem Press.

MARCUS, S. (1984) *Sigmund Freud and the Culture of Psychoanalysis.* London: George Allen & Unwin.

MARROW, A.J. (1968) *The Practical Theorist. The Life and Work of Kurt Lewin.* New York: Teachers College Press.

MAZZIOTTA, J.C., Phelps, M.E. and Kuhl, D.E. (1982) Tomographic mapping of human cerebral metabolism. *Neurology, 32,* 921–937.

MEAD, M. (1973) *Blackberry Winter: My Earlier Years.* London: Angus & Robertson.

MELVIN, K.B., BRODSKY, S.L. and FOWLER, R.D.Jr (Eds) (1977) *Psy Fi One: An Anthology in Science Fiction.* New York: Random House.

MODELL, J. (1984) *Ruth Benedict: Patterns of a Life.* London: Chatto & Windus/Hogarth Press.

MYERS, G. (1986) *William James: His Life and Thought.* New Haven: Yale University Press.

NAPOLETANO, M.A. (1988) Teaching adolescent psychology using popular song lyrics. *Psychological Reports, 62,* 975–978.

NICHOLLS, P. (Ed.) (1976) *Science Fiction at Large.* London: Gollancz.

NICHOLLS, P. (Ed.) (1982) *The Science in Science Fiction.* London: Michael Joseph.

NISBETT, A. (1976) *Konrad Lorenz.* London: Dent.

NIXON, L.L. and WEAR, D. (1991) 'Home Burial' and 'Dead Baby': Poetic perspectives in medical education. *Omega: Journal of Death and Dying, 23,* 241–247.

ORWELL, G. (1948) *1984.* Harmondsworth: Penguin.

OSTBYE, T. and ROCHON, J. (1993) An early 'clinical trial' as a teaching exercise: the Book of Daniel 1.1–15 (1.1–20). *Medical Education, 27,* 97–101.

OWEN, A.R.F. (1971) *Hysteria, Hypnosis and Healing: The Work of J.M. Charcot.* London: Dennis Dobson.

PANSHIN, A. and PANSHIN, C. (1989) *The World Beyond the Hill: Science Fiction and the Quest for Transcendence.* Los Angeles: Jeremy P. Tarcher Inc.

PEARSON, A. (1977) More firsthand accounts of coping with handicap, illness and deviance. *Psychology Teaching, 5,* 145–148.

PEARSON, A. (1980) Summarized firsthand accounts of coping with life crises and handicap. *Psychology Teaching, 8,* 10–21.

PEARSON, K. (1914–1930) *The Life, Letters and Labours of Francis Galton.* Cambridge: CUP.

PETERS, V.H. (1985) *Anna Freud: A Life Dedicated to Children.* London: Weidenfeld & Nicholson.

PITT-AIKENS, T. and ELLIS, A.T. (1990) *Loss of the Good*

Authority. The Cause of Delinquency. Harmondsworth:
Penguin.
POLYSON, J. (1985) Students' peak experiences: A written
exercise. *Teaching of Psychology, 12,* 211–213.
POTTER, J., STRINGER, P. and WEATHERELL, M. (1984)
Social Text and Context: Literature and Social Psychology.
London: Routledge and Kegan Paul.
PRINGLE, D. (1985) *Science Fiction: The 100 Best Novels.*
London: Xanadu.
QUINN, S. (1988) *A Mind of Her Own: The Life of Karen Horney.*
London: Macmillan.
RADFORD, J. (1980) Introduction. In J. Radford and D. Rose
(Eds) *The Teaching of Psychology: Method, Content and
Context.* Chichester: Wiley.
RADFORD, J. (1985) Psychology and science fiction. *Bulletin
of The British Psychological Society, 38,* 113–115.
RADFORD, J. (1988) Sherlock Holmes and the history of
psychology. *The Psychologist, 1*(4), 143–146.
RADFORD, J. (1990) The intelligence of Sherlock Holmes.
*Changes: An International Journal of Psychology and
Psychotherapy, 8,* 90–95.
RADFORD, J. and KIRBY, R. (Eds) (1973) *Psy Fi: The First
Volume of Psychological Science Fiction.* Unpublished.
RADFORD, J. and SMITH, D. (Eds) (1991) *Uses of Literature in
Understanding and Teaching Psychology.* Occasional papers
of the Group of Teachers of Psychology Vol 11. Leicester:
British Psychological Society.
READ, S. (1989) *Only for a Fortnight: My Life in a Locked
Ward.* London: Bloomsbury.
REED, E.S. (1989) *James J. Gibson and the Psychology of
Perception.* New Haven: Yale University Press.
REICH, I.O. (1969) *Wilhelm Reich.* London: Elek.
REICH, W. (1988) *Passion in Youth: An Autobiography 1897–
1922.* London: Penguin.
RICKMAN, H.P. (1979) *Wilhelm Dilthey: Pioneer of the Human
Studies.* London: Paul Elek.
RIDGWAY, J. and BENJAMIN, M. (1987) *PsiFi: Psychological
Theories and Science Fictions.* Leicester: BPS Books (The
British Psychological Society).
RIPPERE, V. (1976) First hand accounts of coping with an ill,
handicapped or deviant child. A short bibliography for use
in psychology teaching. *Psychology Teaching, 4,* 158–159.
RIPPERE, V. (1977) Personal accounts of mental disorder and
its treatment: a short bibliography for use in psychology
teaching. *Psychology Teaching, 5,* 26–29.
RIPPERE, V. (1978) Experience of illness, disability and
treatment: a short bibliography of personal accounts for
use in psychology teaching. *Psychology Teaching, 6,* 57–66.
RIPPERE, V. (1979a) Training and practice in the helping
professions. A short bibliography of personal accounts for
use in psychology teaching. *Psychology Teaching, 7,* 23–27.
RIPPERE, V. (1979b) Bereavement, grief and mourning. A

short bibliography of personal accounts for use in psychology teaching. *Psychology Teaching, 7*, 143–146.

RIPPERE, V. (1980) Working with children. A short bibliography of personal accounts for use in psychology teaching. *Psychology Teaching, 8*, 35–39.

ROSE, D. and RADFORD, J. (1981) The use of literature in teaching psychology. *Bulletin of The British Psychological Society, 34*, 453–455.

RUBIN, D.C. (Ed.) (1986) *Autobiographical Memory*. Cambridge: Cambridge University Press.

RUBINS, J.K. (1978) *Karen Horney: Gentle Rebel of Psychoanalysis*. New York: Dial.

SACHS, H. (1945) *Freud, Master and Friend*. London: Imago.

SACKS, O. (1984) *A Leg to Stand On*. London: Duckworth.

SACKS, O. (1985) *The Man who Mistook his Wife for a Hat*. London: Duckworth.

SAEGER, W. (1977) Science fiction as a teaching tool in social and environmental psychology. *Psychology Teaching, 5*, 154–157.

SAEGER, W. (1979) Literature and learning: the art of the state. *Psychology Teaching, 7*, 3–12.

SARASON, S.B. (1988) *The Making of an American Psychologist: An Autobiography*. San Francisco: Jossey-Bass.

SCHELLENBERG, J.A. (1978) *Masters of Social Psychology: Freud, Mead, Lewin and Skinner*. New York: Oxford University Press.

SCHROEDER, C., VAN GRUNDY, J. and HUSBAND, R.W. (Eds) (1943) *Psychology Through Literature*. New York: Oxford University Press.

SEAGOE, M.V. (1975) *Terman and the Gifted*. Los Altos, CA: William Kaufmann Inc.

SEBEOK, T.A. and UMIKER-SEBEOK, J. (1979) 'You know my method': A juxtaposition of Charles S. Pierce and Sherlock Holmes. *Semiotica, 26*, 203–250.

SEDERBERG, P.V. and SEDERBERG, N.B. (1975) Transmitting the non transmissible. The function of literature in pursuit of social knowledge. *Philosophy and Phenomenological Research, 36*, 173.

SHARAF, M. (1983) *Fury on Earth: A Biography of Wilhelm Reich*. London: Andre Deutsch.

SHEPHERD, M. (1985) *Sherlock Holmes and the Case of Dr. Freud*. London: Tavistock.

SKINNER, B.F. (1948) *Walden Two*. New York: Collier Macmillan.

SKINNER, B.F. (1975) *Particulars of my Life*. New York: New York University Press.

SKINNER, B.F. (1975) *The Shaping of a Behaviourist*. New York: New York University Press.

SKINNER, B.F. (1985) *A Matter of Consequences*. New York: New York University Press.

SMITH, N.D. (Ed.) (1982) *Philosophers Look at Science Fiction*. Chicago: Nelson-Hall.

SNO, H.N., LINZSEN, D.H. and DE JONGHE, F. (1992) Art imitates life: *Deja vu* experiences in prose and poetry. *British Journal of Psychiatry, 160,* 511–518.

SPINRAD, N. (1990) *Science Fiction in the Real World.* Carbondale and Edwardsville: Southern Illinois University Press.

STAFFORD, C.H. (1986) A biblical approach to anger management training. *Journal of Psychology and Christianity, 5*(4), 5–11.

STONE, A.A. and STONE, S.S. (Eds) (1966) *The Abnormal Personality Through Literature.* Englewood Cliffs, NJ: Prentice-Hall.

SULLOWAY, F.J. (1979) *Freud, Biologist of the Mind.* New York: Basic Books.

SUTHERLAND, N.S. (1987) *Breakdown: A Personal Crisis and a Medical Dilemma,* 2nd edn. London: Weidenfeld & Nicholson.

SWAIN, R. (1977) Psychological thrillers: An Irish list. *Bulletin of The British Psychological Society, 30,* 135–137.

VANDE KEMP, H. (1980) Teaching psychology through the case study method. *Teaching of Psychology, 7,* 38–40.

WEATHERELL, M., POTTER, J. and STRINGER, P. (1983) Psychology, literature and texts. *Bulletin of The British Psychological Society, 36,* 377–379.

WEHR, G. (1985, trans. 1987) *Jung: A Biography.* Boston: Shambhala.

WERTSCH, J.V. (1985) *Vygotsky and the Social Formation of Mind.* Cambridge, Mass.: Harvard University Press.

WHITE, R.W. (1952) *Lives in Progress. A Study of the Natural Growth of Personality.* New York: Holt, Rinehart and Winston (3rd edn, 1975).

WHITE, R.W. (1974) Teaching personality through the histories. *Teaching of Psychology, 1,* 69–71.

WIGODER, D. (1987) *Images of Destruction.* London: Kegan Paul.

WILLIAMS, M.H. and WADDELL, M. (1991) *The Chamber of Maiden Thought: Literary Origins of the Psychoanalytic Model of the Mind.* London: Tavistock / Routledge.

WINGROVE, D. (Ed.) (1984) *The Science Fiction Sourcebook.* New York: Van Nostrand.

WOLF, M.A. (1987) Human development, gerontology and self-development throught the writings of May Sarton. *Educational Gerontology, 13*(4), 289–295.

WRIGHT, N. (1988) *Mrs. Klein.* London: Walker Books.

WRIGHTSMAN, L.S. (1981) Personal documents as data: conceptualizing adult personality development. *Personality and Social Psychology Bulletin, 7*(3), 367–385.

YOUNG-BRUEHL, E. (1988) *Anna Freud: A Biography.* New York: Summit Books.

THE LITERATURE ON THE TEACHING OF PSYCHOLOGY

David Rose and Deana Smith

❏ *the main literature sources • literature from other countries • areas of development in the literature • specific psychology teaching contexts*

The following pages contain an update of our earlier listings of the literature on the teaching of psychology (Rose, 1984; Rose and Smith, 1989). However, this literature has now become so voluminous that an exhaustive list is no longer possible within a chapter of reasonable length. We have revised our objectives accordingly. First and foremost we have sought to provide a guide to the main literature sources: a way into the literature for those new to the field of psychology teaching. Secondly, we have tried to highlight particular areas of growth and development within this literature. Finally, and providing continuity with our earlier chapters, we have extended our listing of references relevant to particular teaching contexts.

There are some categories of literature we have excluded from the present chapter. For example, we have omitted articles concerned with counselling. As we observed in the last edition of this volume, although many of these are relevant to the teaching of psychology, they constitute a much wider literature which spans many disciplines and merits its own annotated bibliography. We are not aware of the existence of such a document but hope the gap will be filled in due course. However, we do make mention of training in counselling psychology later in this chapter. On this occasion, and unlike our chapter in the last edition of this volume, we have omitted articles concerned with teaching psychology to non-psychologists (nurses, teachers, etc.). There has been a significant increase in this area of the literature and this has been recognized in the present volume by creating a new chapter devoted to this aspect of the teaching of psychology.

THE MAIN LITERATURE SOURCES

For those joining the ranks of psychology teachers for the first time, the nature and range of relevant literature will be apparent from an examination of a relatively small number of sources.

Books

Although extensive, the literature on the teaching of psychology includes few books. The first book published in the UK devoted entirely to the teaching of psychology was: RADFORD, J. and ROSE, D. (1980) *The Teaching of Psychology. Method, Content and Context.* Chichester: John Wiley & Sons. Within its 17 chapters are to be found discussions of methods of teaching psychology (conventional, experiential, experimental and alternative), teaching different areas of psychology (biological, cognitive, social, developmental, practical psychology and statistics, and integrative and ethical issues) and teaching psychology in various contexts (academic, liberal sciences, medical, social work, educational, industrial, commercial and public service, and Third World).

A rather wider ranging view of the teaching of psychology is taken in: RADFORD, J. and ROSE, D. (Eds) (1989) *A Liberal Science. Psychology Education Past, Present and Future.* Milton Keynes: Society for Research into Higher Education and Open University Press. Here the history of teaching psychology, its present status as seen by eight contributing authors, and its future prospects are reviewed. The book's general thesis is that psychology, as a discipline, is a particularly good basis for an education that is of both practical and public use as well as being of personal value.

Practical guidance, tips and ideas for teachers at all levels are to be found in: ROSE, D. and RADFORD, J. (Eds) (1984) *Teaching Psychology. Information and Resources.* Leicester: BPS Books and: THE BRITISH PSYCHOLOGICAL SOCIETY (1990) *Teaching Psychology. A Handbook of Resources.* Leicester: BPS Books. These are earlier editions of the present book.

There is one further book on teaching psychology currently available and aimed at the UK market: HARTLEY, J. and McKEACHIE, W.J. (Eds) (1990) *Teaching Psychology. A Handbook.* Hillsdale, NJ: Lawrence Erlbaum Associates. This book contains 64 articles taken from the American Psychological Association's journal *Teaching of Psychology.* The selection is divided into 12 sections, each prefaced by an introduction. In making some of the American literature more accessible to the British market, this is a welcome addition to the still small selection of books on the teaching of psychology.

Journals and Occasional Papers

The main journal sources of literature on the teaching of psychology are the publications of The British Psychological Society (BPS) Special Group of Teachers of Psychology and the Association for the Teaching of Psychology (ATP).

Since 1987 the BPS Group of Teachers of Psychology has published 13 sets of Occasional Papers on various aspects of teaching psychology, all but two of which are relevant to our present interests. More recently (March 1992) the BPS Group of Teachers of Psychology has launched *Psychology Teaching Review*. At the time of writing, this journal is still in its infancy (Volume 2 number 1 has just appeared), but it promises to be a major source of relevant material on all aspects of psychology teaching.

Psychology Teaching, the journal of the ATP, has a much longer, if occasionally interrupted history (beginning in May 1973). In recent years it has focused almost exclusively on the teaching of psychology at pre-college level (A-level, A/O-level, GCE/GCSE). Again it merits the attention of anyone wanting to keep up-to-date with the literature on the teaching of psychology.

As well as the journals and occasional papers mentioned above, the BPS house journal, *The Psychologist*, carries teaching-related articles and, from time to time, the BPS publishes reports, statements and discussion documents on particular aspects of psychology teaching.

Articles from all these sources are listed under the appropriate teaching context headings later in this chapter.

Literature From Other Countries

In earlier versions of this chapter (Rose, 1984; Rose and Smith, 1990) we have mentioned the sizeable American literature on the teaching of psychology. This is a rich resource for teachers in the UK, as Hartley and McKeachie have acknowledged in preparing their handbook (see earlier). For those wishing to find additional US sources, the following annotated bibliographies will be useful:

DANIEL, R.S. (1981) Annotated bibliography on the teaching of psychology: 1980. *Teaching of Psychology, 8*(4), 249–253.

MOSLEY, C.E. and DANIEL, R.S. (1982) Annotated bibliography on the teaching of psychology: 1981. *Teaching of Psychology, 9*(4), 250–254.

BERRY, K.A. and DANIEL, R.S. (1985) Annotated bibliography on the teaching of psychology: 1984. *Teaching of Psychology, 12*(4), 231–236.

WISE, P.S. and FULKERSON, F.E. (1986) Annotated bibliography on the teaching of psychology: 1985. *Teaching of Psychology, 13*(4), 223–227.

FULKERSON, F.E., WISE, P.S. and ANCELET, B.A. (1988) Annotated bibliography on the teaching of psychology: 1987. *Teaching of Psychology, 15*(4), 215–222.

FULKERSON, F.E. and WISE, P.S. (1990) Annotated bibliography on the teaching of psychology: 1989. *Teaching of Psychology, 17*(4), 264–272.

WISE, P.S. and FULKERSON, F.E. (1991) Annotated bibliography on the teaching of psychology: 1990. *Teaching of Psychology, 18*(4), 252–260.

For those prepared to hunt for it there is also some literature on the teaching of psychology in Australia, New Zealand and Japan, but particularly welcome in the UK literature is evidence of growing interest in the teaching of psychology elsewhere in Europe. The BPS Special Group of Teachers of Psychology held a symposium entitled 'European Perspectives in Teaching Psychology' during the Society's Annual Conference in April 1992. A brief report of the symposium, compiled by John Radford, is to be found in *Psychology Teaching Review* (1992), *1*(2), 82–86. Also of interest are:

McPHERSON, F.M. (1988) Psychologists and the EEC. Background to the draft directive on the recognition of qualifications. *The Psychologist, 1*(9), 353–355.

McPHERSON, F.M. (1989) Psychologists and the EEC (II). The provisions of the directive on the recognition of qualifications. *The Psychologist, 12*(9), 382–383.

European developments in education and training generally will have major implications for the teaching of psychology in coming years and the 'European perspective', as defined by John Radford, is likely to represent a rapidly expanding area of the literature on the teaching of psychology.

AREAS OF DEVELOPMENT IN THE LITERATURE

Since we last reviewed the literature on the teaching of psychology there have been some areas of notably increased activity.

Perhaps the most prominent expansion has been in the number of publications on the use of computers in teaching psychology. This is not a new area of literature, of course. Chapters devoted to it are to be found in both the earlier editions of the present volume. Also for many years the *Bulletin of The British Psychological Society* had a regular 'Software Review' section, which became the 'Computer Column' when the *Bulletin* was incorporated into *The Psychologist* in 1988. This column has reviewed numerous software packages for use in the teaching of psychology. However, in 1990, a journal appeared devoted entirely to discussion of the use of computers in psychology teaching. *Psychology Software News* is produced by the Computers in Teaching Initiative (CTI) Centre for Psychology at the University of York. This contains articles, software and book reviews, letters and general comment. We have not listed all the articles and software reviews which have appeared in *Psychology Software News*, but this thrice-yearly publication, together with the annual *Directory of Psychology Software*, also produced by the CTI, is clearly a 'must' for anyone wanting to keep up-to-date with the use of computers in psychology teaching (see also chapter by Colbourn in this volume). Further information is available from the editors:

Nick Hammond and Annie Trapp
Psychology Software News
Department of Psychology
University of York
York YO1 5DD

Health psychology has been one of the most exciting areas of development within psychology in recent years, and we are now beginning to see articles about how health psychology should be taught. Consequently, we have added a specific health psychology context to the next section of this chapter. Also included in the next section are articles on training in counselling psychology, another area of significant growth within psychology (see the special issue of *The Psychologist*, 1990, *13*(12)).

A final area of literature meriting special mention is that of continuing professional development. Post-vocational training has for a long time been a concern within clinical, educational and occupational psychology, but the introduction of chartering by the BPS and the quality control that it implies, has given the whole issue of continuing professional development additional and wider impetus. It is gratifying to see the literature on this beginning to extend beyond BPS Division newsletters into more generally available publications. For example, there has recently been a special issue of *The Psychologist* concerned with continuing professional development (1992, *5*(11)), but see also Hayes in *The Psychologist* (1990, *3*(3)). Facilitating and supporting continuing professional development is obviously an important area of psychology teaching and an area of the literature where we expect to see further developments. In recognition of this we have added continuing professional development as a specific teaching context in the next section of this chapter. This listing is far from comprehensive, but will give the reader an introduction to the area.

Finally, since the last edition of *Teaching Psychology*, a new qualification has been launched by The British Psychological Society: a Diploma in the Teaching of Psychology. Further information about this important development for teachers of psychology is to be found in HAYES, N., LUNT, I. and NEWSTEAD, S.E. (1990) A BPS teaching diploma. *The Psychologist*, *3*(8), 371.

SPECIFIC PSYCHOLOGY TEACHING CONTEXTS

Here we list references relevant to teaching psychology in particular contexts: pre-college, undergraduate, postgraduate, educational, clinical, occupational, health, counselling and continuing professional development. Where a reference has relevance to several contexts we have placed it under the heading to which it is primarily relevant, but marked it with an asterisk. Our list also contains some references to newsletters of BPS Sections, Special Groups and Divisions. These may be consulted by anyone in the BPS library at Senate House, Malet Street, London WC1 7HU and can be obtained through inter-library loan. The Occasional Papers are available from the BPS at a cost of £5.00 each. On this occasion we list references from 1986 onwards but would urge readers to refer to our earlier chapters (Rose, 1984; Rose and Smith 1990) if they wish to trace the literature beyond that.

Pre-college   GCSE, A-level and other pre-degree psychology courses

THE BRITISH PSYCHOLOGICAL SOCIETY (1987) *Appropriate Qualifications for Staff Intending to Teach Psychology at GCSE Level.* Leicester: BPS.

THE BRITISH PSYCHOLOGICAL SOCIETY (1988) A- and AS-level subjects for a degree in psychology and a note on degree courses. Letter issued by the Executive Secretary of The British Psychological Society. Available from the BPS.

THE BRITISH PSYCHOLOGICAL SOCIETY/COMMITTEE OF THE ASSOCIATION FOR THE TEACHING OF PSYCHOLOGY (1988) Psychology as a secondary examination subject. *The British Psychological Society Group of Teachers of Psychology Newsletter*, 4, April, 5–9.

THE BRITISH PSYCHOLOGICAL SOCIETY (1992) *The future of A level psychology.* Available from the BPS.

DAVIES, G. (1991) Ethical issues in A, AS and GCSE psychology. In L. Jones (Ed.) *The Future of A-Level Psychology.* The British Psychological Society Group of Teachers of Psychology Occasional Papers, No.13, 17–20.

GAMMON, J. (1991) A level and AS psychology: Future directions. In L. Jones (Ed.) *The Future of A-Level Psychology.* The British Psychological Society Group of Teachers of Psychology Occasional Papers, No.13, 7–9.

GROSS, R. (1988) Making connections in the A.E.B. 'A' level psychology syllabus. *Psychology Teaching*, Part 1, 12–19.

HAYES, N. (1987) The role of GCSE psychology. *Bulletin of The British Psychological Society*, 40, 63–64.

HAYES, N., LUNT, I. and NEWSTEAD, S.E. (1990) A BPS teaching diploma. *The Psychologist*, 3(8), 371.

HIGGINS, L. (1989) Psychology in secondary and further education. In J. Radford and D. Rose (Eds) *A Liberal Science: Psychology Education Past, Present and Future.* Milton Keynes: Society for Research into Higher Education and Open University Press.

HUMPHREYS, P. (1991) The interface between A-level psychology and higher education courses. In L. Jones (Ed.) *The Future of A-Level Psychology.* The British Psychological Society Group of Teachers of Psychology Occasional Papers, No.13, 4–6.

JONES, L. (1991) *The Future of A-Level Psychology.* The British Psychological Society Group of Teachers of Psychology Occasional Papers, No.13.

KIRKWOOD, J. (1988) G.C.S.E. – Already time for change. *Psychology Teaching,* Part 1, 20–23.

NEWSTEAD, S. (1990) Chartered status and teachers of psychology. *The Psychologist,* 3(11), 513–514. *

RADFORD, J. (1988) The 'teaching subject' face. In H.J. Wright and J. Radford (Eds) *The Several Faces of Educational Psychology.* The British Psychological Society Group of Teachers of Psychology Occasional Papers, No.2, 8–12.

Undergraduate ARCHER, J. and GLENN, S. (1989) Developmental psychology practicals. In P. Wright (Ed.) *Practical Classes in Psychology.* The British Psychological Society Group of Teachers of Psychology Occasional Papers, No.8, 28–31.

ARNOLD, J. and NEWSTEAD, S. (1989) Working with psychology. In J. Radford and D. Rose (Eds) *A Liberal Science: Psychology Education Past, Present and Future.* Milton Keynes: Society for Research into Higher Education and Open University Press.

ARNOLD, J., NEWSTEAD, S.E., DONALDSON, M.L., REID, F.J.M. and DENNIS, I. (1987) Skills development in undergraduate psychology courses. *Bulletin of The British Psychological Society,* 40, 469–472.

ATKINSON, N. (1991) Psychology students: conceptions, aims and levels of understanding. In J. Radford (Ed.) *The Choice of Psychology.* The British Psychological Society Group of Teachers of Psychology Occasional Papers, No.12, 20–21.

BAYNE, R. (1991) Psychological types and the question "Why choose psychology?" In J. Radford (Ed.) *The Choice of Psychology.* The British Psychological Society Group of Teachers of Psychology Occasional Papers, No.12, 30–34.

BEAUMONT, J.G. (1990) Registration and the undergraduate degree. In F.N. Watts (Ed.) *The Undergraduate Curriculum in Psychology.* The British Psychological Society Group of Teachers of Psychology Occasional Papers, No.9, 30–34.

THE BRITISH PSYCHOLOGICAL SOCIETY (1988) *The Future of the Psychological Sciences.* A report prepared for the Scientific Affairs Board. Available from the BPS. *

BURTON, A. (1990) Literacy skills and the psychology student. *The Psychologist,* 3(10), 441–443.

BUSHNELL, I.W.R. and MULLIN, J.T. (1986) Automated laboratory classes in psychology. *Bulletin of The British Psychological Society,* 39, 261–262.

CONNOLLY, K.J. and SMITH, P.K. (1986) What makes a 'good' degree: Variations between different departments. *Bulletin of The British Psychological Society,* 39, 48–51.

CRAWSHAW, M. (1991) Integrating the teaching of occupational psychology into the undergraduate curriculum. In S.E. Newstead (Ed.) *Teaching Occupational Psychology:*

Issues Arising at Pre-Masters Level. The British Psychological Society Group of Teachers of Psychology Occasional Papers, No.10, 4–7. *

CUTHBERT, K. (1992) Can we teach social skills within the undergraduate psychology curriculum? An approach using experimental exercises and promoting reflective awareness. *Psychology Teaching Review*, 1(2), 57–65.

DE ALBERDI, M. and DE ALBERDI, L. (1988) Putting psychology to work: A view of the future of the first degree from industry/commerce. In J. Radford (Ed.) *The Future of the First Degree.* The British Psychological Society Group of Teachers of Psychology Occasional Papers, No.4, 6–12.

FLETCHER, C. (1989) Putting psychology to work. In J. Radford and D. Rose (Eds) *A Liberal Science: Psychology Education Past, Present and Future.* Milton Keynes: Society for Research into Higher Education and Open University Press.*

FLETCHER, C., ROSE, D. and RADFORD, J. (1991) Employers' perceptions of psychology graduates. *The Psychologist*, 4(10), 434–437.

FOOT, H. and GAMMON, J. (1990) A-level psychology and first year undergraduate courses. *The Psychologist*, 3(4), 153–156. *

GALE, A. (1988) Memoirs of an external examiner. In S.E. Newstead (Ed.) *External Examining on Undergraduate Psychology Degrees.* The British Psychological Society Group of Teachers in Psychology Occasional Papers, No.6, 30–38.

GALE, A. (1989) Psychology as God's gift: How ungrateful can you be? A critical evaluation of the psychology degree and its failings. In J. Radford and D. Rose (Eds) *A Liberal Science: Psychology Education Past, Present and Future.* Milton Keynes: Society for Research into Higher Education and Open University Press.

GALE, A. (1990) Applying psychology to the psychology degree: Pass with first class honours, or miserable failure? *The Psychologist*, 3(11), 483–488.

GALE, A. (1990) Psychology as God's gift. In F.N. Watts (Ed.) *The Undergraduate Curriculum in Psychology.* The British Psychological Society Group of Teachers of Psychology Occasional Papers, No.9, 7–11.

HARTLEY, J. and McKEACHIE, W.J. (Eds) (1990) *Handbook for the Teaching of Psychology.* Hillsdale, NJ: Erlbaum. *

HARTLEY, J. and TRUEMAN, M. (1992) Some observations on using journal articles in the teaching of psychology. *Psychology Teaching Review*, 1(1), 46–51.

HAYES, N. (1989) The skills acquired in psychology degrees. *The Psychologist*, 2(6), 238–39.

JEEVES, M.A. (1990) The impact of recent scientific developments on the curriculum. In F.N. Watts (Ed.) *The Undergraduate Curriculum in Psychology.* The British Psychological Society Group of Teachers of Psychology Occasional Papers, No.9, 12–16.

KAGAN, C. (1989) Personal and social skills. In J. Radford and D. Rose (Eds) *A Liberal Science: Psychology Education Past, Present and Future.* Milton Keynes: Society for Research into Higher Education and Open University Press. *

KORNBROT, D.E. (1987) Science and psychology degree performance. *Bulletin of The British Psychological Society, 40,* 409–417.

LEE, M.P. and SOPER, J.B. (1986) Using spreadsheets to teach statistics in psychology. *Bulletin of The British Psychological Society,* 39, 365–367.

LEGGE, D. (1987) Modelling a seamless robe. *Bulletin of The British Psychological Society, 40,* 241–249. *

LEGGE, D. (1989) Psychology at degree level. In J. Radford and D. Rose (Eds) *A Liberal Science: Education in Psychology Past, Present and Future.* Milton Keynes: Society for Research into Higher Education and Open University Press.

McGUIRE, R.J. (1990) The needs of postgraduate applied trainees. In F.N. Watts (Ed.) *The Undergraduate Curriculum in Psychology.* The British Psychological Society Group of Teachers of Psychology Occasional Papers, No.9, 24–29. *

MACLEOD, H. (1989) The computer as catalyst in practical work. In P. Wright (Ed.) *Practical Classes in Psychology.* The British Psychological Society Group of Teachers of Psychology Occasional Papers, No.8, 6–13.

MARGOLIS, J., MANICAS, P.T., HARRE, R. and SECORD, P.F. (1986) *Psychology: Designing the Discipline.* Oxford: Blackwell.*

MARSHALL, H. and NICHOLSON, P. (1991) Why choose psychology? Mature and other students' accounts at graduation. In J. Radford (Ed.) *The Choice of Psychology.* The British Psychological Society Group of Teachers of Psychology Occasional Papers, No.12, 22–29.

MORRIS, P. (1991) How and why applicants choose to study psychology at university. In J. Radford (Ed.) *The Choice of Psychology.* The British Psychological Society Group of Teachers of Psychology Occasional Papers, No.12, 6–8.

MORRIS, P.E., CHENG, D. and SMITH, H. (1992) How and why applicants choose to study psychology at university. *The Psychologist,* 5(6), 247–251.

MULLIN, J.T. and BUSHNELL, L.W.R. (1989) An application of computers to psychology laboratory teaching. In P. Wright (Ed.) *Practical Classes in Psychology.* The British Psychological Society Group of Teachers of Psychology Occasional Papers, No.8, 14–20.

MURPHY, R. (1988) The role of external examiners in improving assessment. In S.E. Newstead (Ed.) *External Examining on Undergraduate Psychology Degrees.* The British Psychological Society Group of Teachers of Psychology Occasional Papers, No.6, 39–44.

NEWSTEAD, S.E. (1988) Skills teaching in undergraduate psychology degrees. In J. Radford (Ed.) *The Future of the First Degree.* The British Psychological Society Group of Teachers of Psychology Occasional Papers, No.4, 14–17.

NEWSTEAD, S.E. (1988) (Ed.) *External Examining on Under-graduate Psychology Degrees.* The British Psychological Society Group of Teachers of Psychology Occasional Papers, No.6.
NEWSTEAD, S.E. (1988) Who needs external examiners? In S.E. Newstead (Ed.) *External Examining on Undergraduate Psychology Degrees.* The British Psychological Society Group of Teachers of Psychology Occasional Papers, No.6, 6–12.
NEWSTEAD, S.E. (1989) Staff evaluation in American universities. *The Psychologist, 2*(3), 95–97. *
NEWSTEAD, S.E. (1989) Guidelines for external examiners on undergraduate psychology degrees. *The Psychologist, 2* (12), 533.
NEWSTEAD, S.E. (1992) The Society: policies on two-year degrees. *The Psychologist, 5*(8), 376.
NEWSTEAD, S.E. (1990) Teaching transferable skills. In F.N. Watts (Ed.) *The Undergraduate Curriculum in Psychology.* The British Psychological Society Group of Teachers of Psychology Occasional Papers, No.9, 17–23.
PHILLIPS, K. (1987) Information and resource centre for teaching psychology involving animals. *The British Psychological Society Psychobiology Section Newsletter*, No.8, 13–14. *
PHILLIPS, K. (1989) Practical classes in psychobiology: why, when and how? In P. Wright (Ed.) *Practical Classes in Psychology.* The British Psychological Society Group of Teachers of Psychology Occasional Papers, No.8, 21–27.
RAAHEIM, A. (1991) Why choose psychology? Some results from a study among new psychology students at the University of Bergen, autumn 1991. In J. Radford (Ed.) *The Choice of Psychology.* The British Psychological Society Group of Teachers of Psychology Occasional Papers, No.12, 38–46.
RADFORD, J. (1987) An education in psychology. *Bulletin of The British Psychological Society, 40*, 282–289.
RADFORD, J. (1988) The other half. In J. Radford (Ed.) *The Future of the First Degree.* The British Psychological Society Group of Teachers of Psychology Occasional Papers, No.4, 18–21.
RADFORD, J. (1991) (Ed.) *The Choice of Psychology.* The British Psychological Society Group of Teachers of Psychology Occasional Papers, No.12.
RADFORD, J. (1991) First-year honours students' choice of psychology. In J. Radford (Ed.) *The Choice of Psychology.* The British Psychological Society Group of Teachers of Psychology Occasional Papers, No.12, 14–19.
RADFORD, J. (1992) The undergraduate curriculum in psychology. *The Psychologist, 5*(6), 273–276.
RICHARDSON, J.T.E. (1989) Cognitive skills and psychology education. In J. Radford and D. Rose (Eds) *A Liberal Science: Psychology Education Past, Present and Future.* Milton Keynes: Society for Research into Higher Education and Open University Press.

ROSE, D. (1988) Psychology graduates and employment: An image problem. In J. Radford (Ed.) *The Future of the First Degree*. The British Psychological Society Group of Teachers of Psychology Occasional Papers, No.4, 22–27.

ROSE, D. and RADFORD, J. (1986) The unemployment of psychology graduates. *Bulletin of The British Psychological Society*, *39*, 451–456.

SHILLITO-CLARKE, C. (1987) Experiential interpersonal skills in the psychology curriculum. "An ounce of practice is worth a pound of theory". *The British Psychological Society Counselling Psychology Section Review*, 2(1), 6–10.

SMITH, P.K. (1990) The distribution of psychology degree classes in the UK. *The Psychologist*, 3(4), 147–152.

SUGARMAN, L. (1987) Interpersonal skills training in a psychology curriculum: Account of an experiment and a compromise. *The British Psychological Society Counselling Psychology Section Review*, 2(2), 8–13.

WARREN PIPER, D. (1988) Good practice for external examiners. In S.E. Newstead (Ed.) *External Examining on Undergraduate Psychology Degrees*. The British Psychological Society Group of Teachers of Psychology Occasional Papers, No.6, 13–29.

WATTS, F.N. (Ed.) (1990) *The Undergraduate Curriculum*. The British Psychological Society Group of Teachers of Psychology Occasional Papers, No.9.

WEST, M. (1991) Bad faith and bad practice: Token occupational psychology in the undergraduate degree. In S.E. Newstead (Ed.) *Teaching Occupational Psychology: Issues Arising at Pre-Masters Level*. The British Psychological Society Group of Teachers of Psychology Occasional Papers, No.10, 8–14. *

WRIGHT, P. (Ed.) (1989) *Practical Classes in Psychology*. The British Psychological Society Group of Teachers of Psychology Occasional Papers, No.8.

Postgraduate MPhil, PhD and taught MSc courses other than clinical, educational, occupational, health and counselling psychology

BOYLE, M., MAY, B., WOLFENDALE, S. and BAKER, M. (1990) Towards training in applied psychology? An experiment in integrated teaching. *The British Psychological Society Division of Educational and Child Psychology Newsletter*, *38*, 31–33.

THE BRITISH PSYCHOLOGICAL SOCIETY (1987) Postgraduate qualifications by courses in psychology. Booklet issued by and available from the BPS.

THE BRITISH PSYCHOLOGICAL SOCIETY (1987) Code of practice on the supervision, preparation and examination of doctoral theses in departments of psychology. *Bulletin of The British Psychological Society*, 40, 250–254.

BROMLEY, D. (1992) Getting a doctorate. *The Psychologist*, 5(11), 513–514.

CULLEN, C. (1988) Doctoral degrees in applied psychology. *The Psychologist*, 1(10), 395–396.

DAVIES, G. (1990) New routes to the PhD. *The Psychologist*, 3(6), 253–255.

McPHERSON, F. (1991) Professional psychology training in Western and Nordic Europe. *Educational and Child Psychology*, 8(4), 56–63.

MORRIS, P.E. (1988) BPS code of practice for the PhD: A personal view. In S.E. Newstead (Ed.) *The Future of the PhD*. The British Psychological Society Group of Teachers of Psychology Occasional Papers, No.5, 7–11.

NEWSTEAD, S.E. (Ed.) (1988) *The Future of The Psychology PhD*. The British Psychological Society Group of Teachers of Psychology Occasional Papers, No.5.

PHILLIPS, E.M. (1988) Taught doctorates: The way forward. In S.E. Newstead (Ed.) *The Future of The Psychology PhD*. The British Psychological Society Group of Teachers of Psychology Occasional Papers, No.5, 19–22.

PHILLIPS, E.M. (1989) The PhD cohort as a recommended alternative to conventional doctoral programmes. *The Psychologist*, 2(6), 226–227.

USSER, J.M. (1986) Postgraduate training: An inside perspective. *The British Psychological Society Social Psychology Section Newsletter*, 15, 34–37.

VAN DEURZEN-SMITH, E. (1988) Integration of students' personal concerns and experiences in the postgraduate psychology curriculum. *The British Psychological Society Group of Teachers of Psychology Newsletter*, No.4, April, 10–15.

Educational Psychology

BICHARD, S.H. and BOWLING, E. (1991) Post-qualifying training in the 1990s: What do child psychologists need? *The British Psychological Society Division of Educational and Child Psychology Newsletter*, 43, 35–41.

BLOOR, M. and LOVELL, R.B. (1988) The teaching face. In H.J. Wright and J. Radford (Eds) *The Several Faces of Educational Psychology*. The British Psychological Society Group of Teachers of Psychology Occasional Papers, No.2, 13–20.

THE BRITISH PSYCHOLOGICAL SOCIETY (1988) The initial training of educational psychologists in England, Wales, Northern Ireland and Hong Kong. A policy statement. *The Psychologist*, 1(12), 508–509.

THE BRITISH PSYCHOLOGICAL SOCIETY (1989) Qualifications to become a Chartered Psychologist specializing in educational psychology. Letter issued by the Scientific and Professional Secretary of The British Psychological Society. Available from the BPS.

CAMERON, S., MYERS, M. and REASON, R. (1986) Advanced professional training for practising educational psychologists. *The British Psychological Society Division of Educational and Child Psychology Newsletter*, 22, 18–21.

CLINE, T. and LUNT, I. (1990) Meeting equal opportunities criteria: A review of progress in educational psychology training. *Educational and Child Psychology*, 7(3), 59–68.

DURBIN, N. (1989) Setting the climate: A trainee's perspective. *The British Psychological Society Division of Educational and Child Psychology Newsletter*, 35, 31–32.

DURBIN, N. (1990) A national curriculum for educational psychologists. *The British Psychological Society Division of Educational and Child Psychology Newsletter*, 37, 28–33.

FREDERICKSON, N. (1987) Post-experience views of a regional sample of principal psychologists. *The British Psychological Society Division of Educational and Child Psychology Newsletter*, 25, 14–19.

GRAY, P. and LUNT, I. (1990) Two different worlds? The ULIE approach to training in professional educational psychology. *Educational and Child Psychology*, 7(3), 31–36.

HUGHES, M., ORTON, D. and VAHEY, R. (1991) Some thoughts on research in educational psychology training and its relevance to professional practice. *Educational and Child Psychology*, 8(1), 62–66.

LINDSAY, G. (1990) Assessment in the training of educational psychologists. *Educational and Child Psychology*, 7(3), 74–81.

LUNT, I. (1991) Training and qualifications in educational psychology: Beyond 1992. *Educational and Child Psychology*, 8 (4), 43–55.

LUNT, I. and GRAY, P. (1990) Theory and practice in professional training: Implications for educational psychology. *Educational and Child Psychology*, 7(3), 23–30.

OSBOURNE, E., LEYDEN, G. and POWELL, M. (1990) Supervision of trainee educational psychologists on fieldwork. *Educational and Child Psychology*, 7(3), 37–43.

PHILLIPS, P. (1989) Setting the climate for successful fieldwork training: Beginning the supervision process. *The British Psychological Society Division of Educational and Child Psychology Newsletter*, 35, 26–30.

POMERANTZ, M. (1990) Fieldwork supervision: A personal perspective on the state of the art. *Educational and Child Psychology*, 7(3), 53–58.

POWELL, M., LEYDEN, G. and OSBOURNE, E. (1990) A curriculum for training in supervision. *Educational and Child Psychology*, 7(3), 44–52.

ROBERTS, M. (1988) Comments from a field educational psychologist. In H.J. Wright and J. Radford (Eds) *The Several Faces of Educational Psychology*. The British Psychological Society Group of Teachers of Psychology Occasional Papers, No.2, 51–52.

SHELLEY, C. (1992) The practice of supervision, 1991. *The British Psychological Society Division of Educational and Child*

Psychology Newsletter, 48, 35–39.
VENABLES, K. (1992) Training educational psychologists: The personal cost. *The British Psychological Society Division of Educational and Child Psychology Newsletter, 48,* 29–33.

Clinical Psychology

ADAMS, M. (1990) Evaluation and assessment of competence. *Educational and Child Psychology, 7*(3), 67–73.
ALLEN, C. (1987) National training needs in clinical psychology: A response from the affiliates group. *Clinical Psychology Forum, 7,* 35–36.
BACON, H. (1992) Supervision in clinical training: The integrative model, or muddling through? *Clinical Psychology Forum, 45,* 24–28.
BERGER, M., COLES, C., KIRK, J., MARZILLIER, J., LAVENDER, A., MORLEY, S., REVELL, J. and WATTS, F. (1988) The assessment of clinical psychologists in training: A discussion document. *Clinical Psychology Forum, 15,* 3–15.
THE BRITISH PSYCHOLOGICAL SOCIETY (1989) Training in psychotherapy. Available from the BPS.
THE BRITISH PSYCHOLOGICAL SOCIETY BOARD OF EXAMINERS FOR THE DIPLOMA IN CLINICAL PSYCHOLOGY (1989) Guidelines for the training of independent candidates. Available from the BPS.
THE BRITISH PSYCHOLOGICAL SOCIETY PROFESSIONAL AFFAIRS BOARD COMMITTEE ON TRAINING IN CLINICAL PSYCHOLOGY (1987) Guidelines on clinical supervision. Available from the BPS.
THE BRITISH PSYCHOLOGICAL SOCIETY PROFESSIONAL AFFAIRS BOARD COMMITTEE ON TRAINING IN CLINICAL PSYCHOLOGY (1988) Criteria for the assessment of postgraduate training courses in clinical psychology. Available from the BPS.
COATE, M.A., CONBOY-HILL, S., KERFOOT, S., MALTBY, M., PARKER, S., POWELL, G. and WYCHERLY, B. (1988) A basic grade training programme. *Clinical Psychology Forum, 14,* 16–19.
COOPER, C.L. (1986) Job distress: Recent research and the emerging role of the clinical occupational psychologist. *Bulletin of The British Psychological Society, 39,* 325–331.
DAVENHILL, R., HUNT, H., PILLAY, H.M., HARRIS, A. and KLEIN, Y. (1989) Training and selection issues in clinical psychology for black and minority ethnic groups from an equal opportunities perspective. *Clinical Psychology Forum, 19,* 13–17.
FROSH, S. (1988) Race equality training in a department of clinical psychology. *Clinical Psychology Forum, 13,* 18–22.
FROSH, S. and LEVINSON, F. (1990) Identifying clinical skill components of training in clinical psychology. *Clinical Psychology Forum, 25,* 20–27.
GRIFFITHS, D. (1987) How successful is research training on clinical courses? *Clinical Psychology Forum, 9,* 16–19.

HALL, J., KOCH, H., PILLING, S. and WINTER, K. (1986) Health services information and clinical psychology. *Bulletin of The British Psychological Society, 39*, 126–130.

HODGETTS, D. (1986) Skills: A personal approach. *Clinical Psychology Forum, 6*, 36–37.

HOOPER, J. (1988) Clinical supervision: Guidelines from trainees. *Clinical Psychology Forum, 15*, 20–26.

HOUSTON, J., REVELL, J. and WOOLLETT, S. (1989) The need for a basic grade training programme: Results of a survey from basic grade psychologists in the SW Thames region. *Clinical Psychology Forum, 19*, 29–32.

HUMPHREY, M. and EDELMANN, R. (1991) The research component of clinical training. *Clinical Psychology Forum, 31*, 25–28.

KENDRICK, D. and TAYLOR, I. (1986) The Humberside clinical psychology training course. *Clinical Psychology Forum, 6*, 21–24.

KENNEDY, P. (1992) Health psychology input to clinical psychology training courses. *Clinical Psychology Forum, 46*, 7–9.*

MACY, C. (1986) Supervision in clinical psychology: The what and the how. *Clinical Psychology Forum, 6*, 31–34.

McPHERSON, F.M. (1992) Clinical psychology training in Europe. *British Journal of Clinical Psychology, 31*, 419–428.

MALTBY, M., LAVENDER, T., FIELD, R., WAINWRIGHT, T. and HODSON, J. (1986) Manpower findings in the South East Thames region. *Clinical Psychology Forum, 6*, 11–15.

MARZILLIER, J.S. (1986) Course accreditation. *Clinical Psychology Forum, 6*, 4–6.

NEWTON, S. and MERIAN, S. (1986) Basic grade training and support: Existing schemes and issues. *Clinical Psychology Forum, 2*, 19–22.

NICHOLS, K., CORMACK, M. and WALSH, S. (1992) Preventive personal support: A challenge to the training courses. *Clinical Psychology Forum, 45*, 29–31.

PHILLIPS, P. (1986) Intervening at the organisational level. *Clinical Psychology Forum, 6*, 37–38.

SHARROCK, R. and HUNT, S. (1986) A national survey of trainees' satisfaction with clinical supervision. *Clinical Psychology Forum, 6*, 27–31.

STURMEY, P. (1986) The case for a skills-based approach. *Clinical Psychology Forum, 6*, 34–35.

WHITEHEAD, T. (1986) National training needs in clinical psychology. *Clinical Psychology Forum, 6*, 7–11.

Occupational Psychology

CRAWSHAW, M. (1988) Postgraduate occupational psychology at Hull. *The Occupational Psychologist, 5*, August, 15–17.

JACKSON, C. (1988) Occupational Psychology in Cardiff. *The Occupational Psychologist, 5*, August, 8–11.

LYONS, P. (1988) MSc in occupational psychology at Hatfield Polytechnic. *The Occupational Psychologist, 5*, August, 11–14.

PHILLIPS, E.M. and COOPEY, J. (1988) Birkbeck College department of occupational psychology. *The Occupational Psychologist*, 5, August, 7–8.

WEST, M. (1988) Innovations in the teaching of occupational psychology at Sheffield and the implications of chartering. *The Occupational Psychologist*, 5, August, 17–19.

Health Psychology

BELAR, C.D. (1990) Issues in training clinical health psychologists. *Health Psychology*, 4(1), 31–37.

KENNEDY, P. (1992) Health psychology input to clinical psychology training courses. *Health Psychology Update*, 10, 23–26.

KENNEDY, P., MARTEAU, T. and WEINMAN, J. (1992) Teaching and training in health psychology: A draft discussion document. *Health Psychology Update*, 10, 27–28.

MAES, S. and KITTEL, F. (1990) Training research health psychologists. *Health Psychology*, 4(1), 39–50.

METHORST, G.J., JANSEN, M.A. and KERKHOF, A.J.F.M. (1990) Training in health psychology: An international look. *Health Psychology*, 4(1), 19–30.

MICHIE, S. and MARTEAU, T. (1993) Health psychology as a science: A reply to Mary Watts. *Health Psychology Update*, 12, 33–34.

VINCK, J. (1988) Training in health psychology in Europe. *The British Psychological Society Health Psychology Section Newsletter*, 1, 18–23.

WATTS, M. (1992) Teaching and training in health psychology: A response to Kennedy, Marteau and Weinman's discussion document. *Health Psychology Update*, 11, 20–24.

WEINMAN, J., EDELMAN, R., MARKS, D. and WATTS, M. (1989) Training in health psychology: An overview of MSc courses in the UK. *The British Psychological Society Health Psychology Section Newsletter*, 3, June.

Counselling Psychology Training

EDGERTON, N. (1990) Counselling psychology: The Polytechnic of East London MSc course. *Counselling Psychology Review*, 5(1), 15–20.

PICKARD, E. (1990) Counselling psychology: From courses to networks. *Counselling Psychology Review*, 5(1), 11–14.

WILSON, J.E. (1992) CPD for counselling psychologists: The Society's "recommended" short courses. *Counselling Psychology Review*, 7(1), 4. *

WOOLFE, R. (1992) The diploma in counselling psychology. *Counselling Psychology Review*, 7(1), 3.

WORKING PARTY OF THE COUNSELLING PSYCHOLOGY SECTION OF THE BRITISH PSYCHOLOGICAL SOCIETY (1986) Training in counselling psychology. *The British Psychological Society Counselling Psychology Section Review*, 1(2), 5–16.

Continuing
Professional
Development

ELTON WILSON, J., HAYES, N., LINDLEY, P., MILLER, R., PERKINS, D. and REASON, R. (1992) Varieties of professional views. *The Psychologist*, 5(11), 507–509.

HAYES, N. (1990) CPD. Continuing professional development. *The Psychologist*, 3(3), 103–105.

HAYES, N. (1992) Keeping up to date. *The Psychologist*, 5(11), 508–509.

LINDLEY, P.A. (1992) Beyond chartered status. *The Psychologist*, 5(11), 504–505.

PERKINS, D. (1992) Talking it over. *The Psychologist*, 5(11), 506.

PUBLISHERS OF BOOKS AND JOURNALS IN PSYCHOLOGY

❏ *general profiles of publishers • journals and their readerships • publishers and their readerships • publishers' addresses*

*T*he aim of this chapter is simply stated: to help you, the reader, to identify and locate all the useful books and journals in your present sphere of psychological interest and for any future searches. But a number of decisions were involved: What should it cover? Whom to include? How to present the information? A short account of the methods used and of the decisions underlying this database should help you to make best use of the material.

The Scope of the Database

Mindful that the readership of this book includes psychologists and non-psychologists, academics and practitioners, and teachers of psychology from school to university level, we cast our net wide and assessed not only psychology lists but also medical, nursing, paramedical, social work, management and many others. The twin criteria used were 'psychological relevance' and 'usefulness'. We included therefore only English-language publishers in the UK, or with a UK base. Most of the latter are American originating most of their titles in the States; we have tried to indicate where this is the case. Other overseas publishers, who quoted overseas addresses and non-sterling prices only, were excluded. For journals, an exception was made for the American Psychological Association, since many of their journals are too important to omit.

Collecting the Information

The information for this chapter (updated from the 1990 edition) was collected by means of questionnaires and requests for catalogues sent out to all 'significant' psychology publishers towards the end of 1992. ('Significance' was judged by the quality of the list rather than size, and for this reason we included a number of association and society publishers.) Some publishers returned both; others responded with a catalogue only or a questionnaire only. Some questionnaires gave full answers; others the briefest details. Where we had only the latest catalogue (perhaps covering only the last three months) some degree of subjectivity was involved in characterizing the publisher's activities. Where we had only the questionnaire, some degree of trust (and sometimes discretion) was necessary in adapting the information supplied. Within these constraints, we aimed to make the database as comprehensive as possible.

How to Use the Lists

For ease of use and to cater for different needs, the information is presented in three separate lists. List 1 gives all the publishers in alphabetical order with a description of their scope and size. List 2 gives an alphabetical listing of journals by title and indicates their readership categories. List 3 takes the analysis one stage further with a tabular listing of the same publishers divided into six readership categories:

Reference – this includes dictionaries, encyclopaedias and the like and may be of interest to any reader;

Schools – this refers to textbooks and other materials used in the teaching of psychology in schools; also careers material;

Higher education – tertiary level material; largely textbooks and monographs in psychology;

Applied psychologists and other professionals – this includes all the practitioner areas both in psychology, such as clinical, educational etc., and other professions such as social workers, nurses, doctors, teachers and managers;

Trade – these are non-specialist books for the general public usually sold in high street bookshops;

Journals – largely learned and professional journals, but also a few significant weeklies; their readership is indicated in List 2.

There are different ways of approaching these lists, but perhaps the easiest is to turn straight to List 3 and use the column headings to identify your area of interest. Running your finger down the column will give you the names of relevant publishers and the addresses to write to for a catalogue are given at the end of the chapter. (Don't forget to state what subject area(s) you are interested in.)

A word about inspection copies (IC) and desk copies (DC)

Many publishers offer an inspection copy system on selected inspection titles and, where this is known, it is indicated in List 1. But, judging from our experience, the rationale behind this 'generosity' of publishers is not well understood and occasionally gives rise to misunderstandings. It is, of course, part of a marketing strategy. A free copy of a particular title (usually a textbook) is offered to tutors in the hope that they will recommend it to their students for purchase. The publisher recoups the cost of the free one by the sale of 10 or 15. A comments form usually accompanies the inspection copy-book stating that it should be paid for or returned if it is not recommended. Monographs more suitable for library use are not usually available as part of an inspection copy system.

The system of giving away desk copies operates in much the same way, the main difference being that the recipient does not have to recommend the book as a condition of keeping it. The underlying reasoning is the same though. This system is more popular in the States where the potential market for textbooks is ten times larger, though it is used occasionally in the UK.

You will not be surprised to learn that this book is not on IC or DC; none the less, I hope you find it useful.

LIST 1: GENERAL PROFILES OF PUBLISHERS

A B Academic
Publishers of a new series dealing with social/psychological issues during adolescence and youth. [IC]
Three journals for academics and professionals.

Academic Press
Now publish only in cognitive psychology, ergonomics, AI. An imprint of Harcourt Brace & Co. (q.v.).
Also publisher of two psychology journals.

Addison-Wesley
A major publisher of books in psychology, originated both in the UK and the USA. Specialisms include computing and AI, cognition, linguistics and organizational psychology. The list caters for most readerships except schools. [IC, DC]

Airlift Book Company
Distributor for mainly North American publishers, notably Inner City Books (Canada) and Spring Publications (US) as well as Daimon Publishers (Switzerland) who all specialize in Jungian psychology. Also a range of self-help titles.

Allyn & Bacon
See Harvester-Wheatsheaf.

American Psychological Assn
Published some 20 titles in 1992 in all fields, mainly for practitioners and professionals. Distributed by the Eurospan Group (q.v.). [IC]
Publisher of 25 major journals.

Analytical Psychology Club
Publisher of the Journal for Jungian Studies, *Harvest*.

Ann Arbor Publishers Ltd
Publisher and distributor of educational tests and remedial materials (for use in schools) originated in the USA. [IC]

Anna Freud Centre
Publisher of the *Bulletin of the Anna Freud Centre*.

Aquarian Press
A HarperCollins imprint; popular psychology and sexuality.

Edward Arnold
A division of Hodder & Stoughton. List includes books in introductory and general psychology and in social and developmental psychology, mainly for a readership of academics and undergraduate students but with some overlap into A-level studies. [IC]

Artesian Books	Publisher of the *British Journal of Psychotherapy*.
Assn for Humanistic Psychology	Apart from *Self and Society: A Journal of Humanistic Psychology*, the AHP also publishes a few booklets in related fields, principally for practitioners.
Assn of Child Psychotherapists	Publisher of the *Journal of Child Psychotherapy*.
Assn of Educational Psychologists	Publisher (through Longman) of the journal *Educational Psychology in Practice*.
Avenue	Publisher of the *International Journal of Social Psychiatry*.
Baillière Tindall	An imprint of Harcourt Brace & Co. (q.v.).
BILD Publications	A small and specialist list in the field of learning disability mainly for practitioners. Also have three journals (published by Multilingual Matters (q.v.)): *Mental Handicap*, *Mental Handicap Bulletin* and *Mental Handicap Research*.
Blackwell	Major publisher of psychology (17 new titles in 1992): books in most fields especially developmental, social and experimental psychology (but no clinical psychology and psychiatry, health or psychotherapy titles). Mainly for academics, practitioners and professionals. Some reference publishing in general, cognitive and educational psychology. [IC, DC] Blackwell also publish five psychology and psychology-related journals, including *Journal of Family Therapy*, *Mind and Language* and the *Journal of Research in Reading* (the latter aimed at teachers).
Blackwell Scientific	A substantial list in the fields of clinical psychology and psychiatry (with a degree of specialism in child psychiatry), and psychotherapy addressed mainly to a readership of practitioners. [IC]
BPS Books	This is the book publishing arm of The British Psychological Society (q.v.). A wide-ranging list is published with catalogues covering the subject areas of: human resources, helping professions and health care, education, schools and colleges, and careers. Titles range from texts and academic monographs to self-help books. BPS Books caters for many different markets including social workers, health workers and managers, as well as for academic and applied psychologists.
British Assn for Counselling	A range of books (especially reference) and other materials for counsellors, including trainees and trainers. Publisher of *Counselling*, the journal of the BAC.
British Assn of Psychotherapists	Publisher of the *Journal of the British Association of Psychotherapists*.

The British Psychological Society	Publisher of seven major research journals, including the *British Journal of Psychology*. Also publish *Selection & Development Review* and *The Psychologist* (the monthly bulletin of the Society), plus the various newletters from the Divisions, Sections and Special Groups of the Society. See also BPS Books.
British Society for Projective Psychology	Publisher of the *British Journal of Projective Psychology*.
W.C. Brown	US publisher of college-level psychology textbooks and ancillary materials; covering most fields especially introductory and developmental psychology.
Butterworth Heinemann	Emphasis on psychiatry but some psychotherapy and clinical psychology titles. [IC, DC]
Cambridge University Press	One of the major UK publishers of psychology (35 new titles in 1992). Books in all areas of psychology and at all levels, with many titles for practitioners and professionals, but mainly for a readership of high-level research psychologists. CUP also distribute MacKeith Press titles which include clinical psychology (with a special emphasis on childhood), psychiatry and neurology. [IC] CUP psychology journals (ten in all) include *Psychology of Women Quarterly* and *Behavioral and Brain Sciences*.
Carfax	Journals publisher, with ten psychology-related titles (mainly for practitioners), including *Addiction*, the *Journal of Mental Health* and the interdisciplinary journal, *AIDS Care*.
Cassell	An expanding psychology list with particular specialisms in educational psychology, and counselling and special needs. Aimed largely at undergraduates and practitioners in various applied fields. [IC, DC]
Paul Chapman	A substantial education and educational psychology list, primarily for a readership of teachers and student teachers; also titles concerning management and organizational behaviour. [IC]
Chapman & Hall	Publish in clinical, health and other applied fields; directed towards nurses, therapists and health care workers. [IC]
The Children's Society	A range of books and other materials (covering such topics as child abuse, homelessness, leaving care) for childcare professionals including titles of interest to clinical and educational psychologists. The Children's Society is a voluntary society of the Church of England and the Church in Wales.
Churchill Livingstone	See Longman
Community Psychiatric Nurses Assn	Publisher of the *Community Psychiatric Nursing Journal*.

Constable	A small psychology list dominated by titles in counselling and therapy (particularly the works of Carl Rogers).
Current Science	Publisher of *Current Opinion in Psychiatry*.
J.M. Dent	An imprint of Orion Publishing (see also Weidenfeld and Nicolson). Small but various psychology/sociology list (not easy to characterize here). [DC]
Duckworth	Small but eclectic list in psychology and psychiatry, with a bias towards the latter. Includes books for researchers and practitioners. [IC, DC]
Element Books	Publisher and distributor of books on philosophy and religion, among other cognate subjects, with a focus on popular psychology, mainly originated in the USA.
Elsevier	Publishes in the UK under the North-Holland imprint. A major academic psychology publisher (26 new titles in 1992) with a bias towards cognitive psychology, but most fields are covered in the extensive 'Advances in Psychology' series. Also a comprehensive 'Handbook of Neuropsychology' series. Publisher of some 14 psychology or psychology-related journals, including *Acta Psychologica*, *Artificial Intelligence* and *Cognition*.
Lawrence Erlbaum	One of the major UK publishers of books in psychology in all fields and (excepting school texts and general trade) at all levels. Worldwide, 120 new psychology titles published in 1992. Sister company of LEA Inc. (USA), US-originated titles are a substantial part of the list. [IC] LEA Ltd also publish 12 psychology journals (including the *Quarterly Journal of Experimental Psychology*) and handle journals published by LEA Inc.
The Eurospan Group	Distributor of US publishers including the American Psychological Association, American Psychiatric Press (manuals, reference books and textbooks covering clinical practice and psychiatry), New York University Press (15 new titles in 1992 in a wide variety of areas but with a general bias towards psychoanalysis), Jason Aronson (psychotherapy), Praeger Publishers and Greenwood Press (wide range of academic monographs for the social sciences) and Haworth Press (academic and trade titles in psychology and medicine).
Falmer Press	Part of the Taylor & Francis group. Specialist publisher of education books for teachers with a substantial list in educational psychology, as well as general psychology texts for undergraduate psychology students. [IC, DC: some titles]
Fontana	Small list for the general reader with titles in child development, self-help and women's studies.
Fontana Press	A more academic market than Fontana, also focusing on child development, and psychology and philosophy.

Free Association Books	Independent psychology publisher (seven new titles in 1992), specializing in psychoanalysis and psychotherapy. Publisher of the journal *Free Associations*.
W.H. Freeman	Catalogues also contain publications from the imprints Scientific American Books and Scientific American Library. Also UK distributor of books published in the USA by Sinauer Associates Inc. The books in the life and behavioural sciences catalogue are mainly aimed at undergraduates, and include titles in social, developmental and abnormal psychology, learning and cognition, statistics, neuroscience, and general psychology. [IC, DC]
Gaskell	Imprint of the Royal College of Psychiatrists (q.v.).
Gateway Books	Small publisher whose list includes some popular psychology, mainly self-help.
Guilford Press	US-based publisher with a substantial list of psychology titles ranging from clinical psychology, psychotherapy and psychoanalysis to organizational psychology and research. Publisher of several psychology journals.
Harcourt Brace & Co	The American parent company includes the following imprints: Baillière Tindall; The Psychological Corporation; W.B. Saunders; Holt, Rinehart & Winston; Grune & Stratton; and Academic Press. Publishers of large general introductory and child development texts; also some personality, physiological psychology and statistics. A few British authors. Also, high level education books and conference proceedings under Academic Press imprint.
HarperCollins	Psychology publishing is split between a variety of publishing divisions, depending on target audience. Textbooks are available from Collins Educational (GCSE and A-level/16+) and the College Division (16+ and undergraduate texts – US published). College Division also handles Basic Book's large psychotherapy list. [IC]
Harvester-Wheatsheaf	Catalogues also include titles from other publishers in the Simon & Schuster group (Allyn & Bacon, Prentice Hall). Publish in all areas of psychology but specialize in social and developmental psychology (notably the 'Developing Body and Mind' series). The sociology catalogue includes titles of interest (social work and social welfare, family and marriage, criminology), as does the economics catalogue (economic psychology and behavioural economics). Most readerships catered for, but no school texts. [IC]
Harwood Academic	An imprint of Gordon & Breach Science Publishers. Titles in health psychology and addiction research; also educational psychology and criminological and legal psychology. Readership mainly researchers, clinicians and health professionals. [IC] Harwood publish five psychology journals, including *Anxiety Research* and *Psychology and Health*.

Haverstock	Publisher of the *Journal of the Balint Society*, plus the occasional book in Balint-inspired medicine.
Hobsons	Publish a bienniel psychology course guide and the *British Journal of Guidance and Counselling*.
Hodder & Stoughton	Specialize in textbooks for A-level and first year undergraduates. [IC] See also Edward Arnold.
Institute of Psychoanalysis	Publisher of *International Journal of Psychoanalysis*.
IPC Specialist Group	Publisher of *New Scientist*.
JAI	US publisher specializing in research annuals, with particular emphasis on management, cognitive science, educational and developmental psychology. [IC: some titles] Also six psychology journals.
Johns Hopkins University Press	US academic publisher with a list covering clinical and health psychology, cognition, and history and philosophy of psychology. Also specializing in psychoanalysis (including titles for practitioners). [IC, DC: some titles]
Jossey-Bass	US-based publisher with catalogue which includes psychology-related titles in management and education, as well as a social and behavioural sciences list. Titles in the latter category are principally for practitioners. Distributed in the UK by Maxwell Macmillan (q.v.).
Karnac	Specialist publisher of books in psychoanalysis, psychotherapy and analytical psychology. Twenty-five new titles in 1992. Also publish the journal *Winnicott Studies*.
Jessica Kingsley	Emphasis on psychotherapy but also a significant social work list including titles of interest to psychologists and health professionals. [IC: some titles]
John Libby & Company	Small list with specialized titles in clinical psychology and psychiatry. [IC]
Longman	Mainly introductory and general psychology books catering for A-level and GCSE students. No new psychology titles in 1992. Specialized titles in clinical psychology and psychiatry are published through Churchill Livingstone. [IC: some titles]
McGraw-Hill	A substantial textbook list including introductory psychology, child development, personality theory, sexuality, feminist psychology, some clinical psychology and statistics/research methods. Most books originated in the USA. [IC, DC]
Macmillan	Publishes an introductory psychology series for A-level, and a general focus on titles for applied fields (in particular, nursing, education, social work). Co-publishers (with the BPS) of the 'Psychology for Professional Groups' and 'Psychology Applied to Nursing' series. [IC, DC: some titles]

Manchester University Press	A few titles in psychology for practitioners (education, working with the elderly) as well as a medical self-help series, 'Living With'. [IC: some titles]
Maxwell Macmillan	US publisher with substantial psychology list, including titles on counselling and psychotherapy, health psychology and education.
MCB University Press	The initials stand for Management Consultants Bradford. Publisher of more than 100 serials for professionals, including the *Journal of Managerial Psychology*.
MIND	Ten new titles per year in the field of mental health and cognate areas, including criminological and legal psychology. Also publisher of the bi-monthly journal *Openmind*.
MIT Press	US academic publisher (MIT stands for Massachusetts Institute of Technology) specializing in cognitive psychology but with titles in many fields, particularly neuroscience, AI and philosophy of mind. Fifty new psychology titles in 1992. [IC] Three psychology-related journals including the *Journal of Cognitive Neuroscience*.
Multilingual Matters	Specialist publisher of psycholinguistics and education (also published under the Channel View imprint). Act as distributor for the British Institute of Learning Disabilities (BILD). [IC] Publish journals for BILD (q.v.).
National Extension College	Publisher of open learning materials for schools and FE colleges as well as for correspondence students and adult learners. GCSE and A-level psychology packages are available; some titles on health and social issues may also be of interest. [IC: some titles]
Thomas Nelson	Educational publisher whose sociology catalogue includes one introductory psychology textbook. [IC]
NFER-Nelson	Leading UK publisher and supplier of the full range of testing and assessment materials, from developmental and ability tests to selection and recruitment instruments for industry. For use by a wide variety of professionals including the caring professions, not least psychologists (clinical, occupational, educational) and counsellors. Also interdisciplinary training materials for practitioners and professionals. Many materials originate in the USA. ASE is a division of NFER-Nelson which focuses exclusively on tests for occupational use.
North-Holland	The European imprint of Elsevier Science Publishers (q.v.).
Norton	US-based publisher with a clear bias towards psychoanalysis and psychotherapy. Some undergraduate texts. Norton Professional Books covers titles for psychiatrists, counsellors and therapists. [IC, DC: some titles]
Oneworld	Small publisher of general reader psychology, particularly therapy/psychoanalysis. Distributed by Element Books (q.v.).

Open University Press	A substantial psychology list (six new titles in 1992), principally for students and teachers in higher education, and medical and health workers. Specialisms in social, developmental and health psychology as well as psychotherapy and counselling, but also a number of general/introductory texts. [IC]
Oxford University Press	Major international publisher in the life sciences, with 20 new psychology titles in 1992. Specialisms in experimental psychology, clinical psychology and psychotherapy, but with titles in most fields. Most titles for academic/undergraduate or practitioner/professional readership. [IC: some titles] See also OUP's catalogues in medicine, neurosciences, psychiatry, and philosophy. OUP also publishes the *Journal of Psychopharmacology*.
Pan Macmillan	A dozen or so popular psychology titles, mainly general, health, and self-help; also some titles of psychological interest among the business management list. Pan Macmillan comprises Macmillan London, Pan Books, Picador and Sidgwick & Jackson.
Penguin	A large and expanding psychology list, with academic titles (especially undergraduate texts) in introductory; social and developmental; experimental and cognitive psychology; maths and stats/computing and AI; psychoanalysis (inc. the Pelican Freud Library); organizational and management psychology; and history and philosophy of psychology. [IC, DC: some titles]
Pergamon	Major psychology publisher principally for undergraduate and graduate students, and practitioners. Titles in most fields, but especially strong in social and educational psychology, as well as in therapy, neuropsychology and other branches of clinical practice. [IC: some titles] Pergamon also publishes some 22 psychology journals, covering a wide range of research and applied fields.
Pinter Publishers	Pinter's social science catalogue includes titles in the series 'Communication in Artificial Intelligence'. The psychology list will be expanding with a new series in cognitive science. Some of the linguistics titles may also be of interest. [IC: some titles]
Pion	Publisher of the journal *Perception*.
Plenum	US-based publisher of high level monographs and conference proceedings for researchers and practitioners/professionals. Titles in a range of fields, but with a general bias towards behavioural psychology. Strong specialism in social and developmental psychology, also clinical psychology and neuroscience. The vast majority of Plenum's books originate in the USA. [IC, DC: some titles] Plenum publishes some 20 high level psychology journals for researchers and practitioners.

Positive Products	Specialist publisher of a range of materials dealing with teaching and classroom behaviour.
Prentice Hall	See Harvester-Wheatsheaf.
The Psychological Corporation	World's largest publisher of psychological tests for use in: clinical, educational and occupational practice; speech and language therapy; business, industry and government. American company, but since 1987 some of these materials have been designed and produced in the UK. Now an inprint of Harcourt Brace & Co. (q.v.).
Routledge	A major UK psychology publisher (75 new books in 1992), with titles in most fields, principally for a readership of undergraduates, academics and practitioners/professionals. Particularly strong in psychoanalysis, psychotherapy and analytical psychology, but also separate education and health and social welfare lists. Routledge co-publishes and distributes a number of titles from BPS Books (q.v.). [IC, DC: some titles] Routledge also publishes two psychology journals.
Royal College of Psychiatrists	Publishes books under the Gaskell imprint. All publications are in psychiatry, for a practitioner/professional readership. Eight new books in 1992. Two journals including the *British Journal of Psychiatry*.
Royal Society	The *Proceedings of the Royal Society of London*, Series B, is a general biological research journal with occasional papers on animal psychology and behaviour. Likewise the *Philosophical Transactions*, Series B, which also occasionally publishes psychology-related conference reports.
Sage	Basically a US-based social sciences publisher. Books mainly for practitioners (and students) in various applied fields. Apart from psychology per se, the catalogue features psychology-related titles under categories such as: child abuse, counselling and psychotherapy, criminology, education, gender studies, gerontology, social work. UK-originated series include 'Counselling in Practice'. [IC] Major publisher of social science journals. Apart from their 30 psychology titles, there are many psychology-related journals under other heads (as above).
Sheldon Press	An imprint of the Society for Promoting Christian Knowledge. Mainly self-help and popular psychology books.
Souvenir	Some 35 psychology titles, with a focus on humanistic psychology. Most published under the Condor imprint, including the 'Human Horizons' series for people with disabilities.
Springer	International academic publisher with psychology titles in virtually every field. However, no English-language titles were published in 1992. Also publisher of several English-language research journals in psychology, psychiatry and related fields.

Taylor & Francis	Major international scientific and educational publisher (also with an editorial and marketing office in the US). There is a growing psychology list with titles in health psychology, general psychology and social and developmental psychology. Aimed largely at undergraduates, A-level students and practitioners in various applied fields. [IC, DC: some titles] Publisher of several psychology and related journals.
Thomson International	Distributor for US imprints Boyd & Fraser, Brooks/Cole, Van Nostrand Reinhold and Wadsworth which all publish a wide range of psychology texts for students. [IC, DC: some titles]
Thorsons	Mainly for the general reader; popular psychology, personal development and self-help.
Transaction	US publishers, mainly of psychoanalysis, but also a recent volume on social psychiatry. [IC: some titles]
Transworld	Incorporates Bantam Press and Doubleday imprints. A small psychology list for the general reader, mostly originated in the US. [IC]
University Presses of California, Columbia & Princeton	All three publishers have lists of 60 to 80 psychology titles covering psychoanalysis/therapy and developmental, cognitive and legal psychology. Princeton has more academic titles (including a series on Jung), Columbia has a mainly practitioner market, including books for nurses, while California University Press includes titles aimed at the general reader. Distributed in the UK by John Wiley (q.v.).
Weidenfeld & Nicolson	An imprint of Orion Publishing (see also J.M. Dent). A dozen or so miscellaneous psychology titles, including some general/introductory textbooks for schools. [DC: some titles]
Whiting & Birch	Focuses on childhood and health, also titles for social workers. Publisher of three psychology-related journals including *Children and Society*.
Whurr	Titles in psychology and psychiatry, but focus on psychotherapy and counselling. Publish three psychology-related journals.
John Wiley	A subsidiary of John Wiley & Sons Inc., New York. Major international publisher in psychology (40 new titles in 1992), especially for practitioners and professionals but also many academic and reference titles. Books in many fields, but in particular clinical, psychotherapy, organizational and developmental. [IC] Also 17 psychology journals, including the *European Journal of Personality*.
Williams & Wilkins	US medical publisher. A range of titles (some 39) in clinical psychiatry, textbooks as well as books for practitioners. UK distributors for Igaku-Shoin and F.A. Davis (also US medical and health sciences publishers). W & W also publish five psychiatric journals for practitioners.

Winslow	Some psychology books among a range of multi-media therapy/rehabilitation materials for various professional groups, including teachers, nurses, occupational therapists, geriatricians and social workers; also a range of special-needs materials for childcare professionals. [IC: some titles]
Women's Press	Titles in educational, health, and general psychology; also in psychotherapy. Some of interest to practitioners and professionals, and some to teachers of women's studies, but mostly addressed to general readers. [IC]
Yale University Press	US publisher with 19 new titles in 1992, with clear specialisms in psychiatry, psychoanalysis and child development. Readership: primarily academics, psychoanalysts and other practitioners. [IC, DC: some titles]

LIST 2: JOURNALS AND THEIR READERSHIPS

Journals are listed in alphabetical order in the righthand column, where the publisher of each title is also given. The lefthand column gives the readership of each journal, using the category 'R' to indicate research; 'AP' to indicate applied psychologists, such as clinical or educational psychologists; and 'OP' to indicate other interested professionals, such as social workers, nurses, doctors, teachers and managers.

R-AP	*Acta Psychologica* (Elsevier)
R	*Adaptive Behaviours* (MIT Press)
R-AP-OP	*Addiction* (Carfax)
R-AP-OP	*Addiction Research* (Harwood Academic)
R-AP-OP	*Addictive Behaviors* (Pergamon)
R	*Advances in Behavior Research and Therapy* (Pergamon)
R-AP	*Aggressive Behavior* (John Wiley)
R-AP-OP	*AIDS Care: Psychological and Socio-Medical Aspects of AIDS/HIV* (Carfax)
R	*American Behavioral Scientist* (Sage)
AP-OP	*American Psychologist* (American Psychological Assn)
R-AP	*Anxiety, Stress and Coping* (Harwood Academic)
Monthly newsletter of the APA	*APA Monitor* (American Psychological Assn)
R	*Aphasiology* (Taylor & Francis)
R-AP	*Applied and Preventive Psychology* (Cambridge University Press)

R-AP	*Applied Behavioral Science Review* (JAI Press)
R-AP-OP	*Applied Cognitive Psychology* (John Wiley)
R-AP	*Applied Psycholinguistics* (Cambridge University Press)
R-AP-OP	*Applied Psychology: An International Review* (Lawrence Erlbaum Associates)
R	*Archives of Clinical Neuropsychology* (Pergamon)
R	*Artificial Intelligence* (Elsevier)
AP-OP	*The Arts in Psychotherapy* (Pergamon)
R-AP	*Behavior Modification* (Sage)
R-AP	*Behavioral and Brain Sciences* (Cambridge University Press)
R-AP-OP	*Behavioral Assessment* (Pergamon)
R	*Behavioral Ecology and Sociology* (Springer)
R	*Behavioral Neuroscience* (American Psychological Assn)
AP-OP	*Behavioral Residential Treatment* (John Wiley)
AP-OP	*Behavioral Sciences and the Law* (John Wiley)
R-AP	*Behavior and Information Technology* (Taylor & Francis)
R	*Behavior Research and Therapy* (Pergamon)
R-AP	*Behavioural Brain Research* (Elsevier)
R	*Behavioural Processes* (Elsevier)
R-AP	*Biofeedback and Self Regulation* (Plenum)
R	*Biological Psychology* (Elsevier)
R	*Brain Injury* (Taylor & Francis)
R-AP-OP	*British Journal of Clinical Psychology* (British Psychological Society)
R-AP-OP	*British Journal of Developmental Psychology* (British Psychological Society)
AP	*British Journal of Guidance and Counselling* (Hobsons)
R	*British Journal of Mathematical and Statistical Psychology* (British Psychological Society)
R-AP-OP	*British Journal of Medical Psychology* (British Psychological Society)
R-AP	*British Journal of Projective Psychology* (British Society for Projective Psychology)
R-AP	*British Journal of Psychiatry* (Royal College of Psychiatrists)
R-AP-OP	*British Journal of Psychology* (British Psychological Society)
AP	*British Journal of Psychotherapy* (Artesian Books)
R-AP-OP	*British Journal of Social Psychology* (British Psychological Society)

R-AP-OP	*Bulletin of the Anna Freud Centre* (Anna Freud Centre)
AP-OP	*Changes* (Journal of the Psychology and Psychotherapy Association) (Lawrence Erlbaum Associates)
AP-OP	*Child Abuse and Neglect* (The International Journal, Official Publication of the International Society for the Prevention of Child Abuse and Neglect) (Pergamon)
AP-OP	*Child Abuse Review* (John Wiley)
R-AP-OP	*Children and Society* (Whiting and Birch)
AP	*Clinical Psychology and Psychotherapy* (John Wiley)
R-AP-OP	*Clinical Psychology Review* (Official Journal of the Division of Clinical Psychology of the American Psychological Association) (Pergamon Press)
R	*Cognition* (Elsevier)
R	*Cognition and Emotion* (Lawrence Erlbaum Associates)
R	*Cognitive Neuropsychology* (Lawrence Erlbaum Associates)
R-AP	*Cognitive Therapy and Research* (Plenum)
R-AP-OP	*Community Psychiatry Nursing Journal* (Community Psychiatric Nurses Assn)
R-AP-OP	*Computers in Human Behavior* (Pergamon)
R-AP	*Contemporary Hypnosis* (Whurr)
AP-OP	*Contemporary Psychology* (American Psychological Assn)
R-AP	*The Counseling Psychologist* (Journal of the Division of Counseling Psychology of the American Psychological Assn) (Sage)
AP	*Counselling* (British Assn for Counselling)
R-AP-OP	*Counselling Psychology Quarterly* (Carfax)
R-AP	*Criminal Behaviour and Mental Health* (Whurr)
R-AP-OP	*Criminal Justice and Behavior* (Sage)
R-AP	*Current Directions in Psychological Science* (Cambridge University Press)
R-AP-OP	*Current Opinion in Psychiatry* (Current Science)
R-AP-OP	*DATA* (Brown University Digest of Addiction Theory and Application) (Carfax)
AP-OP	*Death Studies* (Taylor & Francis)
AP	*Depression* (John Wiley)
R-AP	*Development and Psychopathology* (Cambridge University Press)
R	*Developmental Psychobiology* (John Wiley)
R	*Developmental Psychology* (American Psychological Assn)

R	*Deviant Behaviour* (Taylor & Francis)
R-AP-OP	*Drug and Alcohol Dependence* (Elsevier)
R-AP-OP	*Early Child Development* (Harwood Academic)
R-AP-OP	*Early Development and Parenting* (John Wiley)
R-AP-OP	*Eating Disorders Review* (Journal of the Eating Disorders Association) (John Wiley)
R-AP-OP	*Educational Psychology* (Carfax)
AP	*Educational Psychology in Practice* (Assn of Educational Psychologists)
R-AP-OP	*Educational Psychology Review* (Plenum)
R	*Environment and Behavior* (Sage)
R	*Ergonomics* (Taylor & Francis)
R-AP	*European Archives of Psychiatry and Clinical Neurosciences* (Springer)
R	*European Journal of Cognitive Psychology* (Lawrence Erlbaum Associates)
R-AP	*European Journal of Disorders of Communication* (Whurr)
R	*European Journal of Personality* (John Wiley)
R	*European Journal of Social Psychology* (John Wiley)
R	*European Review of Social Psychology* (John Wiley)
R	*European Work and Organizational Psychologist* (Lawrence Erlbaum Associates)
R-AP	*Evaluation Practice* (Journal of the American Evaluation Association) (JAI Press)
R	*Feminism and Psychology* (Sage)
R-AP-OP	*Free Associations* (Free Association Books)
R	*Gender Dysphoria* (Whiting and Birch)
R-AP-OP	*Gifted Education International* (A B Academic)
R-AP	*Group Analysis* (Sage)
R-AP	*Group and Organization Management* (Sage)
R	*Harvest* (Analytical Psychology Club)
AP-OP	*Health Psychology* (American Psychological Assn)
R	*Hispanic Journal of Behavioral Sciences* (Sage)
R	*History of the Human Sciences* (Sage)
R	*Human Movement Science* (Elsevier)
R-AP	*Human Relations* (Plenum)
R-AP-OP	*International Journal of Adolescence and Youth* (A B Academic)

R	*International Journal of Behavioral Development* (Lawrence Erlbaum Associates)
R	*International Journal of Clinical and Experimental Hypnosis* (Sage)
AP-OP	*International Journal of Law and Psychiatry* (Pergamon)
R	*International Journal of Personal Construct Psychology* (Taylor & Francis)
R-AP	*International Journal of Psychoanalysis* (Institute of Psychoanalysis)
R	*International Journal of Psychology* (Lawrence Erlbaum Associates)
R	*International Journal of Psychophysiology* (Elsevier)
R-AP	*International Journal of Short-Term Psychotherapy* (John Wiley)
R-AP	*International Journal of Social Psychiatry* (Avenue)
R-AP-OP	*International Review of Industrial and Organizational Psychology* (John Wiley)
R-AP-OP	*International Review of Psychiatry* (Carfax)
R-AP	*International Review of Victimology* (A B Academic)
R	*Journal for the Theory of Social Behaviour* (Blackwell Publishers)
R-AP	*Journal of Abnormal Child Psychology* (Plenum)
R	*Journal of Abnormal Psychology* (American Psychological Assn)
R-AP-OP	*Journal of Adolescence* (Academic Press)
R	*Journal of Adolescent Research* (Sage)
R-AP	*Journal of Affective Disorders* (Elsevier)
R	*Journal of Aging Studies* (JAI Press)
AP	*Journal of Analytical Psychology* (Routledge)
R-AP	*Journal of Anxiety Disorders* (Pergamon)
R-AP	*Journal of Applied Behavioral Sciences* (Sage)
R-AP	*Journal of Applied Psychology* (American Psychological Assn)
R-AP	*Journal of Autism and Developmental Disorders* (Plenum)
R-AP	*Journal of Behavior Therapy and Experimental Psychiatry* (Pergamon)
R-AP	*Journal of Behavioral Medicine* (Plenum)
R	*Journal of Black Psychology* (Sage)
R-AP	*Journal of Child Language* (Cambridge University Press)
R-AP	*Journal of Child Psychology and Psychiatry and Allied Disciplines* (Pergamon)

AP-OP	*Journal of Child Psychotherapy* (Assn of Child Psychotherapists)
AP	*Journal of Clinical Psychopharmacology* (Williams & Wilkins)
R	*Journal of Cognitive Neuroscience* (MIT Press)
R	*Journal of Community and Applied Social Psychology* (John Wiley)
R	*Journal of Comparative Psychology* (American Psychological Assn)
R-AP	*Journal of Consulting and Clinical Psychology* (American Psychological Assn)
R-AP-OP	*Journal of Counseling Psychology* (American Psychological Assn)
R	*Journal of Cross-Cultural Psychology* (Sage)
AP	*Journal of Developmental and Behavioral Pediatrics* (Williams & Wilkins)
R	*Journal of Early Adolescence* (Sage)
R	*Journal of Economic Psychology* (Elsevier)
R-AP	*Journal of Educational Psychology* (American Psychological Assn)
R	*Journal of Experimental and Theoretical Artificial Intelligence* (Taylor & Francis)
R	*Journal of Environmental Psychology* (Academic Press)
R	*Journal of Experimental Psychology* (American Psychological Assn)
R	*Journal of Experimental Psychology: Animal Behavior Processes* (American Psychological Assn)
R	*Journal of Experimental Psychology: Human Perception and Performance* (American Psychological Assn)
R	*Journal of Experimental Psychology: Learning, Memory and Cognition* (American Psychological Assn)
R	*Journal of Experimental Social Psychology* (Academic Press)
R-AP	*Journal of Family Psychology* (American Psychological Assn)
R	*Journal of Family History* (Journal of the National Council of Family Relations) (JAI Press)
R-AP	*Journal of Family Therapy* (Journal of the Association for Family Therapy) (Blackwell Publishers)
R-AP-OP	*Journal of Family Violence* (Plenum)
AP-OP	*Journal of Forensic Psychiatry* (Routledge)
R-AP	*Journal of Humanistic Psychology* (Sage)
R-AP-OP	*Journal of Interpersonal Violence* (Sage)

R-AP-OP	*Journal of Interprofessional Care* (Carfax)
R	*Journal of Language and Social Psychology* (Sage)
AP	*Journal of Managerial Psychology* (MCB University Press)
R-AP	*Journal of Mental Health* (Carfax)
R-AP	*Journal of Mental Health Counseling* (Sage)
AP	*Journal of Nervous and Mental Disease* (Williams & Wilkins)
R-AP	*Journal of Occupational Psychology* (British Psychological Society)
R-AP-OP	*Journal of Organizational Behavior* (John Wiley)
R-AP-OP	*Journal of Pediatric Psychology* (Plenum)
R	*Journal of Personality and Social Psychology* (American Psychological Assn)
R	*Journal of Psychiatric Research* (Pergamon)
R-AP	*Journal of Psycholinguistic Research* (Plenum)
R-AP	*Journal of Psychopathology and Behavioral Assessment* (Plenum)
R	*Journal of Psychopharmacology* (Oxford University Press)
AP	*Psychosomatic Medicine* (Williams & Wilkins)
R	*Journal of Psychosomatic Research* (Pergamon)
R-AP	*Journal of Psychotherapy Integration* (Plenum)
R-AP	*Journal of Research in Reading* (Blackwell Publishers)
R-AP	*Journal of School Psychology* (Pergamon)
R	*Journal of Social and Personal Relationships* (Sage)
R	*Journal of Social Issues* (Plenum)
AP-OP	*Journal of Substance Abuse Treatment* (Pergamon)
AP	*Journal of the American Academy of Child and Adolescent Psychiatry* (Williams & Wilkins)
R-AP-OP	*Journal of the Balint Society* (Haverstock)
AP-OP	*Journal of the British Association of Psychotherapists* (British Assn of Psychotherapists)
R	*Journal of the Society for Psychical Research* (Society for Psychical Research)
R-AP	*Journal of Traumatic Stress* (Plenum)
R-AP	*Journal of Youth and Adolescence* (Plenum)
R	*Language and Cognitive Processes* (Lawrence Erlbaum Associates)
R-AP	*Learning and Individual Differences* (JAI Press)
R-OP	*Learning and Instruction* (The Journal of the European Association for Research on Learning and Instruction) (Pergamon)

R	*Memory* (Lawrence Erlbaum Associates)
R-AP-OP	*Mental Handicap* (Multilingual Matters) (published for the British Institute of Learning Disabilities)
R	*Mental Handicap Research* (Multilingual Matters) (published for the British Institute of Learning Disabilities)
R	*Mind and Language* (Blackwell Publishers)
R-AP	*Motivation and Emotion* (Plenum)
R	*Neural Computation* (MIT Press)
R-AP	*Neuropsychological Rehabilitation* (Lawrence Erlbaum Associates)
R-AP	*Neuropsychology* (American Psychological Assn)
R-AP	*Neuropsychology Review* (Plenum)
R	*New Ideas in Psychology: An International Journal of Innovative Theory in Psychology* (Pergamon)
AP-OP	*New Scientist* (IPC)
AP	*Openmind* (MIND Publications)
R-AP	*Organizational Behavior and Human Decision Processes* (Academic Press)
R	*Perception* (Pion)
R	*Personality and Individual Differences* (Pergamon)
R	*Personality and Social Psychology Bulletin* (Journal of the Society for Personality and Social Psychology of the American Psychological Association) (Sage)
R	*Philosophical Psychology* (Carfax)
R	*Philosophical Transactions of the Royal Society of London,* Series B (The Royal Society)
R	*Philosophy of the Social Sciences* (Sage)
R	*Political Psychology* (Plenum)
R	*Proceedings of the Royal Society of London,* Series B (The Royal Society)
R-AP	*Professional Psychology: Research and Practice* (American Psychological Assn)
R-AP	*Psychiatric Bulletin* (Royal College of Psychiatrists)
R-AP-OP	*Psychiatry Research* (Elsevier)
R-AP-OP	*Psychological Abstracts* (American Psychological Assn)
AP-OP	*Psychological Assessment* (American Psychological Assn)
R-AP	*Psychological Bulletin* (American Psychological Assn)
R-AP	*Psychological Medicine* (Cambridge University Press)

R	*Psychological Research – Psychologische Forschung* (Springer)
R-AP	*Psychological Review* (American Psychological Assn)
R-AP	*Psychological Science* (Cambridge University Press)
Monthly bulletin of the BPS	*The Psychologist* (The British Psychological Society)
R-AP	*Psychology and Aging* (American Psychological Assn)
R	*Psychology and Developing Societies* (Sage)
R-AP-OP	*Psychology and Health* (Harwood Academic)
R-AP-OP	*Psychology, Crime and Law* (Harwood Academic)
AP-OP	*Psychology of Women Quarterly* (Cambridge University Press)
R	*Psychophysiology* (Cambridge University Press)
R-AP	*Psychotherapy Research* (Guilford Press)
R-AP-OP	*PsycSCAN* (American Psychological Assn)
R	*Quarterly Journal of Experimental Psychology: Section A: Human Experimental Psychology; Section B: Comparative and Physiological Psychology* (Lawrence Erlbaum Associates)
AP-OP	*Reading Psychology* (Taylor & Francis)
AP	*Reading and Writing Quarterly* (Taylor & Francis)
R	*Research in Development Disabilities* (Pergamon)
R-AP	*Schizophrenia Research* (Elsevier)
R-AP	*School Psychology International* (Sage)
AP	*Selection & Development Review* (British Psychological Society)
R-AP-OP	*Self and Society: A Journal of Humanistic Psychology* (AHP)
R-AP	*Sex Roles* (Plenum)
R-AP-OP	*Sexual and Marital Therapy* (Carfax)
R	*Small Group Research* (Sage)
R	*Social Cognition* (Guilford Press)
R	*Social Development* (Blackwell Publishers)
R-AP-OP	*Social Justice Research* (Plenum)
R	*Social Psychiatry and Psychiatric Epidemiology* (Springer)
R-AP-OP	*Social Science and Medicine* (Pergamon)
R-AP-OP	*Social Work and Social Sciences Review* (Whiting & Birch)
R	*Symbolic Interaction* (Official Journal of the Society for the Study of Symbolic Interaction) (JAI Press)
R	*Theory and Psychology* (Sage)
AP	*Winnicott Studies* (Karnac Books)
R-AP	*Work and Stress* (Taylor & Francis)

LIST 3: PUBLISHERS AND THEIR READERSHIPS

	REFERENCE	SCHOOLS & FURTHER EDUCATION	HIGHER EDUCATION & ACADEMIC	APPLIED PSYCHOLOGISTS & OTHER PROFESSIONS	TRADE & GENERAL	JOURNALS
A B Academic				●		●
Academic Press	●		●			●
Addison-Wesley	●		●	●	●	
Airlift				●	●	
Allyn & Bacon				●		
American Psychological Assn	●		●	●		●
Analytical Psychology Club						●
Ann Arbor				●		
Anna Freud Centre						●
Aquarian Press					●	
Edward Arnold		●	●			
Artesian Books						●
Assn for Humanistic Psychology				●		●
Assn of Child Psychotherapists						●
Assn of Educational Psychologists						●
Avenue						●
Baillière Tindall				●		
BILD Publications				●		●
Blackwell	●		●	●		●
Blackwell Scientific	●			●		
BPS Books	●	●	●	●	●	
Br. Assn for Counselling	●			●		●
British Assn of Psychotherapists						●
The British Psychological Society						●

	REFERENCE	SCHOOLS & FURTHER EDUCATION	HIGHER EDUCATION & ACADEMIC	APPLIED PSYCHOLOGISTS & OTHER PROFESSIONS	TRADE & GENERAL	JOURNALS
Br. Soc. for Projective Psychology						•
W. C. Brown		•	•			
Butterworth Heinemann			•			
Cambridge Univ. Press	•		•	•	•	•
Carfax						•
Cassell		•	•	•		
Paul Chapman			•	•		
Chapman & Hall				•		
The Children's Society				•	•	
Churchill Livingstone				•		
Community Psychiatric Nurses Assn						•
Constable				•	•	
Current Science						•
J.M. Dent				•		
Duckworth			•	•		
Element Books				•		
Elsevier	•			•	•	•
Erlbaum	•		•	•		•
Eurospan	•		•	•	•	
Falmer			•	•		
Fontana				•	•	
Fontana Press				•	•	
Free Association Books	•			•		•
W.H. Freeman			•		•	
Gaskell				•		
Gateway					•	
Guilford Press	•			•		•
Harcourt Brace & Co.		•	•	•		
HarperCollins		•	•	•		

	REFERENCE	SCHOOLS & FURTHER EDUCATION	HIGHER EDUCATION & ACADEMIC	APPLIED PSYCHOLOGISTS & OTHER PROFESSIONS	TRADE & GENERAL	JOURNALS
Harvester-Wheatsheaf	●		●	●		
Harwood Academic			●	●		●
Haverstock						●
Hobsons			●			●
Hodder & Stoughton		●	●			
Institute of Psychoanalysis						●
IPC						●
JAI	●		●	●		●
Johns Hopkins Univ. Press			●	●	●	
Jossey-Bass			●	●		
Karnac			●			●
Jessica Kingsley	●		●	●		
John Libby			●			
Longman		●				
MacGraw-Hill			●	●		
Macmillan		●	●	●		
Manchester Univ. Press				●	●	
Maxwell Macmillan				●		
MCB Univ. Press						●
MIND				●		●
MIT	●		●	●	●	●
Multilingual Matters				●		●
National Extension Coll.		●				
Thomas Nelson		●				
NFER- Nelson				●		
W. W. Norton			●	●		
Oneworld					●	
Open Univ. Press			●	●		
Oxford Univ. Press	●		●	●		●
Pan Macmillan					●	
Penguin	●		●	●	●	

	REFERENCE	SCHOOLS & FURTHER EDUCATION	HIGHER EDUCATION & ACADEMIC	APPLIED PSYCHOLOGISTS & OTHER PROFESSIONS	TRADE & GENERAL	JOURNALS
Pergamon			●	●		●
Pinter Publishers	●			●		
Pion						●
Plenum			●	●		●
Positive Products				●		
Prentice Hall			●			
Psychology Corp.				●		
Routledge	●	●	●	●	●	●
Royal Coll. of Psychiatrists						●
Royal Society						●
Sage	●		●	●		●
Sheldon					●	
Souvenir			●	●		
Springer-Verlag				●		●
Taylor & Francis		●	●	●		●
Thomson International	●		●			
Thorsons					●	
Transaction				●		
Transworld					●	
Univ. Presses of California, Columbia & Princeton			●	●	●	
Weidenfeld & Nicolson		●		●	●	
Whiting & Birch				●		
Whurr				●		●
John Wiley	●		●	●	●	●
Williams & Wilkins				●		●
Winslow Press				●		
Women's Press				●	●	
Yale Univ. Press	●		●	●		

Publishers' Addresses

A B Academic Publishers
PO Box 42
Bicester
Oxon OX6 7NW

Academic Press
see Harcourt Brace & Co.

Addison-Wesley Publishers Ltd
Finchampstead Road
Wokingham
Berks RG11 2NZ

Airlift Book Company
26/28 Eden Grove
London N7 8EF

Allyn & Bacon
see Harvester-Wheatsheaf

American Psychological Association
750 First Street, NE
Washington DC 20002–4242
USA

Analytical Psychology Club
37 York Street Chambers
London W1H 1DE

Ann Arbor Publishers Ltd
PO Box 1
Belford
Northumberland NE70 7JX

Anna Freud Centre
21 Maresfield Gardens
London NW3 5SH

Aquarian Press
see HarperCollins

Edward Arnold
see Hodder & Stoughton

Artesian Books
18 Artesian Road
London W2 5AR

Association for Humanistic
  Psychology in Britain
BM Box 3582
London WC1N 3XX

Association of Child Psychotherapists
Burgh House
New End Sqare
London NW3 1LT

Association of Educational
  Psychologists
3 Sunderland Road
Durham DH1 2LH

Avenue Publishing Co.
55 Woodstock Avenue
London NW11 9RG

Baillière Tindall
see Harcourt Brace & Co.

BILD Publications
see Multilingual Matters

Blackwell Publishers
108 Cowley Road
Oxford OX4 1JF

Blackwell Scientific Publications Ltd
Osney Mead
Oxford OX2 0EL

BPS Books
see The British Psychological Society

British Association for Counselling
1 Regent Place
Rugby
Warks. CV21 2PJ

British Association of
  Psychotherapists
21 Cantelowes Road
London NW1 9XR

The British Psychological Society
St Andrews House
48 Princess Road East
Leicester LE1 7DR

British Society for Projective
  Psychology
Tavistock Centre
120 Belsize Lane
London NW3 5BA

W.C. Brown Publishers
Holywell House
Osney Mead
Oxford OX2 0ES

Butterworth Heinemann
Linacre House
Jordan Hill
Oxford OX2 8DP

Cambridge University Press
The Edinburgh Building
Shaftesbury Road
Cambridge CB2 2RU

Carfax Publishing Co.
PO Box 25
Abingdon
Oxon OX14 3UE

Cassell plc
Villiers House
41–47 Strand
London WC2N 5JE

Paul Chapman Publishing
144 Liverpool Road
London N1 1LA

Chapman & Hall
2–6 Boundary Row
London SE1 8HN

The Children's Society
Edward Rudolph House
Margery Street
London WC1X 0JL

Churchill Livingstone
Robert Stevenson House
1–3 Baxter's Place
Leith Walk
Edinburgh EH1 3AF

Community Psychiatric Nurses
  Association
44 Dartford Road
Sevenoaks
Kent TN13 3TQ

Constable Publishers
3 The Lanchesters
162 Fulham Palace Road
London W6 9ER

Current Science
34–42 Cleveland Street
London W1P 5FP

J.M. Dent & Sons Ltd
see Weidenfeld & Nicolson

Duckworth
48 Hoxton Square
London N1 6PB

Element Books
Longmead
Shaftesbury
Dorset SP7 8PL

Elsevier Science Publishers B.V.
PO Box 103
1000 AC Amsterdam
The Netherlands

Lawrence Erlbaum Associates Ltd
27 Church Road
Hove
East Sussex BN3 2FA

The Eurospan Group
3 Henrietta Street
Covent Garden
London WC2E 8LU

Falmer Press
Rankine Road
Basingstoke
Hants RG23 0PR

Fontana
see HarperCollins

Fontana Press
see HarperCollins

Free Association Books
26 Freegrove Road
London N7 9RQ

W.H. Freeman & Co. Ltd
20 Beaumont Street
Oxford OX1 2NQ

Gaskell
see Royal College of Psychiatrists

Gateway Books
The Hollies
Mill Hill
Wellow
Bath BA2 8QJ

Guilford Press
UK distribution:
27 Palmeira Mansions
Church Road
Hove
East Sussex BN3 2FA

Harcourt Brace & Co.
24–28 Oval Road
London NW1 7DX

HarperCollins Publishers
77–85 Fulham Palace Road
Hammersmith
London W6 8JB

Harvester-Wheatsheaf
Simon & Schuster International
  Group
Campus 400
Maylands Avenue
Hemel Hempstead
Herts. HP2 7EZ

Harwood Academic Publishers
PO Box 90
Reading
Berks RG1 8JL

Haverstock Publications
249 Haverstock Hill
London NW3 4PS

Hobsons Publishing plc
Bateman Street
Cambridge CB2 1LZ

Hodder & Stoughton Publishers
Mill Road
Dunton Green
Sevenoaks
Kent TN13 2YA

Institute of Psychoanalysis
63 New Cavendish Street
London W1M 7RD

IPC Specialist Group
King's Reach Tower
Stamford Street
London SE1 9LS

JAI Press Ltd
The Courtyard
28 High Street
Hampton Hill
Middx TW12 1PD

Johns Hopkins University Press
101 Beckett House
14 Billing Road
Northampton NN1 5AW

Jossey-Bass Publishers
see Maxwell Macmillan

Karnac Books
58 Gloucester Road
London SW7 4QY

Jessica Kingsley Publishers
116 Pentonville Road
London N1 9JB

John Libby & Company Limited
13 Smiths Yard
Summerley Street
London SW18 4HR

Longman
Longman House
Burnt Mill
Harlow
Essex CM20 2JE

McGraw-Hill Book Company Europe
Shoppenhangers Road
Maidenhead
Berks SL6 2QL

Macmillan Press
Houndmills
Basingstoke
Hants RG21 2XS

Manchester University Press
Oxford Road
Manchester M13 9PL

Maxwell Macmillan International
Little Baldon House
Nuneham Courtenay
Oxford OX44 9PU

MCB University Press
60–62 Toller Lane
Bradford BD8 9BY

MIND Publications
Kemp House, 1st Floor
152–160 City Road
London EC1V 2NP

The MIT Press
14 Bloomsbury Square
London WC1A 2LP

Multilingual Matters
Frankfurt Lodge
Clevedon Hall
Victoria Road
Clevedon
Avon BS21 7SJ

National Extension College
18 Brooklands Avenue
Cambridge CB2 2HN

Thomas Nelson & Sons Ltd
Nelson House
Mayfield Road
Walton-on-Thames
Surrey KT12 5PL

NFER-Nelson
Darville House
2 Oxford Road East
Windsor
Berks SL4 1DF

North-Holland Publishing Co.
see Elsevier Science Publishers

W.W. Norton & Company
10 Coptic Street
London WC1A 1PU

Oneworld Publications
185 Banbury Road
Oxford OX2 7AR

Open University Press
Celtic Court
22 Ball Moor
Buckingham MK18 1XW

Oxford University Press
Walton Street
Oxford OX2 6DP

Pan Macmillan Ltd
18–21 Cavaye Place
London SW10 9PG

Penguin Books
27 Wrights Lane
London W8 5TZ

Pergamon Press Ltd
Headington Hill Hall
Oxford OX3 0BW

Pinter Publishers
25 Floral Street
Covent Garden
London WC2E 9DS

Pion Ltd
207 Brondesbury Park
London NW2 5JN

Plenum Publishing Co. Ltd
88/90 Middlesex Street
London E1 7EZ

Positive Products
PO Box 45
Cheltenham GL52 3BX

Prentice Hall
see Harvester-Wheatsheaf

The Psychological Corporation
Foots Cray High Street
Sidcup
Kent DA14 5HP

Routledge
11 New Fetter Lane
London EC4P 4EE

The Royal College of Psychiatrists
17 Belgrave Square
London SW1X 8PG

The Royal Society
6 Carlton House Terrace
London SW1Y 5AG

Sage Publications
6 Bonhill Street
London EC2A 4PU

Sheldon Press
Holy Trinity Church
Marylebone Road
London NW1 4DU

Souvenir Press Ltd
43 Great Russell Street
London WC1B 3PA

Springer-Verlag London Ltd
8 Alexander Road
London SW19 7JZ

Taylor & Francis Ltd
Rankine Road
Basingstoke
Hants RG24 0PR

Thomson International Publishing
2–6 Boundary Row
London SE1 8HN

Thorsons
see HarperCollins

Transaction Publishers UK
c/o Plymbridge Distributors Ltd
Estover
Plymouth PL6 7PZ

Transworld Publishers
61–63 Uxbridge Road
London W5 5SA

University Presses of California,
  Columbia and Princeton Ltd
1 Oldlands Way
Bognor Regis
West Sussex PO22 9SA

Weidenfeld & Nicolson
Orion Publishing Group
5 Upper St Martins Lane
London WC2H 9EA

Whiting & Birch Ltd
PO Box 872
London SE23 3HL

Whurr Publishers Ltd
19b Compton Terrace
London N1 2UN

John Wiley & Sons Ltd
Baffins Lane
Chichester
West Sussex PO19 1UD

Williams & Wilkins Ltd
Broadway House
2–6 Fulham Broadway
London SW6 1AA

Winslow Press
Telford Road
Bicester
Oxon OX6 0TS

The Woman's Press Ltd
34 Great Sutton Street
London EC1V 0DX

Yale University Press
23 Pond Street
London NW3 2PN

TEACHING OF PSYCHOLOGY TO OTHER PROFESSIONALS

Alastair G. Gale and Leslie J. Francis (Editors)

❏ *health: medicine, nurse training, radiography, physiotherapy, sport and exercise, music therapy, pharmacy, chiropody • management • helping professions: clergy, social work, teaching • other professions: law, engineering, architecture*

In 1990 the British Psychological Society set up the Standing Committee on Teaching Psychology to Other Professional Groups. The committee began its work by identifying some of the professions to which psychology might reasonably be brought to make a significant contribution. Surveys and reviews were undertaken to establish how psychology is currently taught to students studying within these professional areas and to gain both a quantitative and qualitative view of the current status of psychology teaching in these professions.

One of the most important challenges of teaching psychology to professional groups is to teach psychology in a way in which it can be readily applied to what the student does in day-to-day practice and integrated with other disciplines which inform that practice. The major challenge facing teachers of psychology to other professional groups is to teach it in a way which helps the student to apply and integrate psychological knowledge and skills.

This chapter presents a selection of some of the many areas where psychology is relevant. These areas are grouped into four broad categories. Consideration is given for each to aspects of psychology which may be taught. The key research journals and a selection of the important references are cited.

Taken together this sample demonstrates how important psychology is to other professions. In many instances the subject is taught by members of those professions who have some psychological knowledge rather than primarily being taught by psychologists per se.

HEALTH

The role of psychology in health and health-related fields is being increasingly recognized. The importance of psychological factors in physical well-being and recovery from illness is now widely acknowledged, as well as the positive effect of good communication and counselling skills on the part of the health professional. Professional bodies in fields as diverse as chiropody and pharmacy are advocating the importance of including psychology in the curriculum. The application of theories of developmental psychology is particularly useful when dealing with client groups such as children, the elderly and people who are disabled; theories of interpersonal communication are especially relevant to health care professionals who need to explain treatment methods or who are frequently dealing with people in shock or distress; the growing field of health psychology, concerned primarily with the relationship between psychological factors and physical health, is finding its place on training courses in a wide variety of health-related areas.

Readings

BRANNON, L. and FEIST, J. (1992) *Health Psychology: An Introduction to Behaviour and Health*. London: Edward Arnold.

BROOME, K. (Ed.) (1989) *Health Psychology: Processes and Applications*. London: Chapman and Hall (new edition due 1993).

BURNS, R.B. (1991) *Essential Psychology: For Students and Professionals in the Health and Social Services*, 2nd ed. London: Kluwer.

DI MATTEO, M.R. (1991) *The Psychology of Health and Illness: An Individual Perspective*. Monterey, California: Brooks/Cole.

HARVEY, P. (1988) *Health Psychology*. London: Longman.

MAES, S. (1992) *International Review of Health Psychology*, Vol 1. Chichester: John Wiley.

MORRISON, P. (1992) *Professional Caring in Practice: A Psychological Analysis*. Aldershot: Avebury.

SARAFINO, E.P. (1990) *Health Psychology: Biopsychosocial Interactions*. Chichester: John Wiley.

TAYLOR, S. (1987) *Health Psychology*. New York: Random House.

WINETT, R.A., KING, A.C. and ALTMAN, D.G. (1989) *Health Psychology and Public Health: An Integrative Approach*. New York: Pergamon.

MEDICINE
Charles Abrahams and Lorraine Sherr

Medicine is an example of an applied area where psychology interacts at a variety of levels. These include the following. First, psychology illuminates the behavioural change associated with the normal course of development, or interruptions in this course such as illness or impairment. Second, there is the contribution of psychological factors (such as stress) to the expression and manifestation of illness (such as asthma or migraine). Psychology also applies when illness is acquired through behaviours such as drug use or sexual intercourse. A third area concerns interactions between patients and medical staff. These include communicating with patients, interviewing them and understanding the psychological/ physiological effect of pain, anxiety, fear or environmental constraints.

Fourth, patients' reactions to medical intervention and the role such reactions have in the course of treatment and prognosis is also important. This area can encompass factors involved in acceptance of and compliance with treatment, adherence to drug regimens, coping and adjustment, as well as tolerance to and use of medication, effects of length of stay in hospital, etc.

A fifth area is that of psychological models of care and treatment. These interact with medical models, often separate and yet sometimes indistinguishable and integrated. Psychosocial models are most prominent in areas where medical interventions are limited (such as AIDS, psychosomatic problems, death and dying), but are more commonly utilized in holistic medical approaches which mark a change of approach in medicine generally. References which can be used here include those relating to the specific issues involved when treating people who are disabled, people with terminal illness, children, the elderly, mothers-to-be, etc.

Sixth, health education is an area which provides an avenue for prevention and management of disease. Issues commonly addressed are smoking, diet, alcohol, drug abuse and behaviour changes. Health education can also extend to ameliorate negative societal reaction to disability or disease such as AIDS.

Finally, medical systems describe how the implementation of medicine can be understood from a psychological point of view. This can range from areas as diverse as management, recruitment and interviewing to decision-making, change, and staff stress and burnout. Such an understanding can contribute directly or indirectly to patient management and care.

This growing body of knowledge has now been integrated, to varying degrees, both into medical education and continuing medical practice and training. General texts on psychology in medicine include Mathews and Steptoe (1988), Pearce and Wardle (1989), Robbins and Cooper (1988), Weinman (1987) and Rachman (1984). Some texts with specific reference to communicating with patients include Enelow and Fisher (1986), Green and McCreaner (1989), Kübler Ross (1970), Ley (1988), Pendleton and Hasler (1983), Sherr (1989), Stroebe and Stroebe (1987), and Worden (1983). A new series `Communication and Counselling in Health Care' (editor: Hilton Davis) is published by BPS Books (The British Psychological Society).

Journals

There is a number of relevant articles in both mainstream medical and psychological journals. In addition some specialist journals have now evolved which are of particular interest. Psychology is often closely linked with sociology in its contribution to medical education; hence the existence of general social science journals such as *Social Science and Medicine*.

Psychology usually appears under the headings of `medical psychology', `behavioural medicine' or `health psychology'. These sub-disciplines overlap extensively and reflect a difference in emphasis rather than content. Behavioural medicine is the broadest of the three defining an interdisciplinary field encompassing all aspects of behaviour which relate to health, illness and treatment (see *Journal of Behavioural Medicine*). Medical psychology is limited to the work of psychologists, but also covers a broad field of application (see *British Journal of Medical Psychology*).

Health psychology is a more recent development initiated in the United States. It has the advantage of shifting psychological research away from categories derived from medical practice. Thus, health psychology textbooks are less likely than behavioural medicine texts to group research around diagnostic terms. Health psychology also incorporates a focus on prevention and public health and illness, and responses to treatment (see *Health Psychology* and *Psychology and Health*). Psychology is also involved with research into psychological disorders where it overlaps with psychiatry (see *Psychological Medicine*). Other journals include *Journal of Psychosomatic Research, AIDS Care, British Journal of Addiction, Journal of Reproductive and Infant Psychology, Psychosomatic Research, Medical Education, Sociology of Health and Illness* and *Medical Teacher*.

Readings

ENELOW, A.J. and FISHER, S.N. (1986) *Interviewing and Patient Care*. Oxford: Oxford Press.
GREEN, J. and McCREANER, A. (1989) *Counselling in AIDS and HIV Infection*. Oxford: Blackwell Scientific Publications.
KÜBLER ROSS, E. (1970) *On Death and Dying*. London: Macmillan.
LEY, P. (1988) *Communicating with Patients: Improving Communication Satisfaction and Compliance*. London: Chapman and Hall.
MATHEWS, A. and STEPTOE, A. (1988) *Essential Psychology for Medical Practice*. Edinburgh: Churchill Livingstone.
PEARCE, S. and WARDLE, J. (1989) *The Practice of Behavioural*

Medicine. Oxford: Oxford University Press and BPS Books (The British Psychological Society).

PENDLETON, P. and HASLER, J. (Eds) (1983) *Doctor–Patient Communication*. London: Academic Press.

RACHMAN, S. (1984) *Contributions to Medical Psychology*, Vols 1–3. Oxford: Pergamon Press.

ROBBINS, T.W. and COOPER, P. (1988) *Psychology for Medicine*. London: Edward Arnold.

SHERR, L. (1989) *Death, Dying and Bereavement*. Oxford: Blackwell Scientific Publications.

STROEBE, W. and STROEBE, M.S. (1987) *Bereavement and Health*. Cambridge: Cambridge University Press.

WEINMAN, J. (1987) *An Outline of Psychology as Applied to Medicine*, 2nd ed. London: Wright.

WORDEN, J. (1983) *Grief Counselling and Grief Therapy*, 2nd ed. London: Routledge.

Please also refer to those publications listed under `Health'.

NURSE TRAINING
Paul Morrison

The number of nursing degree courses in the UK has increased rapidly over the last 30 years. Psychology forms an important facet of most nurse training programmes at diploma and degree level. A common trend observed in the BPS survey was the emphasis on applied social psychology and health psychology issues. The main areas of psychology being taught to nurses are: introduction to psychology, developmental psychology, social psychology, health psychology, learning theory, counselling, interpersonal relationships, anxiety and stress. There is a large literature available in all these areas, which often directly relates psychology and psychosocial issues to nursing practice.

Only two methods of *applying* psychology to the practice situation were mentioned consistently in the survey. These were providing nursing examples of psychological principles during the teaching session, and expecting the clinical lecturers to apply principles in practice.

One particularly useful approach through which specific principles in psychology can be integrated into nursing training is the `problem-based' model of curriculum design (see Boud, 1985; Boud and Feletti, 1991; Colby *et al.*, 1986; Neame, 1981). The major emphasis here is on the `problems' which professionals face on a day-to-day basis. The curriculum is structured around these problems, and the information students need to solve these problems forms the basis of teaching. This has the effect of highlighting for the student how psychology can be applied to real world settings. Some medical and nursing schools in the UK already run this type of course.

Journals

Journals which publish articles on research, many of which span both nursing and psychology include: *Nursing Research, Journal of Advanced Nursing, International Journal of Nursing Studies, Image: The Journal of Nursing Scholarship, Nursing Science Quarterly, Research in Nursing and Health, Western Journal of Nursing Research, Advances in Nursing Science, Qualitative Health Research, Issues in Mental Health Nursing, Journal of Clinical Nursing, British Journal of Nursing, Nursing Times, Nursing Standard, Nurse Education Today, Journal of Holistic Nursing, Archives of Psychiatric Nursing, Health Visitor, Hospital and Community Psychiatry, Intensive Care Nursing, Journal of Advances in Health and Nursing Care, Journal of Nursing Administration, Paediatric Nursing* and *Journal of Gerontological Nursing.*

Readings

ABRAHAM, C. and SHANLEY, E. (1992) *Social Psychology for Nurses.* London: Edward Arnold.

ALTSCHUL, A. and SINCLAIR, H. (1986) *Psychology for Nurses,* 6th ed. London: Ballière Tindall.

BOUD, D. (1985) Problem-based learning in perspective. In D. Boud (Ed.) *Problem-Based Learning in Education for the Professions.* Sydney: Higher Education Research and Development Society of Australasia.

BOUD, D. and FELETTI, G. (Eds) (1991) *The Challenge of Problem-Based Learning.* London: Kogan Page.

BURNARD, P. and MORRISON, P. (1990) *Nursing Research in Action: Developing Basic Skills.* Basingstoke: MacMillan.

COLBY, K., ALMY, T.P. and ZUBKOFF, M. (1986) Problem-based learning approach in baccalaureate role nursing: How effective is it? *Nursing Papers, 19, 2,* 17–26.

HYLAND, M.E. and DONALDSON, M.L. (1989) *Psychological Care in Nursing Practice.* London: Scutari.

LINGIAH, D. (1988) *Social Policy in Nursing.* Glasgow: Lingiah.

McGHIE, A. (1986) *Psychology as Applied to Nursing,* 8th ed. Edinburgh: Churchill Livingstone.

MORRISON, P. and BURNARD, P. (1991) *Caring and Communicating: The Interpersonal Relationship in Nursing.* London: Macmillan.

NEAME, R.L.B. (1981) How to construct a problem-based course. *Medical Teacher, 3,* 94–99.

NIVEN, N. (1989) *Health Psychology: An Introduction for Nurses and Other Health Care Professionals.* Edinburgh: Churchill Livingstone.

NYE, R. (1986) *Three Psychologies.* Monterey, California: Brooks/Cole.

SKEVINGTON, S. (Ed.) (1984) *Understanding Nurses: The Social Psychology of Nursing.* Chichester: Wiley.

WALLIS, D. AND DE WOLFF, C.J. (Eds) (1988) *Stress and Organisational Problems in Hospitals: Implications for Management.* London: Croom Helm.

RADIOGRAPHY
Alastair Gale

The major radiographic qualifications have been the Diploma of the College of Radiographers (DCR) and the Higher Diploma (HDCR). These are gradually being phased out and replaced by degree and postgraduate qualifications respectively. As a subject radiography encompasses two complimentary areas: diagnostic radiography and therapeutic radiotherapy. Psychology is applicable in diagnostic radiography to understanding both the processes involved in the examination of the medical image (Gale *et al.*, 1979) as well as the interpersonal factors important when dealing with patients (Hegarty and DeCann, 1986). In radiotherapy the emphasis is on the latter as patients undergo a course of treatment and often need counselling and support.

The 1991 BPS research indicated that behavioural and cognitive models in psychology were addressed to some extent in courses (as well as perceptual issues in diagnostic radiography), but emphasis was placed primarily on topics relevant to dealing adequately with patients. These include: communication, interpersonal skills, effects of illness on the family, hospitalization, anxiety, stress, dying, the effects of life events, dealing with aggression and body image. Courses also focused on counselling skills, the use of role play, research skills and how to deal with specific groups such as the elderly.

Journals
The main radiography journal is *Radiography Today*. This together with *Rad Magazine* cover all of the radiographic areas. Both sometimes address psychological topics. Nursing journals such as *Nursing Times* are also applicable. Whilst dealing primarily with radiology, the following journals are occasionally relevant to radiographers: *Radiology*, *British Journal of Radiology* and *Clinical Radiology*.

Readings
GALE, A.G., JOHNSTON, F. and WORTHINGTON, B.S. (1979) Psychology and radiology. In D.J. Oborne, M.M. Gruneberg and J.R. Eiser (Eds) *Research in Psychology and Medicine*. London: Academic Press.
HEGARTY, J.R. and DeCANN, R.W. (1986) *Psychology in Radiography*. Stoke: Change.

Please also refer to those publications listed under `Health'.

PHYSIOTHERAPY
John Hegarty and Marian Whittaker

Physiotherapy (`physical therapy' in the USA) is one of the `professions supplementary to medicine' and is regulated in the UK by the Chartered Society of Physiotherapy (CSP) and the Council for Professions Supplementary to Medicine. Training (from 1992) is at degree level with the former schools of physiotherapy teaching alongside university departments.

Physiotherapists use a variety of techniques and work, as part of a multidisciplinary team, in a range of settings with many client groups, including people with minor injuries, patients recovering from surgery, and individuals with severe intellectual or physical disabilities.

Psychology is considered by the profession to be an important subject to include in training courses and particular areas are suggested (Chartered Society of Physiotherapy, 1991). One reason is undoubtedly that physiotherapy relies heavily on the cooperation of the patient for treatments to be successful. Often, patients are not inclined to cooperate, being not at their best after surgery or injury. Therefore, it is helpful for physiotherapists to be aware of factors affecting self-esteem and body image, motivation, and interpersonal communication.

A knowledge of stages and processes in child development is broadly valuable when working with youngsters and with people who have developmental disorders. Especially relevant is cognitive psychology, particularly those aspects which underpin the development of skilled performance. Many aspects of health psychology impinge on the work, including behavioural alternatives to the medical model, effects of institutional care, stress and anxiety, and the psychology of pain. There are perspectives within counselling and psychotherapy which physiotherapists find personally valuable and which enhance their skill base, including behavioural relaxation training, therapeutic imagery work, basic Rogerian counselling skills (Grant, 1979) and an understanding of loss and bereavement. Basic texts for psychology and physiotherapy include Dunkin (1981), and French (1992). Pratt (1978) gives a psychological view of the physiotherapist's role.

The research skills of psychologists are prized, although there is already a strong research element within the profession (Rothstein, 1985; Hicks, 1988). Techniques of single case research (Ottenbacher, 1986) are important for assessing interventions, and group comparison designs are vital in assessing the relative efficacy of different physiotherapy methods.

Whilst physiotherapy values and benefits from input from psychology, there is considerable potential gain for psychology in extended collaboration since the profession is working with a wide range of clients in many settings. Studies of patients in the context of physiotherapy will, as just one example, contribute to the relatively sparse knowledge about gross motor skill development.

Readings   CHARTERED SOCIETY OF PHYSIOTHERAPY (1991) *Curriculum of Study*. London: C.S.P.

DUNKIN, N. (1981) *Psychology for Physiotherapists*. Basingstoke: Macmillan.

FRENCH, S. (1992) *Physiotherapy: A Psychosocial Approach.* Oxford: Butterworth-Heinemann.
GRANT, D. (1979) The physiotherapist as patient counsellor. *Physiotherapy, 65,* 218–220.
HICKS, C.M. (1988) *Practical Research Methods for Physiotherapists.* London: Churchill Livingstone.
OTTENBACHER, K.J. (1986) *Evaluating Clinical Change.* Baltimore: Williams & Wilkins.
PRATT, J.W. (1978) A psychological view of the physiotherapist's role. *Physiotherapy, 64,* 241–243.
ROTHSTEIN, J.M. (1985) *Measurement in Physical Therapy.* New York: Churchill Livingstone.

SPORT AND EXERCISE
Stuart Biddle

During the 1980s there was a rapid increase in the number of undergraduate degree courses in the UK in fields related to sport. Prior to this, the academic study of sport and physical activity was restricted to BEd degrees for pre-service physical education teachers.

The teaching of psychology in sport and related fields has also expanded, to include masters degrees in sports science, exercise and health science, and exercise and sport psychology. The teaching of psychology in sport-related courses ('sport science') has included three main areas: motor learning, sport psychology and exercise psychology. 'Motor learning' refers to the acquisition and control of physical actions relevant to sport. 'Sport psychology' is often used as a generic term to refer to sport psychology, exercise psychology and motor learning. Adopting a more specific definition, Rejeski and Brawley (1988) suggest that sport psychology is the contribution of psychology to the promotion, maintenance and enhancement of sport-related behaviour. 'Exercise psychology', a relatively new term, refers to the contribution of psychology to the 'promotion, explanation, maintenance and enhancement of behaviours related to physical work capacity' (Rejeski and Brawley, 1988, p.239). Usually this means exercise for health and fitness rather than competitive performance. The BPS survey indicated that popular areas of teaching on psychology in sport science include psychological preparation and mental skills, acquisition of skill and health/exercise psychology.

The key textbooks tend to be from North American authors (for example, Dishman, 1988; Gill, 1986; Horn, 1992; Schmidt, 1988; Silva and Weinberg, 1984), although recently British authors have contributed with texts in stress and performance in sport (Jones and Hardy, 1990), exercise psychology (Biddle and Mutrie, 1991) and applied sport psychology (Bull, 1991; Terry, 1989). In addition, an international text has also appeared (Singer, Murphey and Tennant, 1993).

Journals   Key journals specializing in the field, or which publish rele-
vant articles on a regular basis, include *International Journal of
Sport Psychology, Journal of Sport and Exercise Psychology,
Journal of Applied Sport Psychology, Journal of Sports Science,
Journal of Motor Behavior, Journal of Sport Behavior, Medicine and
Science in Sports and Exercise, Research Quarterly for Exercise and
Sport*, and *The Sport Psychologist*.

Readings   BIDDLE, S.J.H. and MUTRIE, N. (1991) *Psychology of Physical
Activity and Exercise: A Health-Related Perspective*. London:
Springer-Verlag.
BULL, S.J. (Ed.) (1991) *Sport Psychology: A Self-Help Guide*.
Marlborough: The Crowood Press.
DISHMAN, R.K. (Ed.) (1988) *Exercise Adherence: Its Impact on
Public Health*. Champaign, IL: Human Kinetics.
GILL, D.L. (1986) *Psychological Dynamics of Sport*. Champaign,
IL: Human Kinetics.
HORN, T.S. (Ed.) (1992) *Advances in Sport Psychology*.
Champaign, IL: Human Kinetics.
JONES, J.G. and HARDY, L. (1990) (Eds) *Stress and
Performance in Sport*. Chichester: Wiley.
REJESKI, W.J. and BRAWLEY, L.R. (1988) Defining the
boundaries of sport psychology. *The Sport Psychologist*, 2,
231–242.
SCHMIDT, R.A. (1988) *Motor Control and Learning*.
Champaign, IL: Human Kinetics.
SILVA, J.S. and WEINBERG, R.S. (Eds) (1984) *Psychological
Foundations of Sport*. Champaign, IL: Human Kinetics.
SINGER, R.N., MURPHEY, M. and TENNANT, L.K. (Eds)
(1993) *Handbook of Research on Sport Psychology*. New York:
Macmillan.
TERRY, P. (1989) *The Winning Mind*. Wellingborough:
Thorsons.

MUSIC THERAPY
John Sloboda

There are currently approximately 200 professional music
therapists working in the UK.

The Association of Professional Music Therapists (APMT)
regulates the training of music therapists through its Courses
Liaison Sub-Committee. All entrants to professional training
must have studied music for at least three years at degree or
diploma level. The qualifying training is provided through a
postgraduate diploma in music therapy. For most trainees,
their postgraduate diploma will contain their first formal
exposure to psychology as a discipline. There are currently
four accredited courses in the UK.

It is stipulated by the APMT that any course must contain
a minimum of 44 contact hours of `medical/psychological
studies'. The main areas covered by all four courses are:
developmental psychology, psychiatry and psychotherapy.

There is a wide range of mainstream texts to choose from. Issues of most importance are those which relate to the main client groups of music therapists, namely, people with mental or physical disability including neurological conditions; those with mental illness or emotional disturbances; children with multiple disabilities or autism; people with speech and language or sensory impairment; the elderly.

There is a number of books on wider psychological aspects of music which can inform discussions of therapy (Hargreaves, 1986; Wilson and Roehmann, 1990; Miller, 1989; Moog, 1976; Shuter-Dyson and Gabriel, 1980; Sloboda, 1985). More than one course leader has commented that a textbook on psychology for music therapists is long overdue.

Journals Almost no literature exists which specifically relates psychology to music therapy, and the reading lists of the four courses refer on the whole to mainstream psychology and psychiatry texts. However, the following journals occasionally publish material at the psychology/music-therapy interface: *Psychology of Music, Journal of Music Therapy, Journal of British Music Therapy*. A special issue of *Psychology of Music* was devoted to music therapy (Vol 16.1, 1988, for example, Bunt, *et al.*).

Readings BUNT, L., CLARKE, E., CROSS, I. and HOSKYNS, S. (1988) A discussion of the relationship between music therapy and the psychology of music. *Psychology of Music*, 16, 62–70.

HARGREAVES, D. (1986) *The Developmental Psychology of Music*. Cambridge: Cambridge University Press.

MILLER, L.K. (1989) *Musical Savants: Exceptional Skill in the Mentally Retarded*. Hillsdale, NJ: Erlbaum.

MOOG, H. (1976) *The Musical Experience of the Pre-School Child*. London: Schott.

SHUTER-DYSON, R. and GABRIEL, C. (1981) *The Psychology of Musical Ability*, 2nd ed. London: Methuen.

SLOBODA, J.A. (1985) *The Musical Mind: The Cognitive Psychology of Music*. London: Oxford University Press.

WILSON, F. and ROEHMANN, F. (Eds) (1990) *Music and Child Development*. St Louis, MS: MMB Inc.

PHARMACY
Donald Pennington

The Royal Pharmaceutical Society of Great Britain published a report on a working party on social and behavioural sciences in June 1989. This report identified areas of psychology that should feature on all pharmacy courses and optional recommended areas.

The core area of psychology specified was interpersonal communication dealing specifically with: verbal and non-verbal communication, social skills, client–practitioner communication, social perception and communication, and dyadic and small group communication.

The optional areas of psychology deemed to be of special relevance were: patient compliance/adherence, models of illness and wellness, and understanding specific client groups (for example, the elderly, mothers and young children, people with learning disabilities, ethnic minorities, etc.). Pharmacy courses are also looking to the growing field of health psychology for input.

CHIROPODY
Donald Pennington

Most chiropody courses are moving from diploma to degree status, and there is a number of honours degree courses by part-time study for practising chiropodists. Some courses include a considerable psychology component taught by qualified psychologists, others have little explicit psychology taught. However, the trend is towards developing psychology for training and experienced chiropodists.

To date three themes or areas have been emphasized. At first-year level a short life span module is taught to make students aware of the person on the 'end of the foot'. Given that the majority of clients of state-registered chiropodists are elderly people, the psychology of ageing is included at second-year level, along with a course in health psychology.

MANAGEMENT
Barrie Brown, Rhona Flin, Georgina Slaven and Stefan Wills

There are estimated to be around 2.4 million managers in the UK out of a total working population of 17.8 million, that is approximately one in eight of those in employment are regarded as managers (Employment Department Training Agency, 1989, *Management Challenge for the 1990s*). In the 1980s there was growing concern that British managers were not equipped with sufficiently sophisticated skills in what was becoming an increasingly competitive international market. Following the publication of two influential reports, *The Making of Managers* (Handy, 1987) and *The Making of British Managers* (Constable and McCormick, 1987), the Management Charter Initiative (MCI) was established. Its objective is to increase the quantity, quality, relevance and accessibility of management education and development and the MCI is now the leading body responsible for the development of national standards of performance for managers and supervisors. As one of the main areas of competence in all their management standards relates to managing people, psychology has an important contribution to make to these national management training initiatives.

At present, managers and prospective managers are trained on the job and on a wide variety of courses from one day programmes through to degree awarding courses. Most of the undergraduate programmes in business studies, commerce or marketing and the postgraduate management programmes such as Master of Business Administration include a psychological component, typically within generic subjects such as organizational behaviour or consumer behaviour. As there is a wide variety of university and college courses in business and management and a multitude of different commercial and in-house training packages, it is not feasible to present a list of teaching materials that would suit all courses and levels of students. We have concentrated instead on teaching psychology to managers at a postgraduate and post-experience level and on the training of personnel managers. However, most of the sources listed are also suitable for teaching psychology to undergraduate business students or to managers on specialist short courses.

The degree of Master of Business Administration (MBA) is recognized as the principle postgraduate qualification specific to business and management. There is a wide range of MBA programmes available in the UK, including part-time, full-time, distance learning and company-specific programmes. The information presented has been compiled on the basis of our own experience teaching MBA students and the results of a recent survey of MBA programmes.

Personnel professionals are managers who address themselves to the task of balancing the needs of those who work in organizations with the aims of the organization itself. Their core interest is in managing the human resource. There is, therefore, a significant overlap in the content and orientation of the role of personnel managers on the one hand and general managers on the other. The education and training of more than 40,000 personnel professionals who currently work in the UK is the responsibility of the Institute of Personnel Management (IPM).

The following topics with a definite psychological component are covered (under a number of different guises) on MBA programmes. Analysis of the IPM syllabus and course materials for selected courses reveal a similar list. There is now a vast literature in the area of human resources and management and the references cited do not constitute a comprehensive overview of this material. They provide only a starting point for those beginning to explore the area: motivation/job satisfaction (Pinder, 1984; Robertson *et al.*, 1992), leadership in organizations (Yukl, 1989), group behaviour/team building (Belbin, 1981; Brown, 1988; Hastings *et al.*, 1986), recruitment and selection (Cook, 1988; Herriott, 1989; Shackleton and Newall, 1991), attitudes to work (Walters, 1990), personality/individual differences (Furnham, 1992), psychometric testing (British Psychological Society, 1989), occupational stress (Fontana, 1989; Leatz and Stolar, 1992), thinking and decision-making (de Bono, 1985; Heirs, 1986), communication (Rakos 1991; Raspberry and

Lemoine 1986; Reddy, 1987), culture and power (Morgan, 1986), managing change (Buchanan and Boddy, 1992), safety (Reason, 1990), research methods (Bryman, 1989; Hutton, 1988; Philips, 1987), training and development (Wille, 1990), consumer behaviour (Schiffman and Kanuk, 1987; Chisnall, 1989; Engel *et al.*, 1990; Foxall, 1991).

Journals

Journals which can provide useful articles in managerial psychology include: *Journal of Occupational and Organizational Psychology, Journal of Organizational Behaviour, Journal of Applied Psychology, Journal of Managerial Psychology, Management Today* and *Work and Stress.*

Journals which can provide useful articles in consumer behaviour include: *Journal of Advertising Research, Journal of Consumer Research, Journal of Marketing Research* and *Journal of the Market Research Society.*

Journals which can provide useful articles in personnel management include: *Personnel Management, Personnel Today, IPM Magazine* and *Personnel Review.*

Other journals which regularly contain articles of interest to personnel professionals are: *Administrative Science Quarterly, Academy of Management Review, American Sociological Review, British Journal of Industrial Relations, Harvard Business Review, Human Relations, Human Resource Management, Journal of General Management, Journal of Management Studies, Journal of Occupational Psychology, Personnel Administrator, Personnel, Personnel Journal, Sloan Management Review, Strategic Management Journal, The Magazine for Human Resources Development, Training* and *Training & Development Journal.*

Readings

BARON, R.A. and GREENBURG, J. (1990) *Behaviour in Organisations.* Boston, Mass: Allyn and Bacon.
BELBIN, M. (1981) *Management Teams: Why They Succeed or Fail.* Oxford: Heinemann.
THE BRITISH PSYCHOLOGICAL SOCIETY (1989) *Psychological Testing: Guidance for Users.* Leicester: BPS.
BROWN, R. (1988) *Group Processes.* Oxford: Basil Blackwell.
BRYMAN, R. (1989) *Doing Research in Organizations.* London: Routledge.
BUCHANAN, D. and BODDY, D. (1992) *The Expertise of the Change Agent.* London: Prentice Hall.
CHERRINGTON, D. (1989) *Organizational Behavior.* Boston, Mass: Allyn and Bacon.
CHISNALL, P. (1989) *Marketing: A Behavioural Analysis*, 2nd ed. London: McGraw Hill.
CONSTABLE, J. and McCORMICK, R. (1987) *The Making of British Managers.* London: British Institute of Managers.
COOK, M. (1988) *Personnel Selection and Productivity.* Chichester: Wiley.
DAWSON, S. (1992) *Analysing Organizations*, 2nd ed. London: Macmillan.

DE BONO, E. (1985) *Lateral Thinking for Managers*. London: Pan.

ENGEL, J., BLACKWELL, R. and MINIARD, P. (1990) *Consumer Behaviour*, 6th ed. Hillsdale: Dryden.

FONTANA, D. (1989) *Managing Stress*. Leicester: BPS Books (The British Psychological Society) and Routledge.

FOXALL, G. (1991) *Consumer Psychology in Behavioural Perspective*. London: Routledge.

FURNHAM, A. (1992) *Personality at Work*. London: Routledge.

GUEST, D. (1989) Personnel and HRM – Can you tell the difference? *IPM Magazine*, January.

HANDY, C. (1985) *Understanding Organizations*, 3rd ed. London: Penguin.

HANDY, C. (1987) *The Making of Managers*. London: National Economic Development Office.

HASTINGS, C., BIXBY, P. and CHAUDHRY-LAWTON, R. (1986) *Superteams*. London: Fontana.

HEIRS, B. (1986) *The Professional Decision Thinker*. London: Sidgwick and Jackson.

HERRIOTT, P. (1989) *Assessment and Selection in Organisations*. Chichester: Wiley.

HERSEY, P. and BLANCHARD, K. (1988) *Management of Organizational Behavior*, 5th ed. New York: Prentice Hall.

HUCZYNSKI, A. and BUCHANAN, B. (1991) *Organizational Behaviour*, 2nd ed. London: Prentice Hall.

HUNT, J. (1992) *Managing People at Work*, 3rd ed. London: McGraw Hill.

HUTTON, P. (1988) *Survey Research for Managers*. London: Macmillan.

LEATZ, C.A. and STOLAR, M.D. (1992) *Career Success: Personal Stress*. New York: McGraw-Hill.

LUTHANS, F. (1992) *Organizational Behavior*, 6th ed. New York: McGraw Hill.

MACKAY, L. and TORRINGTON, D. (1986) *The Changing Nature of Personnel Management*. London: IPM.

McKENNA, E. (1987) *Psychology in Business*. London: LEA.

MAKIN, P., COOPER, C. and COX, C. (1989) *Managing People at Work*. Leicester: BPS Books (The British Psychological Society) and Routledge.

MILLS, D.Q. (1985) Planning with people in mind. *Harvard Business Review*, 63, 97–105.

MORGAN, G. (1986) *Images of Organisation*. London: Sage.

PHILIPS, J.J. (1987) *Handbook of Training Evaluation and Measurement Methods*. Houston: Gulf.

PINDER, C. (1984) *Work Motivation*. New York: Scott Foresman.

RAKOS, R. (1991) *Assertive Behaviour*. London: Routledge.

RASPBERRY, R. and LEMOINE, L. (1986) *Effective Managerial Communication*. Boston: Kent.

REASON, J. (1990) *Human Error*. Cambridge: Cambridge University Press.

REDDY, M. (1987) *The Manager's Guide to Counselling at Work.* Leicester: BPS Books (The British Psychological Society) and Methuen.

ROBERTSON, I.T., SMITH, M. and COOPER, D. (1992) *Motivation: Strategies, Theory and Practice.* London: IPM.

SCHIFFMAN, R. and KANUK, P. (1987) *Consumer Behavior,* 3rd ed. New York: Prentice Hall

SHACKLETON, V. and NEWALL, S. (1991) Management selection: A comparative survey of methods used in top British and French companies. *Journal of Occupational Psychology, 64,* 23–36.

SISSON, K. (1989) *Personnel Management in Britain.* Oxford: Blackwell.

SMITH, M. (1991) *Analyzing Organisational Behaviour.* London: Macmillan.

STEERS, R. (1991) *Introduction to Organizational Behaviour,* 4th ed. New York: HarperCollins.

VECCHIO, R. (1991) *Organizational Behavior,* 2nd ed. Hillsdale: Drysdale.

WALTERS, D. (1990) *What About the Workers? Making Employee Surveys Work.* London: IPM.

WARR, P. (1987) *Psychology at Work.* London: Penguin.

WILLE, E. (1990) *People Development and Improved Business.* Berkhamsted: Ashridge Management Research Group.

WILSON, D. and ROSENFELD, R. (1990) *Managing Organisations.* London: McGraw Hill.

YUKL, G. (1989) *Leadership in Organisations.* New York: Prentice Hall.

HELPING PROFESSIONS

CLERGY
Leslie Francis and Fraser Watts

Provision for the initial training of Christian clergy varies widely from denomination to denomination and within denominations according to the personal characteristics of the candidates, including age, previous academic and professional experience and intention to enter stipendiary or non-stipendiary ministry.

While specific curriculum requirements will vary from institution to institution, the following topics can properly benefit from informed psychological perspective. Although the relevant literature is vast, the following references provide useful pointers: religious development (Slee, 1990), faith development (Fowler, 1981; Astley and Francis, 1992), religious experience (Hay, 1990; Hay and Morisy, 1985), religious perspectives (Batson and Ventis, 1982; Kirkpatrick and Hood, 1990), psychology of religion (Brown, 1985, 1988; Paloutzian, 1983), personality types (Briggs-Myers and Myers, 1980; Osborn and Osborn, 1991), personality and prayer (Michael and Morrisey, 1984; Keating, 1987), personality and ministry (Oswald and Kroeger, 1988; Francis, 1991; Malony and Hunt, 1991), congregational life (Hopewell, 1987), clergy as counsellors (Domino, 1990), teenage church participation (Francis, 1984), clergy stress (Fletcher, 1990; Dewe, 1987), religion and mental health (Schumaker, 1992), psychoanalysis and religion (Meissner, 1984).

Clergy will often have to deal with subjects such as: relationships, marital problems, sexual problems, difficult children, growing old, bereavement, depression, fear and anxiety, alcoholism, physical illness, psychiatric disorders and community care. A number of general texts is available to assist with these areas.

Journals

While no journals exist exclusively to discuss the relevance of psychology for Christian ministry, the following journals carry relevant material from time to time: *International Journal for the Psychology of Religion, Journal of Empirical Theology, Journal for the Scientific Study of Religion, Journal of Pastoral Care, Journal of Psychology and Christianity, Journal of Psychology and Theology, Pastoral Psychology, Review of Religious Research,* and *Sociological Analysis.*

Readings

ASTLEY, J. and FRANCIS, L.J. (Eds) (1992) *Christian Perspectives on Faith Development: A Reader.* Leominster: Gracewing.

BATSON, C.D. and VENTIS, W.L. (1982) *The Religious Experience: A Social Psychological Perspective.* New York: Oxford University Press.

BRIGGS-MYERS, I. and MYERS, P.B. (1980) *Gifts Differing.* Palo Alto: Consulting Psychologists Press.

BROWN, L.B. (Ed.) (1985) *Advances in the Psychology of Religion.* Oxford: Pergamon Press.

BROWN, L.B. (1988) *The Psychology of Religion: An Introduction.* London: SPCK.

DEWE, P.J. (1987) New Zealand ministers of religion: identifying sources of stress and coping processes. *Work and Stress, 1,* 351–364.

DOMINO, G. (1990) Clergy's knowledge of psychopathology. *Journal of Psychology and Theology, 18,* 32–39.

FLETCHER, B. (1990) *Clergy Under Stress.* London: Mowbray.

FOWLER, J.W. (1981) *Stages of Faith: The Psychology of Human Development and the Quest for Meaning.* San Francisco: Harper and Row.

FRANCIS, L.J. (1984) *Teenagers and the Church: A Profile of Church-Going Youth in the 1980s.* London: Collins Liturgical Publications.

FRANCIS, L.J. (1991) The personality characteristics of Anglican ordinands: feminine men and masculine women? *Personality and Individual Differences, 12,* 1133–1140.

HAY, D. (1990) *Religious Experience Today: Studying the Facts.* London: Mowbray.

HAY, D. and MORISY, A. (1985) Secular society/religious meanings: a contemporary paradox. *Review of Religious Research, 17,* 179–188.

HOPEWELL, J.F. (1987) *Congregations: Stories and Structures.* London: SCM.

KEATING, C.J. (1987) *Who We Are is How We Pray.* Mystic, CT: Twenty-Third Publications.

KIRKPATRICK, L.A. and HOOD, R.W. (1990) Intrinsic – extrinsic religious orientation: the boon or bane of contemporary psychology of religion. *Journal for the Scientific Study of Religion, 29,* 442–462.

MALONY, H.N. and HUNT, R.A. (1991) *The Psychology of Clergy.* Harrisburg, PA.: Morehouse Publishing.

MEISSNER, W.W. (1984) *Psychoanalysis and Religious Experience.* Yale: Yale University Press.

MICHAEL, C.P. and MORRISEY, M.C. (1984) *Prayer and Temperament.* Charlottesville, Virginia: The Open Book Inc.

OSBORN, L. and OSBORN, D. (1991) *God's Diverse People.* London: Daybreak.

OSWALD, R.M. and KROEGER, O. (1988) *Personality Type and Religious Leadership.* Washington, DC: The Alban Institute.

PALOUTZIAN, R.F. (1983) *Invitation to the Psychology of Religion.* Glenview, Illinois: Scott, Foresman and Company.

SCHUMAKER, J.F. (Ed.) (1992) *Religion and Mental Health.* Oxford: Oxford University Press.

SLEE, N.M. (1990) Getting away from Goldman: changing perspectives on the development of religious thinking. *Modern Churchman, 32,* 1–9.

SOCIAL WORK
Carole Sutton

The professional qualification for social work is the Diploma in Social Work (DipSW) which is awarded by the professional body, the Central Council for Education and Training in Social Work (CCETSW).

A typical course is two years and comprises one year of theory and practice common to all students, and a second year of specialization, also containing theory and substantial field practice in one of several fields including: children and families; care in the community; probation; group care; residential care. Most students study law, social policy, sociology and psychology as these disciplines have relevance to social work, but although psychology is an implicit component of all courses, it is not always easy to separate from the teaching of applied social work.

All social workers need a wide repertoire of skills, working as they do with many client groups, both individually and as part of interdisciplinary teams. An understanding of interpersonal relationships, as well as the skills of effective communication, interviewing and assessment are a vital part of the social worker's day-to-day work. So too is an under-standing of factors which increase vulnerability, such as poor self-esteem, stress and depression.

Most social workers have some training in counselling; basic Rogerian skills can be supplemented by training in an appropriate area – such as family therapy or group work – or in more specific methods such as problem-solving, goal-set-ting or assertion training. In addition, social workers draw on psychology for keeping up with current research, and are now recognizing the need to become more research-oriented within their own work. They should also be aware of their own personal needs.

Social workers practising in the area of *children and families* carry major responsibilities which include the investigation of, and intervention in, cases of suspected child abuse; the support of parents and their children in accordance with the Children Act 1989; the placement of children, often distressed or unmanageable, in foster homes; and the carrying out of supervision orders placed by the courts upon, for example, young offenders.

Key areas of psychology needed by social workers in this field include a thorough knowledge of child development, including signs of delay and neglect, indicators of disturb-ance arising from child abuse, as well as the specific signs and characteristics of failure to thrive and emotional and conduct disorders. A knowledge of social learning theory and its application can help social workers to support parents who cannot control their children and intervene in the cycle of vio-lence and aggression which occurs in such families.

Social workers involved in *care in the community* imple-ment the National Health Service and Community Care Act 1990 and are concerned with the support of people with dis-abilities, elderly people, those with mental health difficulties, people who are ill, and those with learning disabilities. Practitioners in these fields need a knowledge of psychology as it pertains to each of these groups, together with an aware-ness of the growing associated research fields. Much information can be obtained through keeping abreast of developments as reported in relevant journals and newslet-ters.

Probation officers work mainly with offenders but also with families who need support in planning child care arrange-ments when parents are separating. The ability to train people in anger and aggression management, as well as strategies for dealing with alcohol or drug abuse are valuable. Such strategies frequently involve the application of cognitive and behavioural approaches in psychology.

Social workers practising in *group care settings* include those in family centres, in day-care provision for elderly or disabled people, and those working in centres for psychiatric patients. In each case a knowledge of developmental psychol-ogy, supplemented, as appropriate, with a familiarity of aspects of abnormal psychology (for example, signs of depression and acute anxiety), is required.

There is a major initiative to ensure that social workers practising in *residential child care* settings are suitably qualified and experienced. For the extremely demanding task of caring for disturbed and often disruptive children and young people in such settings, workers need both a knowledge of developmental and applied psychology, as well as practical skills of management and planning. This field is likely to grow.

Finally, it is emphasized that white/western modes of psychology are not adequate for practice, and that a knowledge of cultural differences, and an ability to communicate and work effectively with all people in a multi-racial, multi-cultural society, are essential.

Journals

The *British Journal of Social Work, Community Care* and *Behavioural Psychotherapy* will all carry relevant articles. Many other useful journals can be found in the listing in the chapter on publishers of books and journals.

Readings

The following books can be used also as sources for further reading.

HERBERT, M. (1981) *Psychology for Social Workers*. Leicester: BPS Books (The British Psychological Society) and Macmillan.

HERBERT, M. (1993) *Working with Children and the Children Act*. Leicester: BPS Books (The British Psychological Society).

HUDSON, B. and MCDONALD, G.M. (1986) *Behavioural Social Work*. Basingstoke: Macmillan.

SUTTON, C. (1987) *A Handbook of Research for the Helping Professions*. London: Routledge & Kegan Paul.

SUTTON, C. (in preparation) *Social Work, Community Work and Psychology*. Leicester: BPS Books (The British Psychological Society).

TEACHING
Roger Merry

The vast majority of British teachers now achieve `Qualified Teacher' status either by taking a first degree in education (BEd) or a degree in another subject plus a one year Postgraduate Certificate in Education (PGCE).

Psychology has traditionally played a major part in initial teacher training, and many student teachers have regarded it as one of the most interesting and useful parts of their courses (Bernbaum, 1985). There are several well-established books on psychology and education, including British ones such as those by Child (1986) or Fontana (1988), and comprehensive American texts such as Gage and Berliner (1992). Contents obviously vary, but most cover a wide range, including topics like motivation, assessment, language, individual differences, social groups, the self, learning, memory and child development. Psychologists have also recently made a strong bid to be involved in setting up competencies for beginning teachers (Tomlinson *et al.*, 1993).

However, trends in teacher education, partly reflecting radical changes in schools themselves, have caused concern among some psychologists who feel that the shift towards more instrumental, school-based courses has been achieved at the expense of the contribution of psychology and other disciplines (for example, Tomlinson, 1992). Such reactions can be seen as part of a wider debate about whether teachers should be taught psychology in order to apply it, or whether educational researchers should develop their own theories from classroom experience.

Both sides of this debate are to some extent represented in books and courses at initial and in-service levels. On the one hand, coverage of `child development' or `motivation', for example, tends to support the view that `pure' psychology can be applied, while the treatment of topics such as `classroom management' or `personal and social education', though clearly based on psychological principles, usually also rests heavily on classroom experience.

Child development has long been seen as a particularly relevant area of psychology, and the traditional reliance on Piagetian models has now given way to views placing more emphasis on the context of learning, and its meaning for the child. The recognition that not all factors affecting learning lie `within the child' has major implications for the role of the teacher, so that students now study authors such as Vygotsky, Bruner and Feuerstein, as much as Piaget. Similarly, teachers' reliance on psychometric models involving assumptions about intelligence has now been at least partly replaced by an interest in areas like metacognition and social cognition.

Conversely, many practical ideas currently offered to teachers to improve children's learning or behaviour can be traced directly back to the behaviourists, but they have also taken on board other techniques simply because experience shows that they work. Teachers are also increasingly expected to be aware of a range of affective factors in learning which psychologists have studied. Growing recognition of the importance of motivation, self-esteem and individual differences, for example, has resulted in teachers working in areas such as counselling, pastoral care, personal and social education, and individual Records of Achievement. Similar psychological principles are also evident in studies of teacher stress, for example, or in developing whole-school responses to problems like bullying.

Psychology has also been recognized as particularly relevant to the education of children with special needs, and educational psychologists usually play a major part in assessment and provision for children with learning or emotional difficulties. Teachers now generally accept that other children, including the `gifted' and physically and sensorily disabled, may also have psychological problems. All educational psychologists, therefore, must have a recognized degree in psychology, qualified teacher status and at least two years' teaching experience, as well as an advanced qualification in educational psychology.

Educational researchers have often applied techniques developed by psychologists to look in depth at what actually happens in classrooms (for example, Galton, 1989) and many teachers on in-service courses have themselves carried out small-scale studies which are firmly based on psychological principles. Writers such as Schwieso *et al.* (1992) argue that classroom-based studies should be recognized by academic psychologists as well as vice versa, and it is therefore likely that psychology will continue to have a major, if indirect, effect at various levels on the professional development of teachers who are genuine `reflective practitioners'.

Journals

The British Psychological Society's *British Journal of Educational Psychology* as well as the *Education Section Review* are particularly relevant, though the more general journals such as *Cambridge Review of Education* and *Education 3–13* often publish articles involving psychological research. In the area of special educational needs, British journals include *Support for Learning, Special Children* and *The British Journal of Special Education*.

Readings

BERNBAUM, G. (1985) Psychology in initial teacher education. In M. Francis (Ed.) *Learning to Teach – Psychology in Teacher Training*. Lewes: Falmer.

CHILD, D. (1986) *Psychology and the Teacher*, 4th ed. London: Holt.

FONTANA, D. (1988) *Psychology for Teachers*, 2nd ed. Leicester: BPS Books (The British Psychological Society) and Macmillan.

GAGE, N.L. and BERLINER, D.C. (1992) *Educational Psychology*, 5th ed. Boston: Houghton Mifflin.

GALTON, M. (1989) *Teaching in the Primary School*. London: David Fulton.

SCHWIESO, J.J., HASTINGS, N.J. and STAINTHORP, R. (1992) Psychology in teacher education: A response to Tomlinson. *The Psychologist*, 5(3), 112–113.

TOMLINSON, P. (1992) Psychology and education: What went wrong – or did it? *The Psychologist*, 5(3), 105–109.

TOMLINSON, P., EDWARDS, A., FINN, G., SMITH, L. and WILKINSON, E. (1993) Psychological aspects of beginning teacher competence. A submission by The British Psychological Society to the Council for the Accreditation of Teacher Education. *Education Section Review*, 17(1), 1–19.

OTHER PROFESSIONS

LAW
Lorraine Sherr

Psychology has long been taught within law courses, but it is often informal or not recognized as such. Recent moves within the legal profession have promoted the application of psychology in three main areas. The first area concerns skills and the needs of practising professionals. These would include interpersonal skills such as communication (Sherr, 1986; Binder *et al.*, 1991), interviewing (Watson, 1976; Goodpaster, 1975), management, advocacy (Sherr, 1993), counselling (Redmount, 1976; Schaffer and Redmount, 1980), memory (Kahnemann *et al.*, 1982), criminal conduct (Gudjonsson, 1992; Blackburn, 1993), self-presentation and assertiveness, as well as issues concerned with staff burnout and stress.

Secondly, there are the legal processes and issues which involve a psychological component. Psychology has made a major contribution in the understanding of such areas as jury decision-making, eye witness testimony (Buckhout, 1974; Loftus, 1979), child witnesses (Dent, 1978, 1992), and mental health, criminal justice (Stephenson, 1992), judgement (Abercrombie, 1960) and the law.

The third area encompasses specialist witnesses and reports. Psychologists often supplement legal cases with specialist knowledge and understanding. They may provide expert opinion or act as expert witnesses. Training here would be to sensitize legal practitioners to these areas and familiarize them with the procedures regarding referral to, or consultation with, psychologists.

Psychology is relevant to a broad range of legal practitioners including solicitors, barristers, the judiciary, as well as those who work in legal advice or Citizens Advice Bureaux and law centres.

Journals

Some articles appear in mainstream law journals and others within mainstream psychology journals. A number of more specialized sources have emerged recently. These include: *Journal of the Legal Profession; Psychology, Crime and Law; Behavioural Sciences and the Law; International Journal of the Law and Psychiatry*.

Readings

ABERCROMBIE, M.L.J. (1960) *The Anatomy of Judgement: An Investigation into the Process of Perception and Reasoning*. Harmondsworth: Penguin.

AINSWORTH, P. and PEASE, K. (1987) *Police Work*. Leicester: BPS Books (The British Psychological Society) and Routledge.

BERGMAN, P. (1989) *Trial Advocacy*. St Paul, Minnesota: West Publishers.

BINDER, D., BERGMAN, P. and PRICE, S. (1991) *Lawyers as Counsellors*. St Paul, Minnesota: West Publishers.
BLACKBURN, T. (1993) *The Psychology of Criminal Conduct: Theory, Research and Practice*. Chichester: John Wiley.
BUCKHOUT, R. (1974) Eyewitness testimony. *Scientific American, 231*, 23.
CHARROW, R.P. and CHARROW, V.R. (1979) Making legal language understandable: a psycholinguistic study of jury instructions. *Columbia Law Review, 79*, 1306.
DENT, H. (1978) *Interviewing Child Witnesses in Practical Aspects of Memory*. London: Academic Press.
DENT, H. (1992) *Children as Witnesses*. Chichester: John Wiley.
GOODPASTER, G.S. (1975) The human arts of lawyering. *Journal of Legal Education, 27*, 33.
GUDJONSSON, G.H. (1992) *The Psychology of Interrogations, Confessions and Testimony*. Chichester: Wiley.
KAHNEMANN, D., SLOVIK, P. and TVERSKY, A. (1982) *Judgement under Uncertainty: Heuristics and Biases*. Cambridge: Cambridge University Press.
KING, M. (1986) *Psychology In and Out of Court*. Oxford: Pergamon Press.
LLOYD-BOSTOCK, S. (1988) *Law in Practice*. Leicester: BPS Books (The British Psychological Society) and Routledge.
LOFTUS, E. (1979) *Eyewitness Testimony*. Cambridge, Mass: Harvard University Press.
REDMOUNT, R.S. (1976) An enquiry into legal counselling. *Journal of the Legal Profession, 1*, 181.
SCHAFFER, T.L. and REDMOUNT, R.S. (1980) *Legal Interviewing and Counselling*. Albany, NY: Matthew Bender.
SHERR, A. (1986) Lawyers and clients: the first meeting. *Modern Law Review, 49*, 323.
SHERR, A. (1986) *Client Interviewing for Lawyers: An Analysis and Guide*. London: Sweet and Maxwell Publishers.
SHERR, A. (1993) *Advocacy*. London: Blackstone Press.
STEPHENSON, G.M. (1992) *The Psychology of Criminal Justice*. Oxford: Blackwell.
TYLER, T.R. (1992) *Why People Obey the Law*. New Haven, CT: Yale University Press.
WATSON, A.S. (1976) *The Lawyer in the Interviewing and Counselling Process*. New York: Bobbs-Merrill.

ENGINEERING
John MacDonald

In the UK the provision of undergraduate degree education in engineering is strongly influenced by the guidelines produced by the various professional bodies, for example, the Institution of Electrical Engineers (IEE). Graduates from accredited courses meet one of the requirements to become a Chartered Engineer. A continuing concern of the professional bodies has been the aim of broadening student education and training. For instance, the IEE guidelines include reference to providing the potential chartered engineer with an awareness of the constraints imposed on engineering activities by physical, human and financial resources and by economic, environmental and safety considerations. Some of these issues are explicitly the province of the psychological and behavioural sciences, the human side of engineering practice. From these objectives and guidelines, two themes emerge that have psychological import.

The first is that the education and training of prospective engineers should equip them to take a broad view of the design and production of engineering artifacts. They should not only consider meeting a narrow functional specification, but also consider the usage of such artifacts. The contribution that psychology makes here are topics that come under the heading of `ergonomics' or `human factors' (Oborne, 1987), which include perceptual processing (Wickens, 1992), vigilance and attention (Warm, 1984), memory (Baddeley, 1990), skill and performance (Holding, 1989), problem-solving and decision-making (Edwards, 1987), displays (Lintern *et al.*, 1990; Sorkin, 1987), controls (Norman, 1988), accidents and safety (Reason, 1990), environmental effects (Hamilton and Warburton, 1984), models of behaviour (Elkind *et al.*, 1990), task analysis (Burgess, 1990) and user-centred evaluation (Cushman and Rosenberg, 1991).

The second feature is that the education process should also introduce students to the non-engineering aspects of the job functions and roles they will be required to perform. Contributions here are from two areas. The first area is `organizational psychology' (for example, Huczynski and Buchanan, 1991), including motivation, group processes and leadership, decision-making, intergroup processes, conflict and power, industrial relations, gender issues, change, innovation and resistance to change. The second area is `personal and social skills', including interpersonal skills, self-awareness and self-presentation, group and team working, communication and influence, self-efficacy, stress and stress management (see management section for references).

Journals A number of journals exist which publish relevant articles: *Ergonomics, International Journal of Man–Machine Studies, Behavior and Information Technology, Journal of Applied Psychology, Human Factors, IEEE Transactions on Systems, Man and Cybernetics, Personnel Review, British Journal of Occupational Psychology, Journal of Management Studies* and *Journal of Organizational Behavior.*

Readings BADDELEY, A.D. (1990) *Human Memory: Theory and Practice.* New York: Lawrence Erlbaum.
BURGESS, J.H. (1990) *Human Factors in Industrial Design.* New York: TAB Inc.
CUSHMAN, W.H. and ROSENBERG, D.J. (1991) *Human Factors in Product Design.* New York: Elsevier.

EDWARDS, W. (1987) Decision making. In G. Salvendy (Ed.) *Handbook of Human Factors*. Chichester: Wiley.

ELKIND, J., CARD, S., HOCHBERG, J. and HUEY, T.S. (1990) *Human Performance Models for Computer-Aided Engineering*. London: Academic Press.

HAMILTON, V. and WARBURTON, D.M. (Eds) (1984) *Human Stress and Cognition: An Information Processing Approach*. Chichester: Wiley.

HOLDING, D. (Ed.) (1989) *Human Skills*, 2nd ed. Chichester: Wiley.

HUCZYNSKI, A.A. and BUCHANAN, D.A. (1991) *Organisational Behaviour: An Introductory Text*. Englewood Cliffs, NJ: Prentice Hall.

LINTERN, G., ROSCOE, S.N. and SIVIER, J. (1990) Display principles, control dynamics, and environmental factors in pilot performance and transfer of training. *Human Factors, 32*, 299–317.

NORMAN, D.A. (1988) *The Psychology of Everyday Things*. New York: Basic Books.

OBORNE, D. (1987) *Ergonomics at Work*. Chichester: Wiley.

REASON, J. (1990) *Human Error*. Cambridge: Cambridge University Press.

SORKIN, R.D. (1987) Design of auditory and tactile displays. In G. Salvendy (Ed.) *Handbook of Human Factors*. Chichester: Wiley.

WARM, J.S. (Ed.) (1984) *Sustained Attention in Human Performance*. Chichester: Wiley.

WICKENS, C.D. (1992) *Engineering Psychology and Human Performance*. London: HarperCollins.

ARCHITECTURE
Johnathan Sime

Architectural or environmental psychology addresses the relationship between people and the physical environment and in this sense is in tune with the growing public concern with environmental issues. While the 1970s indicated an evolving interest in integrating architecture and the social sciences through teaching, this declined in the 1980s. Pressures on accountability, frequently from outside the discipline of architecture, new interest in the impact of the environment on people and the 1985 EC Directive on architectural design (likened to a `Social Charter for Architecture' by Marcus, 1990), have rekindled the prospect of psychology making a significant contribution to architectural training. The notion that `users' are also `consumers' of a product (RIBA, 1991) reflects current economic constraints which are likely to encourage the integration of design and the needs of users. There are parallels in integrating architecture with environmental sociology, anthropology and economics, as well as ergonomics, human geography and human factors.

While architectural/environmental psychology is implicit in much of architectural education, it is only taught explicitly by psychologists in a handful of architectural schools in the UK. It is usually taught if at all by psychologists at the degree level in lectures, rather than being fully integrated into studio design work especially at the postgraduate diploma level. In contrast environmental psychology is taught on psychology courses primarily as a postgraduate subject, both in the UK and internationally.

An enormous environmental psychology and interdisciplinary research literature has evolved over the past 20 years or so. General texts or edited books cover themes such as privacy (Altman, 1975), colour and visual perception (Prak, 1977), post-occupancy design evaluation (POE) (Friedman *et al.*, 1978), aesthetics (Nasar, 1988), safety (Sime, 1988), wayfinding and spatial orientation (Arthur and Passini, 1992), and building types, including housing (Cooper Marcus and Sarkissan, 1986; Lawrence, 1987) and offices (Wineman, 1986). The approach is primarily empirical, with an increasing interest in a phenomenological perspective in relation to subjects such as `place' attachment (for example, Seamon and Mugerauer, 1985). There is also a wide range of research at a macro scale concerning the landscape, public settings and urban environments in different cultures, where psychology overlaps with other social science, architectural, engineering and planning concerns. Other key texts include Altman (1976–92), Canter (1974), Fisher *et al.* (1984), Gifford (1987), Holahan (1982), Lee (1978), Levy-Leboyer (1982), Proshansky *et al.* (1970), Stokols and Altman (1987) and Zube and Moore (1987).

Journals

Relevant journals include *Environment and Behaviour, Journal of Environmental Psychology, Journal of Architectural and Planning Research, Design Studies, Architecture et Comportement* and *People and Physical Environment Research*.

Readings

ALTMAN, I. (1975) *The Environment and Social Behaviour: Privacy, Personal Space, Territory and Crowding*. Monterey, California: Brooks/Cole.

ALTMAN, I. (Ed.) (1976–1992) *Human Behaviour and Environment* (edited series). New York: Plenum Press.

ARTHUR, P. and PASSINI, R. (1992) *Wayfinding: People, Signs and Architecture*. Toronto: McGraw-Hill Ryerson.

CANTER, D. (1974) *Psychology for Architects*. London: Applied Science.

COOPER MARCUS, C. and SARKISSAN, W. (1986) *Housing as if People Mattered*. Berkeley: University of California Press.

FISHER, J., BELL, P. and BAUM, A. (1984) *Environmental Psychology*, 2nd ed. New York: Holt, Rinehart and Winston.

FRIEDMAN, A., ZIMRING, C. and ZUBE, E. (Eds) (1978) *Environmental Design Evaluation*. New York: Plenum.

GIFFORD, R. (1987) *Environmental Psychology: Principles and Practice*. London: Allyn and Bacon.

HOLAHAN, C. (1982) *Environmental Psychology*. New York: Random House.

LAWRENCE, R. (1987) *Housing, Dwellings and Homes*. Chichester: Wiley.

LEE, T. (1978) *Psychology and the Environment*. London: Methuen.

LEVY-LEBOYER, C. (1982) *Psychology and Environment*. London: Sage.

MARCUS, T. (1990) A social charter for architecture. *Architecture Today*, July.

MIKELLIDES, B. (Ed.) (1980) *Architecture for People*. London: Studio Vista.

NASAR, J.L. (Ed.) (1988) *Environmental Aesthetics*. Cambridge: Cambridge University Press.

PRAK, M. (1977) *The Visual Perception of the Built Environment*. Delft: Delft University Press.

PROSHANSKY, H.M., ITTELSON, W.H. and RIVLIN, L.G. (Eds) (1970) *Environmental Psychology*, 1st ed. New York: Holt, Rinehart and Winston.

RIBA (1991) *Schools of Architecture 1991–1992*. London: RIBA Publications.

SEAMON, D. and MUGERAUER, R. (Eds) (1985) *Dwelling, Place and Environment*. Dordrecht: Martinus Nijhoff.

SIME, J.D. (Ed.) (1988) *Safety in the Built Environment*. London: E. and F. N. Spon.

STOKOLS, D. and ALTMAN, I. (Eds) (1987) *Handbook of Environmental Psychology*, Vols 1 and 2. New York: Wiley.

WINEMAN, J. (Ed.) (1986) *Behavioral Issues in Office Design*. New York: Van Nostrand Reinhold.

ZUBE, E. and MOORE, G. (Eds) (1987) *Advances in Environment Behaviour and Design*, Vols 1–3. New York: Plenum.

Acknowledgements

We gratefully acknowledge the editorial assistance of Rochelle Serwator in shaping this collaborative chapter. The secretarial work of Sarah Rivington and Anne Rees is greatly appreciated.

Contributors

Dr Charles Abrahams
Epidemiology and Public Health
University of Dundee

Dr Stuart Biddle
School of Education
University of Exeter

Dr Barrie Brown
Ashridge Management College
Berkhamsted, Hertfordshire

Dr Rhona Flin
Business School
The Robert Gordon University, Aberdeen

Revd Prof. Leslie J. Francis
Trinity College
Carmarthen

Prof. Alastair G. Gale
Applied Vision Research Unit
University of Derby

Dr John R. Hegarty and Ms Marian Whittaker
Keele University
Keele, Staffs

Dr John MacDonald
Department of Psychology
University of Portsmouth

Dr Roger Merry
School of Education
University of Leicester

Dr Paul Morrison
School of Nursing Studies
University of Wales College of Medicine
Cardiff

Dr Donald Pennington
School of Health and Social Sciences
Coventry University

Dr Lorraine Sherr
St Mary's Hospital
London

Dr Johnathan D. Sime
JSA Research Consultants and School of Architecture
Kingston University, Surrey

Ms Georgina Slaven
Business School
The Robert Gordon University, Aberdeen

Prof. John Sloboda
Department of Psychology
University of Keele

Dr Carole Sutton
Department of Health and Community Studies
De Montfort University
Scraptoft Campus, Leicester

Revd Dr Fraser N. Watts
MRC Applied Psychology Unit
Cambridge

Mr Stefan Wills
Ashridge Management College
Berkhamsted, Hertfordshire

PSYCHOLOGICAL TESTS

Donald McLeod

❏ why bother to teach about tests? • what is a psychological test? • competence • test procedures • test content • ethical issues • qualifying as a user

WHY BOTHER TO TEACH ABOUT TESTS?

*T*here is a curious contrast in the attitude of psychologists
to psychological tests. On the one hand, there is great
concern about the validity and utility of the psychological
abstractions that tests provide, to the extent that some would
advocate not using tests at all. On the other hand, a great
deal of the subject matter of psychology courses relies on
research that has included the use of test instruments.
Additionally, many of the members of specialist professional
groups – clinical, educational and occupational psychologists
– use tests routinely. In the occupational field in particular,
where the use of tests by non-psychologists is probably greatest, the 1980s saw the development of a substantial market for
test developers and publishers.
  In psychology teaching, however, testing is often neglected.
An examination of university brochures and prospectuses is
not likely to produce much evidence of assessment and testing being treated at the level of an individual topic.
Prospectuses will typically refer to the study of 'individual
differences' or 'cognitive psychology', but will not be explicit
about whether the measurement aspects of these are covered.
A-level syllabuses make some mention of testing, either
specifically in relation to intelligence tests or in contrast to
school attainment tests. The 1992 report of the Chief
Examiner in Clinical Psychology noted that 'few candidates
answered questions involving psychometric testing [and] in
those cases when candidates did answer such questions, the
quality was generally low'. This is just one in a long line of
such findings, with the 1989 report, for instance, commenting
on candidates' reluctance to deal with matters concerning
assessment and the 'details of commonly used tests or basic
psychometry and measurement issues'.

[Editorial comment: This chapter is based on the chapter written by Chris Whetton in the previous edition]

So, why bother to teach about tests? First, because if students continue with psychology as a profession, it is highly likely that they will have to administer tests at some point or, more importantly, to interpret the results. Closely related to this is the fact that, with developments in the ways in which people may be considered qualified to use tests competently, the simple possession of a first degree in psychology will come less and less to be deemed adequate. Then, much psychological theory and debate is reliant for its information on the measures used and these are often psychometric tests of some description. Further, there are those who argue that a particular form of test, the intelligence test, has been one of the most persuasive inventions of psychology and that it has probably exerted greater influence on the social life of the UK through its use in an educational context than any other practical application of psychology. Even after the decline of the eleven plus, tests remain one of the areas where members of the public encounter psychology, through occupational selection or other assessments and now again, increasingly, with formal attainment assessments in the schoolroom.

For all these reasons, psychology students ought to be taught about tests to an appropriate extent. The depth of knowledge that they need will depend on the level at which they are studying psychology and the purposes for which they will use them. Up to now, systems of qualification for the supply of tests have been largely based on the formal qualifications of the prospective purchaser. For professional psychologists, this has been typically taken to mean the possession of a first or a postgraduate degree in psychology. For non-psychologists in, for example, the occupational area, 'formal qualification' for many years meant successful completion of a course in test use, where that course had itself been accredited by The British Psychological Society (BPS). Recent and prospective developments in these kinds of process are described further on in this chapter. But in all cases, where reliance was or still is placed upon the sort of formal qualification just mentioned, it is on the basis of assuming that appropriate education about the administration and interpretation of tests will have been provided on the course concerned. Thus, it is expected that postgraduate students of educational psychology will have been taught the theory and practice of using and interpreting individually administered test batteries with many sub-scales – for example, the WISC-R or BASR. Similarly, postgraduate students in clinical or occupational psychology need training in the use of the assessment techniques that they are likely to employ in their professional work.

At the undergraduate level there are two issues. One – does the student intend seriously to go on to advanced study and the pursuit of psychology at a professional level? If so, providing teaching to qualified user status (to the BPS's relevant certification level, that is) might well be considered at that undergraduate stage. Two – does formal assessment feature as no more than something that the well-rounded individual with a first degree in psychology might be expected to know about? In which case, some less intensive programme could be considered. Taken together, the two would suggest an 'options' or 'elective' approach for the more intensive work, laid over a basic foundation provided for all, where the focus is more on assessment as a contribution to knowledge than as an activity in its own right.

For A-level students of psychology and for general interest courses, the more intensive approach will also be inappropriate and other methods must be considered. The section on ethical issues, further on, also has a bearing here.

WHAT IS A PSYCHOLOGICAL TEST?

A psychological test may be broadly defined as a standard assessment procedure that measures individual differences in some psychological function. Many professional groups use assessment procedures and it is sometimes difficult to decide whether or not these can be called 'psychological tests'. There is such a diversity in their usage and content that an all-inclusive definition is impossible. Any definition, however, would have to emphasize both the procedures involved in assessment and the actual content of the tests.

In the BPS booklet 'Psychological Testing – A Guide' (1990), two definitions of a psychological test are offered:

> an instrument designed to produce a quantitative assessment of some psychological attribute or attributes;

and:

> any procedure on the basis of which inferences are made concerning a person's capacity, propensity or liability to act, react, experience, or to structure or order thought or behaviour in particular ways.

The two crucial elements are that a test is a procedure, and that it is a procedure that provides a basis for inference concerning matters of psychological importance. An inference may be drawn from some non-standard, non-predetermined activity – professional observation, say, or extended questioning – but one would not want to call that kind of assessment a 'test'. And where a standardized activity does *not* lead to inferences being drawn, then it remains at the level of a report of events, or a description – and again the term 'psychological test' would not seem appropriate. But the 'Guide' also goes on to emphasize the limits to the kinds of inference that may be drawn and characterizes the typical test as 'a portable aid to decision-making'.

An earlier attempt at a legal definition (the BPS Working Party on Competence in Psychological Testing, 1983) gave a list of content or subject areas, which included tests of intelligence, ability, aptitude, language development and function, perception, personality, temperament and disposition, interests, habits, values and preferences. It excluded educational attainment tests and non-standardized attitude inventories, among other assessments. In contrast, the technical recommendations for psychological tests (the BPS Professional Affairs Board, 1980) emphasized the procedures involved in the assessment, advising that the term 'test' should be used only for techniques that yield ratings or scores derived from procedures clearly described in a manual and based on adequate standardization data – in other words, the procedure and the inference again. They emphasized the technical aspects of tests, their construction and item analysis, norms, reliability and validity. Both of these approaches – test content and test usage – are brought together in the 1990 guidance which, nevertheless, has properly to be viewed in the context of the further developments with respect to qualification in test usage that have already been referred to and which are expanded later in this chapter.

There are, then, two aspects to education about tests: first, the procedures on which assessment and inference are based; and second, their content. The first of these involves statistical considerations that may prove difficult for some students, and the second can be complicated by ethical considerations.

COMPETENCE

This is the point at which it will be useful to turn to those recent and prospective developments in the ways in which people can achieve 'formal qualification' in test use. It is an important point because as the BPS's certification scheme develops and spreads, access to test material will increasingly require specific attention to demonstrable competence in the prospective user – non-psychologist and psychologist alike.

Test publishers are unusual in that it is in their own interests to limit their markets. Selling test materials to anyone who wanted to buy would quite quickly lead to a situation where tests were routinely being used incompetently by incompetent people, with all the consequences for the reputation of tests and testing. Thus publishers would find themselves out of business. A crude argument, maybe, but a compelling one, especially when set alongside the ethical standards of professional publishers. So, publishers traditionally limit their markets and do so by maintaining their own lists of qualified customers – the qualification having been up to now that either the prospective purchaser has at least a first degree in psychology, or that he or she has undergone approved training.

The new scheme, launched in 1991, does two things that are different from the old. Under the old scheme, the BPS

maintained standards by means of accrediting training courses in test use – in the main, and particularly where
occupational usage was the issue, for non-psychologists.
Under the new, it is the individual user him or herself who
comes under the spotlight, and it applies as much to those
who already have a degree in psychology as it does to those
who do not. Under the old, that accreditation was directly in
the hands of the BPS in the form of its Test Standards committee. Under the new, the model is one where 'affirmation of
competence' is the direct responsibility of any Chartered
Psychologist who is him or herself registered as a competent
test user and, further, whose skill and experience in assessing
others' competence has itself been verified. Complicated?
Not really. But let us look briefly at what is in fact involved.

Moving from a training course accreditation process to one
where individual users may themselves apply for certification as competent test users has involved starting with
occupational usage. This was partly on the grounds that this
seems likely to have been the area where the scope for
improper or inexpert application was greatest, and partly
because it is the area where the issues were most clear-cut.
Ability and aptitude testing form the focus for the first developments. Personality enquiry and assessment follow on.
Ability testing is designated Level A, personality Level B.
They are 'levels' because it is considered essential that users
gain competence and confidence in the use of ability testing
practice and procedure before embarking on the more complex issues associated with personality enquiry. So Level A
precedes B, and introduces concepts of measurement and
scaling. ('A' and 'B' are used, rather than '1' and '2', to avoid
confusion with the numerical levels of competence associated
with National Vocational Qualifications – which might at
some point be incorporated.) As an adjunct to certification
there is an additional registration facility, the Register being
an on-line database that allows enquirers to check to see if a
person claiming competence is or is not 'on the Register'. The
procedures for certification and registration of competence in
occupational testing provide a model for extension, in an
appropriate manner, into educational and clinical usage.

The bare bones are: publishers agree to recognize the BPS
certificate of competence in test usage; that competence may
be acquired in whatever way is most appropriate for the individual concerned – most often a training course of some kind,
but not ruling out self study, study as part of further or higher education, or 'sitting by Nellie' in their job; competence is
affirmed by a fully competent Chartered Psychologist signing
the individual's application; application and affirmation are
checked and a certificate of competence is issued, for a fee; on
payment of a further fee element, entry is made in the
Register of Competence.

The Level A competence framework (ability testing):

Unit 1 – *Defining assessment needs.* The Unit deals with the general categorization of types of assessment instrument and covers the underlying psychological theory and background to ability testing. Issues of job and task analysis are covered in so far as they relate to the delineation of assessment, as opposed to training, needs. Competence in job analysis is *not* assumed, though an ability to evaluate critically the results of job analyses is. (10 elements)

Unit 2 – *Basic principles of scaling and standardization.* This deals with the fundamental statistical concepts required to use psychological tests. Most undergraduate psychology courses will have covered this material, as will some other social science degree courses. (12 elements)

Unit 3 – *The importance of reliability and validity.* Considerable stress is placed on understanding a number of essential concepts in psychometrics. (17 elements)

Unit 4 – *Deciding when psychological tests should or should not be used as part of an assessment process.* (11 elements)

Unit 5 – *Administering tests to one or more candidates and dealing with scoring procedures.* This is very much a skills-based unit with the stress on people's competence to follow good professional practice in test administration, ensuring the maintenance of standard conditions and fairness. (23 elements)

Unit 6 – *Making appropriate use of test results and providing accurate written and oral feedback to clients and candidates.* Stress is placed on competence in the interpersonal skills required to provide face-to-face feedback of test results as well as the oral and written communication skills required to convey highly technical information in lay terms without distortion or exaggeration. (18 elements)

Unit 7 – *Maintaining security and confidentiality of the test materials and the test data.* This deals with issues of security and confidentiality which are of central importance in the professional relationship between test user, candidate and client. (6 elements)

Unit 1 is thus a general, scene-setting unit. Units 2 and 3 concern the relevant underpinning knowledge and understanding required to make proper use of psychological tests. The remainder focus on practical issues relating to test administration, relationships with clients and candidates, use of test information and issues of that sort. They are inter-related, except to the extent that Unit 5 is designed for stand-alone use when training, say, support staff in test administration.

The Level B framework (personality testing) sets out to follow very much the same kind of pattern as Level A. The Units are:

Unit 1 – *Approaches to the assessment of personality and interests.* In addition to a variety of approaches, attention is directed to 'type versus trait' approaches and to the major personality theories.

Unit 2 – *Measurement issues relating to the assessment of personality and interests.*

Unit 3 – *Reliability and validity.* Applying Level A concepts of reliability to personality assessment; stability issues; content, construct, and criterion-referenced validity.

Unit 4 – *When and how to use personality and interest assessment.* This includes fairness and equal opportunities issues.

Unit 5 – *Carrying out the assessment process.*

Unit 6 – *Making appropriate use of results and providing accurate feedback.*

Unit 7 – *Maintaining security and confidentiality.*

These, then, define the area on which training and education in testing and the use of tests should focus. Clearly, educational and clinical usage can be expected to differ in a number of specific respects. At the time of writing, a start has been made on defining the respective competence frameworks for these two broad areas – and the criminological usage closely associated with clinical applications. Differences of emphasis and, to some extent, structure seem likely to focus on whether or not it makes practical sense to separate out test use into the two 'levels' adopted for occupational usage, and on the implications for competence where testing procedures are exclusively individual, with no group testing applications at all. Other than that, there is clear agreement as to the shared value of the kinds of basic issue set out above.

TEST PROCEDURES

Teaching about tests and testing, therefore, needs to take account of what it is that assessment of this sort is about, and what the tools or instruments themselves typically look like. We have just looked at the basics of competent assessment, so how do we go about teaching it? It will be helpful once again to take the case of testing for occupational purposes as a kind of model and to work from there. Notice, by the way, that the term used is 'occupational *testing*' and not 'occupational *tests*'. This is for the very good reason that when one starts to try and classify tests themselves in terms of the use to which they are going to be put, it quickly becomes an impossible task.

Within limits, almost any test might be used for almost any purpose. So the focus is on *usage*, not on the tests themselves. How is this supported?

First, the BPS publishes a small handbook for people who are going to be asked to affirm competence – Chartered Psychologists with their own Certificate of Competence in Occupational Testing and who are listed as 'verified affirm-ers'. (It is not possible to do more than make general reference to 'verification' at the time of writing, as the process itself is only at the design and planning stage. Suffice to say that when it is in place, there will be a sub-register of affirm-ing signatures, and only those will be recognized.) The small handbook is titled 'Certificate of Competence in Occupational Testing (Level A) – Guidance for Assessors'. Its main aims are: to help trainers devise suitable course materials and activities; to help assessors (that is, those affirming compe-tence in the applicant for certification) to set their level of assessment appropriately and help them devise appropriate forms of assessment activity; and to speed the evolution of a dependable, uniform standard of competence associated with holders of the Certificate.

'Guidance for Assessors' deals with what methods are suitable for assessing each element in each unit of compe-tence – the elements being grouped together in loose, topic categories; with what depth of knowledge or level of skill is required; what range of knowledge is required; and what constitutes sufficient evidence of competence.

So, an example, dealing with some of the elements from the unit on reliability and validity is:

* breadth – 'general – all tests with quantifiable reliability estimates'

* depth – 'know that reliability increases as the standard deviation of the sample increases (other things being equal); be aware of the method for computing effects of change in variance on reliability . . . etc'

* assessment – 'the assessee (that is, the trainee in test use) should be able to correct a split-half correlation to give a reliability estimate using the Spearman-Brown formula; given standard deviation and reliability, compute the stan-dard error of measurement . . . etc'

* amount of evidence required – basic questioning and knowledge-testing for short-term assessment, and over the longer term; evidence of understanding from project work; critical comment on case studies; and so on.

A further development is an extensive modular training package, again focusing exclusively on competence in occu-pational testing and, so far, on ability rather than personality usage. *BPS Training Modules for Psychological Testing* (Bartram and Lindley) is, at the time of writing, still in preparation.

When complete it will provide, in the form of 12 separate but interdependent modules, a complete course in test use at this level and in this area. Naturally, it will not transfer unmodified into other areas and other levels. Personality testing will require its own set of modules. Educational and clinical usage will each require theirs in due course. But again, it serves not only as a distinctive publication in its own right but as an example of what can be done and how best to do it – until something better comes along.

It is intended for use in a whole range of settings, from out-and-out open or distance learning, through to the provision of support material in class. Further, in its final form it will provide various 'routes' through the material so that needs of differing levels can be met.

Looking briefly at what the modules cover – not one-by-one, but under broad groupings – should help to focus on what teaching in this area could sensibly be about.

* An introduction that deals with three general categories of assessment instrument – namely, ability, interests and personality – and that goes on to cover the underlying psychological theory and background to, in this case, ability testing. The aim is for the individual to be able to describe the distinction between tests that assess *maximum* performance and those that assess *typical* performance; to distinguish between attainment and ability; to give examples of the different types of test used in occupational assessment; to describe and illustrate the differences between measures of general and specific ability; and to describe how such measures may be influenced by environmental factors.

* Measurement. A section that deals with the fundamental statistical concepts required to use psychological tests, and which includes practical work that focuses on developing a sound grasp of scaling and measurement. The various properties of raw scores, standardized scores, percentile-based measures and normalized standardized scores are explored. Practical work associated with this includes the use of various formats of norm table for converting raw scores into these different types of score. The kinds of practical exercise used here cover the following: plotting histograms of raw scores, percentiles, standard score conversions and normalized standard score conversions. The main statistical concepts introduced are: mean, variance and standard deviation, and the normal distribution.

* Reliability. The aim here is to gain understanding of a number of essential concepts in psychometrics – especially correlation and the idea of common variance. The main focus for understanding reliability is on the Standard Error of Measurement (SEm) and related notions such as the Standard Error of Difference (SEd). These are dealt with in the modules from a practical viewpoint. For example, how

does one know whether Person A's score is better than Person B's? How sure can one be that they possess 'more' of the trait or quality being measured?

* Validity – describing and illustrating various sources of information about validity. This thus covers face validity, content validity, construct validity, and criterion-related validity. Problems of carrying out validation studies are discussed and the notion of validity generalization is introduced. Stress is laid on the importance of validity data both for the estimation of utility and for equal opportunity issues.

* Test administration and scoring. This deals with administering tests to one or more candidates and with scoring procedures. It also covers the maintenance of security and confidentiality of test materials and test data. Clearly, this kind of section is very much a skills-based one. It lays stress on people's competence in following good professional practice in test administration and in ensuring that standard conditions and fairness are observed and maintained.

* Interpretation. This covers a variety of issues, from ensuring that correct use is made of norm tables or other standardizing devices, through reporting and feeding 'forward' to the ultimate user or client, to feeding back to the individual being tested or assessed. The overall aim is complete clarity of communication in interpreting assessment results – without either under- or over-informing. Practical exercises form an important part of the teaching.

* Choosing appropriate instruments. A drawing together of principle and practice that focuses on choosing psychological tests – deciding when to use them, choosing which to use, choosing which to buy. Again, the approach is a practical one that requires the trainee to apply some of the more theoretical aspects of the technical work that he or she has done so far. As the answer to the question about whether or not tests should be used for a particular purpose depends on the nature of that purpose and the information that has to be gathered, attention is addressed to issues like: are there qualities here that can potentially be assessed by using psychometric tests? and if so, which, from a suitable range of tests, will be best for the job? The trainee test-user needs access to information about a wide range of tests for this. Test publishers' catalogues are recommended as an important source of such information.

TEST CONTENT

Teaching procedure will not get far without access to test materials. The modular training system just described incorporates examples of selected tests as part of its teaching approach. Great care has to be taken, not only with the obviously justifiable issues like copyright, but with maintaining the kind of security with respect to test material that is so much a feature of information held about test performance by individuals. The modules also have as an integral part of their design test material specifically developed for practice exercises of various kinds.

As mentioned before, publishers' catalogues form a valuable source of information concerning the kinds of instrument that are available for use by the suitably qualified practitioner. You do not have to be a qualified practitioner to obtain the catalogues, and most test training courses will have relied fairly heavily on their availability in some way or another.

However, BPS Books also publishes the *Review of Psychometric Tests for Assessment in Vocational Training* – an updatable manual associated with the developments in test standards and usage that have been described here. This too focuses at present on occupational use. Published in conjunction with the Employment Department Group, it contains general guidance on test use but the core of it is its detailed and impartial assessment of general ability tests and tests of aptitudes and interests in use in vocational guidance, and in training and development. There is naturally a distinct selection-for-recruitment aspect to it too. There are several dozen tests reviewed – the updating aspect of the publication means that the number itself grows over time, but there were 61 in the first edition. Each is analyzed by a team of independent, professional consultants. Guidance is given on the suitability of each test for particular groups and uses. A five-star rating system is applied to background technical information such as various aspects of validity, reliability and norming. An early update extends the scope to cover tests used in graduate recruitment. In due course, critical reviews of instruments used in personality enquiry will also start to appear. For the present, though, the main point is the fact that the *Review* provides another, and very valuable, source of information about the actual tests typically found in use in an occupational setting.

So far, the emphasis here has been on learning about tests and testing almost exclusively from the point of view of the prospective practitioner – with the occupational focus being intended as some kind of a basis from which to extend thinking and practice out to other uses. However, much earlier on in this chapter it was pointed out that tests and test-like procedures have had a considerable part to play down the years in the development of psychological knowledge. So considerations of test content apply not only to teaching *about* tests but to teaching *with* them.

Many concepts measured by tests form the basis of familiar debates at all levels of psychology teaching. Arguments about the heritability of intelligence or the nature of personality are often considered without reference to the characteristics of the tests that have been used in their formulation. Understanding of such debates can often be deepened by a knowledge of the content and technical qualities of psychological tests.

Used in this way, some tests can be valuable as instructional devices. For example, it is often easier for the student to gain an understanding of 'spatial ability' by reference to a few instances of appropriate item types than from a definition such as 'the ability to perceive patterns and to manipulate them or transform them into other arrangements'. The contrast between the formal definition and the attempt at measurement provided by the test can be illuminating to students and may provide a suitable starting point for discussion of the problems of definition in psychology.

As a concept becomes more complex, however, tests tend to become less useful in helping a student's understanding. Administering an intelligence or creativity test would probably not assist a student to understand the nature of intelligence or be helpful in relating definitions to the reasoning processes implied by the test. When a test is used to illustrate a concept, in most cases it is not necessary to administer the full version to provide instances of the types of operation involved, and a few examples of item types would serve just as well. In many ways it is wasteful of valuable teaching time to administer complete psychological tests to a group of students simply to instruct them in the content of tests. There are also likely to be strong ethical objections.

One method of overcoming this is to use the versions of tests available in popular paperbacks. Some of these are:

EYSENCK, H.J. (1962) *Know Your Own IQ*
BUTLER, E. and PIRIE, M. (1983) *Test Your IQ*
DE CARLO, N. (1984) *Psychological Games: A Book of Tests and Puzzles to Teach You More About Yourself and Those Around You*
EYSENCK, H.J. (1986) *Know Your Own PSI-Q*
ANONYMOUS (1987) *Test Your Reasoning*
SULLIVAN, N. (1988) *Test Your Intelligence*

A not immediately obvious further source of such 'tests' is the press, ranging from recruitment advertisements for Mensa to fairly serious stress indicators. Often, particularly in the heavier papers and their magazines, the 'tests' are based on relatively sound research instruments with some academic support and credibility. In other cases, a few ambiguous questions have been thrown together by a journalist for some salacious purpose.

Teachers will appreciate that even the better of popular 'tests' must be used with caution. Evidence of reliability or information on the derivation of the norms is seldom given. Indeed, the shortcomings of such tests would be a good subject for class discussion, or an exercise where students review one of these 'tests' – using the format set out in the *Review of Psychometric Testing*, say.

A related approach may be for the teacher to devise a short test made up of different types of item representative of various approaches to measuring a particular concept. This could be administered to the students and followed by group discussion or review.

Then there are the practice leaflets that are produced by various test publishers to accompany certain tests or to be given to prospective test takers. For example, Saville & Holdsworth make practice leaflets available for many of their test batteries. They are intended as a means of giving prospective 'testees' an opportunity to become familiar with the procedures and the test materials that they are about to undergo. They explain why such tests are used, and provide self-scoring examples of the kinds of item that the individual is going to meet. At the time of writing, Saville & Holdsworth also have a self-contained practice test in preparation.

Similarly, the ASE Occupational Test Series General Ability Tests (ASE, NFER-Nelson) have 'A Test Taker's Guide' that gives examples of item types and advice on taking tests.

Naturally, the main aim of such leaflets and guides is to reduce anxiety and enhance 'test sophistication' in the prospective assessee. But at the same time, they do provide a useful and interesting source of material for thinking about and discussing tests and testing.

Much of the current development work in psychological assessment is concerned with the production of tests for administration by computer. Computerized tests can have great advantages over pencil and paper assessments, since they can measure response times, provide dynamic displays, allow repeated attempts at an item or allow the tailoring of a test to the ability of the assessee. Computers can also cope rapidly with complex scoring methods and provide statistical analyses of test results that are continuously updated after each session. For all these reasons, much of the future of psychological assessment may lie with computer-based applications.

Initially, research in this area tended to concentrate on adaptations of existing pencil and paper tests to be administered by computer. In addition, some popular 'tests' are available as games software for the home computer market, and these might be used for teaching purposes. As with pencil and paper tests, they can be used to illustrate test content, but they may also be used to promote discussion of the problems of transposing a test from one medium to another. This could lead to an exercise in which an experiment is to be designed to gauge the effect of computerization on the tests' reliability, validity and norms.

The emphasis in more recent development work is on using the capabilities of the computer to a much greater extent than that demanded by simply converting paper and pencil forms to computer use. Guidelines for the design of software for computer-based assessment were adopted by the BPS Scientific Affairs Board, summarized by Bartram *et al.* (1987). For further discussion on the use of microcomputers in the area of psychological testing, see Colbourn (this volume).

ETHICAL ISSUES

Any use of a psychological test poses ethical questions for the user. When, in addition, the test is being used not for its intended purpose but as a teaching device, there are further complications. The ethical problems are two-fold. First, there is the confidentiality of the test material and results. Second, there is the possibility of psychological risk to the students taking the tests and the issue of invasion of privacy.

It is the responsibility of the teacher to ensure that the confidentiality of the test material is maintained as its value soon declines if it is widely available. Tests should be locked away when not in use and students should not be allowed to keep copies of the tests or the answer key. This prevents the possibility of tests being inexpertly administered to friends and incorrectly explained and interpreted. The sessions at which the tests are administered should be treated seriously and the reasons for restrictions on test use and the necessity for confidentiality should be explained clearly.

When a particular assessment procedure is to be used by the students in their professional work following completion of the course – where they are postgraduate students on educational or clinical psychology courses, for instance – then it is essential that they be trained to use that procedure and trained to the level of competence appropriate to it. For more general application, though, it is not advisable to allow students to mark their own tests if this involves disclosing correct answers to all items. This will obviously distort the results if the same test later gets administered to the student as part of the selection procedure for entry on to another course, say, or for recruitment into employment. In other cases, revealing the items that reflect a particular personality dimension may enable the individual to fake certain characteristics if, say, they are later presented with the test concerned as part of some kind of clinical assessment. So, when tests are being used simply to educate, it is best for students not to carry out the marking – unless, of course, it is important for some reason or another for them to practise scoring and interpretation.

Even when every effort is made to simulate real life administration, students will be only too aware that the outcome has no real importance for them. Nothing hinges on it. Since the tests are being used out of context, levels of motivation may be so different that the norms in the manual are not appropriate. So the results will be even less reliable than usual. This needs to be explained clearly. But even with this explanation, there may still be some students who take the results very seriously. These are the ones who may be put at psychological risk.

Knowledge of the results of a personality test may have implications for the manner in which students view themselves. For example, those with a real life tendency to 'neuroticism', in its technical sense, may worry considerably if this is revealed to them by the casual use of the Eysenck Personality Inventory. This type of consideration is strongest for personality tests, but knowledge of the results of an ability test may also have untoward and unintended effects. The discovery that an intelligence test score is below average, for example, may lead to loss of self-esteem. Conversely, a student whose scores are extremely high may considerably reduce the effort being put into study. It is, therefore, important to consider the possible effects before giving students their results. If results are to be given, they should be given only to the individual and not to the whole class. If the group's results are presented, they should be given without attribution to individuals.

The individual's right to privacy is extremely important and, in some cases, unthinking use of psychological tests may infringe this right. Again, personality inventories are most invasive since they ask questions that are personal and potentially revealing. They may include questions on sexual habits or relationships with other people, for example. It may be that the student would not wish to disclose such information to the teacher. Similarly, the results of an ability test may cause the teacher to reconsider the student's capabilities and performance, perhaps unconsciously. If the individual reveals information that he or she would have preferred to withhold, then that person's privacy has been invaded. The students should, therefore, always be told the nature of the test, how the results will be used, and who will have access to them. When they have this information, they are in a position to give, or to withhold, informed consent to the administration of the test.

A formal statement of the ethical principles relating to the use of assessment techniques by psychologists can be found in the *Ethical Principles of Psychologists* of the American Psychological Association. The British Psychological Society's *Code of Conduct, Ethical Principles & Guidelines* does not focus on tests and testing specifically, but sets out very clearly what is expected of psychologists in their professional practice and behaviour. Safeguards necessary in teaching about tests and testing at A-level were addressed by Miller in an earlier version of this present publication (Miller, 1976).

The certification scheme described earlier in this chapter in the section sub-headed 'Competence' obviously starts from considerations of ethical usage. Indeed, in the introductory pages from the scheme's 'General Information Pack', reference is made to concern with respect to 'the growing problem of misuse and abuse of psychological testing in industry and commerce'. And the BPS Guide, also referred to earlier, sets out to provide helpful advice of a more general sort on 'quality control' in using tests.

Then, again from the USA, there are two codes of practice for constructing and using tests. One is the 'Standards for Educational and Psychological Testing' (APA), and the other the 'Code of Fair Testing Practices in Education' (Joint Committee on Testing Practices, 1988).

QUALIFYING AS A USER

The BPS's certification scheme is obviously intended to become an over-arching, nation-wide system of qualification, recognized by all publishers and distributors. But it is not at present obligatory. It is possible simply to register with one supplier, in accordance with the qualifications procedures that they themselves operate. Of course, such procedures produce, in virtually all cases, end results that are very similar indeed to those set by the BPS scheme. But the latter is 'portable' in a way that single-supplier qualifications often are not. It may be interesting to look at a typical publisher-based system.

Reputable test suppliers have all operated their own systems for examining the qualifications of prospective purchasers for many years. The BPS scheme, in many respects, draws together best practice from these. A typical supplier-based scheme may depend on the categorization of tests according to the complexity of their administration and interpretation. One such is to have four levels of complexity, as follows:

Level 1 (the lowest level of complexity) includes group tests of general ability that are straightforward to administer and interpret. Examples are attainment tests or simple general ability tests, such as AH2. Usually, these are available to anyone with a teaching qualification. The BPS scheme starts at a point beyond attainment testing.

Level 2 includes group tests of single psychological abilities. These are used mainly in an occupational context. Examples are Graduate and Managerial Assessment (ASE) and the Bennett Mechanical Comprehension Test (Psychological Corporation). The qualification level has typically been the satisfactory completion of a recognized occupational testing course – which would also lead to 'Level A' certification under the BPS scheme – or the possession of a degree in psychology – which would not.

Level 3 includes groups of tests of personality or attitudes and batteries of aptitude tests that include measures of several dimensions. Examples would be the Eysenck Personality Inventory or the Differential Aptitude Test. These tests often require special training before they can be properly interpreted and this will be reflected in the way in which availability is controlled.

Level 4 includes tests that are particularly difficult to administer or interpret. These include individual tests of mental ability – the Wechsler Intelligence Scale for Children (WISC), say, or the British Ability Scales-Revised (BASR) – and various clinical tests. These will typically only be available to professional psychologists – Chartered Psychologists, or those who are members of one of the BPS professional Divisions.

Qualification at a higher level normally means that tests at lower levels are also available. This is, of course, a simplified account of a qualification system and, in practice, the rules operated by individual suppliers are more complex.

Test Suppliers

NFER-Nelson Publishing Co. Ltd
Darville House
2 Oxford Road East
Windsor
Berkshire SL4 1DF   tel. (0753) 850333

Separate catalogues for educational, clinical and occupational tests. Assessment & Selection for Employment (ASE) is a division of NFER-Nelson that focuses exclusively on tests for occupational use. The company offers a wide range of British and American tests. They also act as agents for the Australian and New Zealand Councils for Educational Research.

The Psychological Corporation
Foots Cray High Street
Sidcup
Kent DA14 5HP   tel. (081) 300 3322

A wide range of tests for clinical, occupational and educational use. Mainly American origin, but increasingly with British editions or norms.

Saville & Holdsworth Ltd
3 AC Court
High Street
Thames Ditton
Surrey KT7 0SR   tel. (081) 398 4170

Tests designed for occupational use, generally constructed within SHL, and available singly or grouped into batteries for use with different employment groups.

The suppliers listed on the previous page are three of the larger British organizations involved in test publishing and distribution. The following are either somewhat smaller or are more specialized in what they have to offer.

Educational & Industrial Test
  Services Ltd
83 High Street
Hemel Hempstead
Hertfordshire HP1 3AH
tel. (0442) 56773

Godfrey Thomson Unit for
  Academic Assessment
University of Edinburgh
24 Buccleuch Place
Edinburgh EH8 9JT
tel. (031) 667 10011 x6703

Hodder & Stoughton
PO Box 702
Dunton Green
Sevenoaks
Kent TN13 2YD
tel. (0732) 450111

Knight Chapman
  Psychological Ltd
48 High Street
Lewes
Sussex BN7 2DD
tel. (0273) 471535

Macmillan Education
Houndmills
Basingstoke
Hampshire RG21 2XS
tel. (0256) 29242

Northern Ireland Council for
  Educational Research
The Queen's University of
  Belfast
52 Malone Road
Belfast BT9 5BS
tel. (0232) 245133 x4366

Oxford Psychologists Press
Lambourne House
311–321 Banbury Road
Oxford OX2 7JH
tel. (0865) 510203

Personality Systems Ltd
4 Freeland Road
London W5 3HR
tel. (081) 752 0880

Science Research
  Associates Ltd
Newtown Road
Henley-on-Thames
Oxfordshire RG9 1EW
tel. (0491) 410111

Psytech International
  Limited
Icknield House
Eastcheap
Letchworth
Hertfordshire SG6 3DA
tel. (0462) 482833

Selby MillSmith Ltd
Windmill House
Victoria Road
Mortimer
Reading
Berkshire RG7 3DF
tel. (0734) 333585

The Test Agency
Cournswood House
North Dean
High Wycombe
Buckinghamshire
HP14 4NW
tel. (0240) 243384

The catalogues of all these suppliers are, of course, advertising brochures and should be treated as such.

FURTHER READING

Publications associated with the work of the BPS Steering Committee on Test Standards	*Psychological Testing – A Guide.* (1990) *Certificate, Statement & Register of Competences in Occupational Testing.* (1991) *Certificate of Competence in Occupational Testing (Level A) – Guidance for Assessors.* (1992) BARTRAM, D., LINDLEY, P.A., FOSTER, J. and MARSHALL, L. (1990) *Review of Psychometric Tests for Assessment in Vocational Training* (and *Update '92*). Leicester: BPS Books (The British Psychological Society) published in conjunction with the Department of Employment [with regular updates, and extension into other areas and applications]. BARTRAM, D. and LINDLEY, P. (in preparation) *Training Modules for Psychological Testing.* [Applies initially to Level A testing for occupational purposes].
Other critical reviews	BUROS, O. and his successors (Eds) *Mental Measurements Yearbooks.* [This still rates as the principal source of unbiased information about tests]. SWEETLAND, R.C. and KEYSER, D.J. (Eds) (1986) *Tests: A Comprehensive Reference for Assessments in Psychology, Education and Business.* Kansas City: Test Corporation of America, available from NFER-Nelson. LEVY, P. and GOLDSTEIN, H. (Eds) (1984) *Tests in Education.* London: Academic Press.
Textbooks	ANASTASI, A. (1988) *Psychological Testing.* New York: Macmillan. CRONBACH, L.J. (1984) *Essentials of Psychological Testing.* New York: Harper & Row.
Other books of interest both general and specific	COOK, M. (1988) *Personnel Selection and Productivity.* Chichester: Wiley. INSTITUTE OF PERSONNEL MANAGEMENT (1992) *The IPM Code on Occupational Testing.* London: IPM. LEWIS, C. (1985) *Employee Selection.* London: Hutchinson. PEARN, M.A., KANDOLA, R.S. and MOTTRAM, R.D. (1987) *Selection Tests and Sex Bias.* London: EOC/HMSO. PUMFREY, P. (1985) *Reading: Tests and Assessment Techniques.* London: Hodder & Stoughton. SMITH, M. and ROBERTSON, I. (Eds) (1989) *Advances in Selection and Assessment.* Chichester: Wiley. SUMNER, R. (1987) *The Role of Testing in Schools.* Windsor: NFER-Nelson. SYDNEY, E. (Eds) (1988) *Managing Recruitment.* Aldershot: Gower. TOPLIS, J., DULEWICZ, V. and FLETCHER, C. (1987) *Psychological Testing: A Practical Guide.* London: IPM. WILSON, J.D. and THOMSON, G.O.B. (Eds) (1989) *Assessment for Teacher Development.* London: Falmer. WOOD, R. (1987) *Measurement and Assessment in Education and Psychology.* London: Falmer.

REFERENCES

(publications referred to in the text, but not covered above)

AMERICAN PSYCHOLOGICAL ASSOCIATION (1981)
Ethical principles of psychologists. *American Psychologist,*
36, 633–638.

AMERICAN PSYCHOLOGICAL ASSOCIATION (1985)
Standards for Educational and Psychological Testing.
Washington DC: APA.

ANONYMOUS (1987) *Test Your Reasoning.* Glasgow: Gibson.

BARTRAM, D., BEAUMONT, J.G., CORNFORD, T., DANN,
P.L. and WILSON, S.L. (1987) Recommendations for the
design of software for computer based assessment –
Summary statement. *Bulletin of The British Psychological*
Society, 40, 86–87.

THE BRITISH PSYCHOLOGICAL SOCIETY *Code of Conduct,*
Ethical Principles and Guidelines. Leicester: BPS.

THE BRITISH PSYCHOLOGICAL SOCIETY (annual) *The*
Register of Chartered Psychologists. Leicester: BPS.

THE BRITISH PSYCHOLOGICAL SOCIETY PROFESSIONAL
AFFAIRS BOARD (1980) Technical recommendations for
psychological tests. *Bulletin of The British Psychological*
Society, 33, 244–249.

THE BRITISH PSYCHOLOGICAL SOCIETY WORKING
PARTY ON COMPETENCE IN PSYCHOLOGICAL TEST-
ING (1983) Psychological tests – a legal definition.
Bulletin of The British Psychological Society, 36, 192.

BUTLER, E. and PIRIE, M. (1983) *Test Your IQ.* London: Pan.

DE CARLO, N. (1984) *Psychological Games: A Book of Tests and*
Puzzles to Teach You More about Yourself and Those Around
You. New York: Facts on File.

EYSENCK, H.J. (1962) *Know Your Own IQ.* Harmondsworth:
Penguin.

EYSENCK, H.J. (1986) *Know your Own PSI-Q.* London: Corgi.

EYSENCK, H.J. and WILSON, G.D. (1976) *Know Your Own*
Personality. Harmondsworth: Penguin.

JOINT COMMITTEE ON TESTING PRACTICES (1988) *Code*
of Fair Testing Practices in Education. Washington DC: Joint
Committee on Testing Practices.

MILLER, K. (1976) Teaching tests at A-level. *Psychology*
Teaching, 4, 146–147.

REPORT OF THE CHIEF EXAMINER (1993) Diploma in
Clinical Psychology – Autumn 1992. *The Psychologist, 6* (1),
35–36.

SULLIVAN, N. (1988) *Test Your Intelligence.* London: Javelin.

DESKTOP COMPUTERS: COURSEWARE AND SOFTWARE

Christopher J. Colbourn

❏ *statistical packages • personality, psychometric and other tests • the computer-based laboratory class • computational modelling • multimedia • learning tools • further information • software index • addresses of software agents and suppliers*

The approach taken in this chapter is to look *principally* at what computers are being used for in psychology teaching. Often I have been sidetracked into suggesting useful software packages, or, in the case of multimedia, for instance, I have mentioned a development which can be expected to have an impact upon teaching practices within the next few years. I have focused almost entirely upon the software that is available, mentioning hardware only in the context of which system is necessary to run a particular piece of software. On the principle that one does not need to understand the thermoelectronics of a car's ignition system in order to drive between Nottingham and Derby, there is no argument for dwelling upon the electronic wizardry that lives beneath the computer's bonnet. Nevertheless, occasionally it may be necessary to refer to some aspects of the technical specification of computers (that is, as used when selecting a specific model to purchase) where this is relevant to certain types of usage. For a more general discussion of the issues involved in selecting and supporting desktop computer systems see Colbourn (1991b).

It is necessary to start by defining one term which is central to this review. A *desktop computer* here is regarded as a machine that is relatively small physically, as its name implies, although its processing capability may be considerable. Such machines include *personal computers* (note that while the acronym PC stands for personal computer it is most commonly used to refer to IBM-type machines and their derivatives usually labelled IBM PC-compatibles), the lower specification types, and *workstations*. The latter usually offer powerful multi-task processing facilities especially necessary in handling high quality complex graphics and can offer computing facilities for a number of simultaneously networked users. A desktop computer is usually dedicated to one user who will control its input and output routines. Such machines

[Editorial comment: This chapter is based on the chapter written by Geoffrey Underwood and Jean D.M. Underwood in the previous edition]

have become the most commonly used types, and are now more often than not interconnected in networks to provide distributed processing facilities for departments, research groups, and even whole institutions. The original distinction between microcomputers, minicomputers and mainframes has all but disappeared. However, the large, remote machine, known as a mainframe computer, which serves an institution, and which is managed by a team of computer engineers, is still to be found though less commonly than once was the case. One metric here is the scale of service – the desktop, the department or the institution – and another is the control available to the user. At one end of this continuum the user has total control over when the machine is switched on, as well as over which programs are available, and at the other extreme the user is served by a team of engineers whose job it is to make programs and other facilities available.

The desktop computers primarily discussed in this chapter are IBM PC-compatible machines (hereafter simply referred to as PCs), and the Apple Macintosh series (hereafter referred to as Macs). While BBC microcomputers are still commonly found, they are showing their age and gradually being replaced by PCs and/or Macs as they wear out. Little new software is produced for the BBC machine now and even their current successors, the Acorn Archimedes series, seems to have been largely bypassed by psychological software developers. In fact the majority of psychological software has been developed for Macs and PCs. There is also now a convergence of software for these two platforms, largely fostered by the successful take-up of Microsoft's Windows interface to the DOS operating system on the PC, which shares many of the characteristics of the Mac interface (see, for example, Colbourn, 1991a). In fact many commercial packages are now developed to appear in virtually the same form on both the PC and the Mac, and for that matter also on the powerful desktop workstations that run under the UNIX operating system, and commonly have a form of the mouse/trackball-driven 'graphical user interface' (GUI) somewhat similar to that found on Macs and many PCs.

At the time of writing a new survey on the use of computers in psychology teaching and research in UK higher education institutions is being carried out by the Computers in Teaching Initiative (CTI) Centre for Psychology at the University of York. However, their previous survey carried out in July 1989 (Hammond and Trapp, 1989) showed that while there was a limited smattering of Archimedes, Apple II, RML Nimbus and Sun workstations around, Macs, PCs and BBCs were in widespread use and it was not uncommon to find all three such machines being used in a psychology department.

These personal computers generally cost less than £1,000 for a basic colour machine with hard disc (HD) storage (so that all of our programs, documents and other files can be kept in one place and conveniently accessed), and some can cost considerably less. Costs start to increase, of course, as soon as we need to install printers or graph plotters for publication-quality output, and scanners for inputting photographic or other pictorial material to use as stimuli, etc. Nevertheless, high quality output and input devices of this type can now be purchased for between £300 and £1000.

In order to supplement my own direct experiences of how psychology teachers choose to use computers, as well as other possible ways in which they can be used, I have drawn upon published reviews of software for psychologists. Periodicals like *The Psychologist, Behavior Research Methods, Instruments, and Computers,* and *Psychology Software News* regularly feature software reviews, and are essential reading for anyone requiring updates and opinions on commercially available software. Many of the present comments are based upon reviews in these publications. Underwood and Underwood, the authors of the first edition of this chapter, sent a questionnaire to 25 polytechnic and university psychology departments, and to 25 schools and colleges of further education that teach A-level psychology. The questionnaire asked specifically about computer and software use in teaching statistics, personality and ability testing, laboratory classes, on-line control of apparatus, AI (artificial intelligence) applications and programming, and also asked what else computers were used for. As might be expected, there is both more use and a greater range of use in degree-level institutions. They simply have larger budgets, and a number of A-level teachers commented that they do not have regular access to desktop computers. But one reason given for the slight use of computers in an A-level institution was that psychology is taught in a short course, and this does not give enough time for any study which is not directly applicable in the examination. This is unfortunate, and one of the aims here is to show how computers can be used with commercially available software for the enhanced presentation of materials which are of direct examination relevance (see also the chapter by Haworth in this volume).

A more recent picture was painted by Hammond and Trapp (1992), but this represents more of a view of the good practices emerging in university departments rather than what is in widespread use. Thus it is a valuable summary for those planning the next phase of their 'teaching with computers'.

STATISTICAL PACKAGES

The most common use of computers in undergraduate psychology courses is for the statistical analysis of data collected in experiments, and there are so many general-purpose packages available that choice will frequently be made on the basis of existing hardware, software and the experience of those carrying out the teaching. Because of the huge number of statistical tests and statistics packages, the comments here are restricted to the packages which current users have found to be satisfactory, and particularly to those packages available for several different hardware platforms. Programs which handle only one statistical test have been excluded, simply because teachers and students tend to prefer a general package so that a separate command structure does not have to be learnt for each test. An extremely useful source of information and review of statistical software for psychologists can be found regularly in a special section of the *British Journal of Mathematical and Statistical Psychology*.

The most frequently used packages at undergraduate level are *Minitab* and *SPSS*, particularly in the versions for IBM PC-compatibles, although both packages are also available for Macs, and various other hardware platforms. Whereas *SPSS* is in the 'research-use' category, and is intended for use beyond the teaching of elementary statistics, *Minitab* and its BBC-based offspring can be used for A-level and introductory undergraduate support purposes. There is also a number of statistics packages specific to the Macintosh for use at degree level and beyond.

For many psychologists and other social scientists the most familiar statistical package is *SPSS*, which runs on IBM PC-compatible machines in its *SPSS/PC* + and *SPSS for Windows* forms (for example, Lovie, 1988a; Pickles and Battaglia, 1992). It is very powerful, although the mainframe version is often considered very awkward to use because learning the commands and their structure can be a time-consuming exercise. Users of all versions will find the command syntax the same, but personal computer versions offer interactive use of help screens, menus, a spreadsheet-type data editor and graphics. For teaching purposes, such facilities are extremely valuable in supporting the novice's construction of a set of commands to analyse data. *SPSS* packages do come with back-up texts which can be used as the basis for an entire statistics course at degree level, and cover all of the tests that most of us could imagine using for research purposes, let alone teaching.

SPSS is generally regarded as an 'industry standard' and many teachers of psychological statistics courses, the author included, have come to the opinion that it is worth starting to teach with this package rather than use a so-called 'introductory' package like *Minitab* first. The latter software will rarely be sufficient by the third year of an undergraduate course and this is not the time to have to cope with learning to use a substantial new piece of software. Two recent texts produced by psychologists provide an even more accessible introduction to the use of *SPSS* especially for introductory statistics teaching (namely, West, 1991; Kinnear and Gray, 1992). Also the latest *SPSS for Windows* version provides an extremely usable GUI interface (even better than the current Mac version) overcoming many of the reservations with other versions.

However, it must be noted that *SPSS* is an expensive package even with the favourable discounts available for educational institutions, and it does require a substantial chunk of hard disc storage on your personal computer (although it will run from a fileserver on a network). Since the package is modular, the actual costs and space needed depend on the techniques and facilities required. Nevertheless, this is a thorough, serious statistical package, and many will consider the expense and learning-costs to be worthwhile.

Although most of the other heavyweight statistical packages like *BMDP, SAS,* etc. are now available in personal computer versions, few of them are commonly used in undergraduate teaching, nor are they really suitable for this use. However, a fairly heavyweight alternative to *SPSS* at a relatively 'budget' price, that has been quite well received is *SYSTAT*, available for both PC and Mac platforms (see Barrett, 1991; Lovie, 1991a, 1991b). This package essentially covers all the main univariate and multivariate techniques, and has sound coverage of contingency table analyses. The data graphics module, *SYGRAPH*, is a particularly strong feature. However, the interface is not as smooth as that in the personal computer versions of *SPSS*. A bonus is that the manuals provide good tutorial material on the statistical techniques covered. However, the author would have some reservations about using this as an undergraduate teaching package because of the complexity of its presentation and some idiosyncrasies in the way it handles data entry.

A well-used alternative to *SPSS* on an IBM PC-compatible is *UNISTAT*, available in both DOS and full 'Windows' versions. This advanced package is less than half the price of personal computer versions of *SPSS*. Data entry is straightforward, and processing options are selected from pull-down and pop-up menus. A version of *UNISTAT* is also available to run on BBC machines. Like *SPSS*, the *UNISTAT* packages are powerful enough for research use.

Minitab is the final package which is in frequent use in degree-level teaching. It offers a good range of descriptive statistics, non-parametric and simple parametric tests, with a few more advanced procedures. It is much less sophisticated than *SPSS, SYSTAT* and *UNISTAT,* and priced accordingly. *Minitab* is very usable in introductory statistics and laboratory classes, and with non-computer literate students, as it is operated interactively and with good use of natural language commands. *Minitab* is a serious contender as a support package for pre-degree level courses in psychology and for introductory statistics classes generally. Useful reviews of the *Minitab* software can be found in Kornbrot (1992) and Lovie (1990, 1992). However, it is worth bearing in mind the comments I made earlier about the limited virtues of teaching with introductory packages if the procedures covered are insufficient to last the whole of the student's psychology degree course.

There are some statistics packages worthy of mention here available only for the Macintosh platform. A fuller comparison of these has been prepared by Lehman (1986), although he tested earlier versions of the packages than are now on release, and many of them have since undergone considerable development. The accessibility and usability of the Macintosh is well known, some (including the present author) would say unsurpassed even by Windows-equipped PCs. Statistics packages available for this machine make good use of its user-centred interface.

SuperANOVA is specifically designed to handle all possible general linear model designs including univariate and multivariate analysis of variance, and simple, multiple and polynomial regression. It is the best program for this purpose as measured by the large number of factors it can handle, the range of post-analysis tests available, and the ease of use. It includes a good range of canned models to cover common needs (see Kornbrot, 1991, for a review).

The same producers also offer *StatView*, a general package with a wide range of parametric and non-parametric tests, a good range of options for data handling and description, and good graphics facilities. Both packages have the advantage of being easy to learn how to use, and current versions share the same interface.

DataDesk does not handle non-parametric statistics, but is particularly good for correlation and multiple regression analysis. It also has cluster and principal components analysis facilities, and the graphics are nothing less than magnificent. This package has been designed for research applications where the manipulation of variables could otherwise be a chore. It has an extraordinary number of options available in each product window, and because these options encourage data exploration the package is useful as a teaching tool (see Shrout, 1987, for a review).

Finally, mention must be made of a unique data visualization package, *MacSpin*, which is excellent for the exploration of multivariate data. The really special feature is that the software allows you to rotate 3-D scatterplots in any direction and at any speed, and provides animation facilities for this spinning scatterplot on a fourth variable. The present author has found this to be an excellent method of revealing patterns in data sets for further exploration. Apart from a few clustering algorithms no actual statistical procedures are included. However, the current version (v3.0) of the software does provide most of the standard graphical methods of data display (for reviews see Cook, 1987, and Hinde, 1988). Similar facilities have now been incorporated into *SPSS for Windows* although the implementation is not as good as in *MacSpin*.

It worth noting here that data visualization techniques and exploratory data analysis (see Lovie and Lovie, 1991, for a review) are becoming increasingly important parts of data analysis and are starting to filter down to undergraduate level. More statistics packages now include some of the necessary tools. Mac packages are especially strong on this point (see review by Marchak and Zulager, 1992), as is *SYSTAT*, and one IBM PC-compatible specific piece of software which should be mentioned in this context is *NCSS* (see Lovie, 1988b, for a review). It is also worth remembering that a substantial amount of descriptive and graphical analysis can be done with standard spreadsheet packages like *Microsoft Excel*, *Lotus 1-2-3*, *Borland Quattro Pro*, etc. Many statistical software packages can directly import data from such spreadsheets and so data entry rarely has to be carried out more than once. However, the attention of users of such data graphics facilities should be drawn to Tufte's (1983) guidelines for excellent, unambiguous and economical graphical representation of data. These are clearly unknown to most producers of the software judged from some of the options offered to end users. The *SYGRAPH* manual, that accompanies the *SYSTAT* package, is a notable exception to this, providing a discussion of not only Tufte's work, but also some of the psychology relevant to the perception of data graphics.

Before leaving this section, brief mention should be made of another burgeoning area of data analysis, and that is qualitative methods. In recent years considerable effort has been made to develop qualitative analysis techniques and provide software tools to support them. While this topic, to my knowledge, still receives relatively little attention in the undergraduate syllabus, postgraduates are often requesting information on the subject. Tesch (1990) provides one of the better sources on qualitative research with special emphasis on appropriate software tools, although Fielding (1991) offers a useful succinct account.

PERSONALITY, PSYCHOMETRIC AND OTHER TESTS

The administration of psychological tests is remarkably easy with a computer, but there is limited evidence of their use in A-level or undergraduate courses on questionnaire and test design, even though they could provide valuable support materials, particularly for undergraduate teaching once the essentials of testing have been dealt with. Indeed there is quite simply little evidence of the use of commercial software packages for psychological testing. One reason might be the high prices charged for these packages which, unlike statistical packages, require the user to buy a separate package for each test.

Automated psychological tests (APTs), such as computer-based questionnaires, have two principle advantages over their pencil-and-paper parents. Administration and scoring are automatic, and are therefore both less tedious and less prone to error. Previous questionnaire responses can be easily accessed, making for simple comparison of individual with sample norms. Discussions of the advantages of computer-based testing can be found in Lockshin and Harrison (1991), Wilson and McMillan (1991), and Wexler (1990). APTs which scale individuals on personality and ability dimensions are in wide use in clinical and industrial personnel settings. Most of them run on IBM PC-compatible machines.

Customized APTs

Many of the traditional pencil-and-paper tests have now been converted, and are listed in the DRAT (1988). The DRAT lists the origins and specifications of a large number of APTs and other psychological diagnostic tests which have been developed 'in-house' by individuals who are, in some cases, prepared to share or sell them. Tests which are mentioned include Mill Hill Vocabulary Scale, Digit Span, Raven's Progressive Matrices, Eysenck Personality Inventory, Bexley-Maudsley Automated Personality Screening, Cattell's 16PF, Myers Briggs Type indicator, and tests of verbal reasoning and verbal fluency. The directory lists the addresses of software writers, the machines on which the software will run, the aim of the software, and research publications relating to its use.

Also worth noting here is O'Carroll *et al.*'s (1993) description of an innovative computer-assisted tutorial package they have developed for teaching psychometrics to undergraduates. The package takes its users through the whole process of developing a psychometric test and would appear to be a valuable supplement to any course in individual differences.

Commercial APTs

Commercial APTS are also available. If those reviewed in the Computer Column of *The Psychologist* in recent years are typical, it may be worth waiting before making an investment. Not one of them received a positive review.

Charles Johnson (1988a) reviewed *Test Plus*, which is based on Cattell's 16PF, and concluded that he 'would not recommend it for serious use'. Under Johnson's pen (1988b) a test of motivation called *Spectrum-1* does not fare any better. This questionnaire scales individuals on sources of motivation – accomplishment, recognition, power and affiliation – and comes from the same software house as *Test Plus*. Johnson's verdict on this one is that it is 'poorly thought out and underdeveloped' and that 'using this package would not advance your understanding of someone's motivation by all that much'. Similarly, a package entitled *IQ-Plus*, purporting to assess and improve users' visuo-spatial abilities was reviewed by Caren Narborough-Hall and Shirley Brennan (1992). While this appeared to involve an interesting and challenging task, no guidance on its use or evidence of the claims made was provided with the software.

A software package which is used in psychological testing and which does seem to be usable is a program called *Circumgrids* (Chambers and Grice, 1986). This is a repertory grid package which allows the analysis and comparison of grids, together with a number of subsidiary analyses. It is usable only by those with a sound knowledge of repertory grid techniques and has a couple of irritating features: input and output are direct, and cannot be made through a file, and secondly it imposes a strict size limitation. It could prove useful for undergraduate teaching purposes however, and has the virtue of being free (see Glendon, 1991, for a brief review). Information on other repertory grid software can be found in Colbourn (1992b) and Jankowicz (1990).

A final package, again of interest to teachers in social psychology, is the *SAMP Survey Sampling* computer-aided learning package reviewed by Dennis Hay (1989). This package allows a survey simulation using the population of an imaginary town. Students can select which of four survey methods will be used (random sampling; clustered random sampling; stratified random sampling; quota sampling), and what sample parameters should be applied. *SAMP* then gives descriptive summary statistics from the selected sample, and these can be compared with summaries from different samples. Hay describes it as a package which 'is professionally presented and provides clear, concise demonstrations' although it is restricted in its scope. This simple simulation tool makes good use of the data-handling capabilities of computers and could be a useful teaching aid.

THE COMPUTER-BASED LABORATORY CLASS

Commercial Packages

There is now a considerable number of software packages that can be used to assist in the running of psychology laboratory classes. Most have been developed by academics and are 'commercial' in the sense that they are marketed via their institutions, companies set up by the authors, or conventional publishers who have diversified into software. The packages can also be broadly divided into three types. First, those providing a collection of 'set piece' experiments allowing the user to gather data and replicate well-documented experimental effects. Some of these allow limited modification of the design parameters. Secondly, there are the 'experiment generator' packages that allow the user to construct just the experiment they desire. These packages are usually also supplied with a library of 'standard' experiments. Finally there are the tutorial and demonstration packages that allow the user to experience various psychological phenomena without actually carrying out full experiments with extensive data gathering.

Not one of the packages of these types that the author has had experience of or has read reviews of can be said to be entirely satisfactory. However, faced with dramatically increased student numbers, many of us may put aside our reservations in order to gain some assistance with practical teaching from the computers! Therefore, I shall briefly comment on some of the widely used software and those packages receiving favourable reviews.

In the first category of collections of 'set piece' experiments, the Glasgow packages are the most comprehensive (Bushnell and Mullin, 1987), and are in use in a number of UK psychology departments to support the teaching of degree-level laboratory techniques. They run on IBM PCs or Apple IIs. There are about a dozen experiments in each package, dealing with topics such as word recognition, mental imagery, memory, visual illusion, and hemispheric asymmetry. Although designed for undergraduate classes, some of the experiments and demonstrations are also appropriate for pre-degree courses in psychology. The two packages are called *Experimental Psychology: A Computerized Laboratory Course* and *Cognitive Psychology: A Computerized Laboratory Course* although most of the experiments could have been presented under either label. They provide a good example of the range of psychology experiments that can be demonstrated on a personal computer. Investing in these programs is a serious decision – they each cost several hundred pounds – but only one copy of each package is required for the laboratory. The supporting texts and workbooks are necessary for each student, but they are more affordable. Underwood (1989) provides a detailed and supportive review of these packages.

There are two somewhat similar packages for PCs that offer smaller sets of experiments than the previously described software. Levy and Ransdell's *Laboratory in Cognition and Perception* consists of 15 experiments covering topics like classical psychophysical methods, sensory memory (Sperling paradigm), activation of long-term memory (priming and lexical decision paradigms), natural concepts (category verification times as a function of typicality ratings), etc. In contrast to Bushnell and Mullin's packages, this one offers three modes of use: demonstration, laboratory and advanced projects where the basic parameters of the standard laboratory experiment can be varied to create new experiments. Smith (1990) gave it a positive review.

Similarly positive was Heard's (1992) review of Henderson's *MindScope*, software that provides some 20 'set piece' unmodifiable experiments. Heard commented that these would be particularly suitable for first year practicals. The range of content available is similar to those packages previously described with some interesting extras like schedules of reinforcement and anxiety hierarchy. An equivalent package for the Mac is *Experiments in Cognitive Psychology* written by Barbara Tversky and her students at Stanford University. Collis (1991) gave this suite of 22 'published' experiments an enthusiastic review, but it is rather expensive and Stanford University were extremely slow in dealing with the present author's enquiries about the software and licensing arrangements (I gave up in the end!).

The second category of 'commercial' software is the 'experiment generator' packages. The major contenders here are *Micro-Experimental Laboratory (MEL)* currently only available for PCs (Mac version said to be imminent), and *SuperLab* for Macs (PC version said to be in development). The latter package was extremely favourably reviewed by Eccleston (1992), and a number of colleagues who have used it have also remarked about its ease of use and amazing flexibility which enables you to create virtually any type of experiment requiring discrete responses using a 'point-and-click' interface. In contrast, there seem to be considerable reservations about the equally, if not more, powerful *MEL* package (Buckley and Green, 1993; Howard and Binks, 1990). However, while *SuperLab* appears to be designed more as a research tool, *MEL* has an optional student package (*MELLAB*) currently consisting of 27 experiments (the producers state that they aim to increase this number dramatically in the next couple of years) covering a similar range to the Bushnell and Mullin software mentioned at the beginning of this section. The advantage of *MELLAB* is that these experiments are modifiable by users to investigate the influence of various parametric values (Hoogland, 1993; St James, 1989).

MEL and *SuperLab* are fairly general purpose experiment generators, but Walter Beagley's *Eye Lines* is a unique and interesting package for designing and running interactive experiments in visual perception. These primarily involve adjusting the size or orientation of one stimulus to match another or some 'standard' orientation, although it is also possible to simulate a four-field tachistoscope. The package is supplied with various demonstrations based around visual illusions and contrast phenomena, and it is available in both Mac and PC versions, interestingly with an identical and non-standard 'pull-down menu' user interface. This package would certainly be a valuable tool in providing a low-cost 'perceptual laboratory' for undergraduate courses and would also be usable in research (see Colbourn, 1992a, for a review).

In the third and final category of software in this section, namely tutorial and demonstration packages, there are many more examples than in the previous two categories. However, a large majority that I have looked at or read about are clearly still in development and are hardly usable in a real teaching environment. Thus, three examples have been singled out that are clearly usable and have received positive reviews. The first of these is Mills and Schiff's *Active Eye* which was reviewed quite enthusiastically by Heard (1991), albeit with some reservations. This Mac only software suite (based on the *HyperCard* and *VideoWorks* applications) contains what is effectively a menu-driven database of 52 dynamic demonstrations, experiments and tutorials in the area of visual perception. It is designed to supplement conventional printed sources and provides lots of follow-up references in the on-screen tutorial material. It comes with a fairly substantial 'guidebook' (Mills and Schiff, 1988) containing further explanatory material (including screen shots to help those perhaps baffled by the on-screen presentation!), further reading, and cross references to other demonstrations in the package. Examples of the content are biological motion perception (based around Johansson's original work using point-light displays and Cutting's developments of this), the Ames trapezoidal window, illusory or subjective contours, social perception (based on Heider's demonstrations), etc.

On the basis of the strong review and the content, I purchased a copy of this package and a licence to run it on our public cluster of networked Mac IIsi computers, and have been using it to support part of the teaching in a first year undergraduate course in cognitive psychology for the past couple of years. Based on this experience I have mixed feelings about its effectiveness. For one thing, some of the modules (stacks) are not bug free and can unpredictably hang the machine. This understandably puzzled and frustrated our student users, and necessitated careful guidance by human tutors during initial sessions with *Active Eye*. Considering this software is sold by a major publisher of psychology textbooks, this is disappointing, and the publishers were unhelpful when we tried to deal with such problems. On the other hand, a substantial number of students enjoyed the computer-based sessions and provided positive feedback about being able to experience many of the phenomena discussed in the course via this medium.

A similar though more limited package is *Insight* by Baro, Lehmkuhle and Sesma of the University of Missouri-St Louis. This software also offers tutorial demonstrations and experiments about perceptual processes on the Mac. Thompson (1992) suggested that it was worth serious consideration though he outlined a number of reservations. It is distributed on the shareware basis (that is, try before you buy) by the authors and is therefore considerably cheaper than *Active Eye*.

In a different topic area, Hall (1993) seemed quite impressed by *Laboratory in Classical Conditioning*, a tutorial/simulation package in animal learning for PCs. Apart from basic Pavlovian conditioning, simulations include conditioned suppression, the Kamin blocking effect, and taste aversion learning. Hall cautions that to make best use of this package, some effort from both students and teaching staff is required. I feel this statement reflects the view of many of us using this type of software.

There are many, many examples of these types of packages and they all share the characteristic that they potentially allow a resource-limited laboratory instructor or tutor to provide demonstrations of a large number of experiments and/or phenomena in psychology. In the prevailing economic and organizational climate it may be that an increasing number of undergraduate departments will take a serious look at the re-organization of their laboratory classes and tutorials. Many packages aim to allow students to use the experiments or demonstrations in the role of participant, with minimal assistance from a class tutor or demonstrator.

Are these packages really usable as the basis of a laboratory class for undergraduate psychologists? The philosophy behind some of these packages indicates that they could provide a 'cafeteria-system' of tuition, but most teachers would regret giving up their close involvement in laboratory class management. Some of this courseware is very good, but more often it leaves much to be desired. A common complaint from reviewers and users is that no opportunity is provided for students to be involved with the decisions about designing experiments. Students are not invited to ask their own questions about human behaviour, and even at an introductory level, it is important that they think about the nature of a good question. There is a place for learning by example, but for many laboratory instructors the use of these packages would place too much distance between the student and the problem of how to go about setting up an enquiry. The real objection is to the whole philosophy of teaching by cafeteria methods which take no account of individual learning difficulties and which set out to teach by example rather than by problem-solving. There is also a potential difficulty in terms of the current coverage of the curriculum since most packages focus on traditional experimental and, particularly, cognitive psychology, leaving significant areas of psychology like developmental, social, and individual differences and their associated methodologies poorly represented.

Issues of teaching philosophy may take second place if you find yourself having to teach laboratory and/or tutorial classes to a couple of hundred students with limited support, and some of the packages mentioned above can certainly provide some useful input to teaching. Many of them could be used for both undergraduate and A-level teaching. However, given the various reservations mentioned here, you would be well advised to either visit a department where the software of interest is already used, or talk to the suppliers about seeing a sample from the packages in operation. With shareware material this is not a problem and free demonstration discs are often available for expensive commercial packages if you ask. Another source of 'try-before-buy' is the Computers in Teaching (CTI) Centre for Psychology where a large collection of psychology software is maintained, all listed in the catalogue (Trapp and Hammond, 1991b). You can try out this software on the regular open days.

Customized Programs

The major alternative to the kinds of packages discussed in the previous section are customized experiment and demonstration programs. A large number of undergraduate departments have written their own software for specific laboratory classes and/or tutorial sessions. In fact the present author spent some time during the mid-80s writing such programs in the BASIC programming language (plus some assembly language) for the BBC B microcomputer to use in some undergraduate laboratory classes. These menu-driven programs are each aimed at a specific topic like choice reaction time or problem-solving behaviour. The programs offer a limited number of menu-selections for items like number of stimuli, number of trials, stimulus-response mapping, etc. However, the student needs to make a number of experimental design decisions, and use the computer like any piece of psychological laboratory equipment. Unlike such equipment, the suitably programmed computer makes the experimenter's life easier by logging responses as the experiment progresses. A disadvantage of this approach is that such software often takes a long time to produce, and it can be considerably more complex to do so with contemporary machines than it was with the relatively simple BBC micro. However, the laboratory 'authoring shell' packages, like *SuperLab* and *MEL* mentioned earlier, offer a solution for certain types of experimental paradigm. Also software tools like *HyperCard* on the Mac and *ToolBook* on the PC can be excellent for rapidly producing small-scale applications, as Macleod *et al.* (1991) have described, although they do have their limitations.

A popular source of customized programs which allow desktop computers to be used as a laboratory is the journal, *Behavior Research Methods, Instruments, and Computers*. These programs occasionally appear as listings, but more usually it is necessary to send the author either an empty floppy disc or a small fee to cover the cost of a new disc. However, increasingly, this software is available for downloading direct to your desktop computer across the academic wide area networks from archive sites (see Huff and Sobiloff, 1993; and also the final section of this chapter).

Typical examples of programs available from this source include various tachistoscopic presentation and timing applications (for example, Doenias *et al.*, 1992), and a program for presenting spoken word lists in short-term memory (STM) experiments (Cox *et al.*, 1992). This STM software is based on the already mentioned *HyperCard* application, a basic version of which is still distributed with every new Macintosh. *HyperCard* has been described as an 'object orientated programming system' (OOPS) in which the objects are buttons, fields, cards, stacks and backgrounds which are displayed on the screen. These screen metaphors are the user-friendly interface to a powerful authoring shell which lends itself to information delivery and educational training applications, but it can also be used in more dynamic ways as a laboratory tool. By 'pressing a button' on screen (that is, pointing at a button using the mouse) a sub-routine in the computer program is initiated, and in laboratory applications this can lead to the presentation of displays of words, sentences, speech or graphics, and the starting of timing routines. Several of my own postgraduate students, some without any previous programming experience, have used *HyperCard* without difficulty to build 'laboratory applications' to run their experiments. There are many texts providing good tutorial courses for those wishing to learn more than the very basics of this application (for example, Coulouris and Thimbleby, 1993). *ToolBook* is a similar application for the PC and it is possible to transfer material between *HyperCard* and *ToolBook*.

A major disadvantage of the in-house approach to writing customized software is that departments up and down this and other countries are duplicating each other's efforts. However, this can be more easily avoided now that we have what can be regarded as a centralized register of psychology software in the form of the directory published by the CTI Centre (Trapp and Hammond, 1991b). Of course, such printed directories tend to become out of date rather quickly. To counter this an electronic version has just been produced, which will be much easier to keep up-to-date, and can also be distributed electronically across the academic networks. The CTI Centre also provides an advice service for computer-based teaching in psychology primarily in the higher education sector, as well as evaluating software and courseware. Queries about the Centre should be sent to Dr Nick Hammond, the director, or Ms Annie Trapp, the manager, at the CTI Centre for Psychology, Department of Psychology, University of York YO1 5DD.

On-Line Control of Laboratory Apparatus Desktop computers are also invaluable as laboratory control devices. Non-computing equipment can be controlled by computers, and data again logged through this storage medium. Most of these applications will be customized, although some companies (for example, Campden Instruments and Electronic Developments) that have traditionally supplied psychology laboratory apparatus are now supplying operant equipment, event recorders, reaction timers, etc. in computer-controllable forms together with the appropriate software. An alternative to pre-designed, off-the-shelf kits is to develop a personal computer system to meet a specific need. This takes us more into the realm of research, but it can be instructive for undergraduate students to get an understanding of the range of behavioural measures that can be taken, and of the flexibility which laboratory computers can provide.

Again, the journal *Behavior Research Methods, Instruments, and Computers* regularly publishes hints about adapting laboratory equipment for computer-control and also provides program listings for the more popular routines such as response timing. Some typical recent examples include Fagot *et al.*'s (1992) description of a PC-controlled apparatus for testing laterality and hand exploratory strategies in haptic processing; and Hawley and Izatt's (1992) account of a voice key for use with experiment generator packages like *MEL*. There is also a number of companies who produce modular psychology laboratory equipment and control software who would be willing to produce special purpose systems on demand. More substantial requirements are involved with psychophysiological work, and on-line control and recording costs commensurately more. However, some impressive laboratory systems have been described involving the use of National Instruments' interface cards that plug inside PCs and Macs and can be programmed, using the *LabVIEW* software package, to control a whole variety of external laboratory equipment (for example, Bates, 1991). The National Instruments' range of products is widely used in university psychology departments.

COMPUTATIONAL MODELLING

Computational modelling, based on artificial intelligence (AI) techniques, is an area that is now included somewhere in most psychology teaching programmes, most usually as one of several approaches to studying human cognition. Increasingly, students are required to carry out some practical work in this area involving the design and production of computer programs aimed to model or simulate some aspect of human behaviour. A range of programming languages is being used – undergraduates are being taught PROLOG, POP and LISP in particular since these are still the major 'research' tools. They are also developing expert systems, and being given introductions to the possibilities available through *HyperCard* techniques. While many departments have developed their own materials (as with most other psychological software), there are now several sets of resources available that make this unnecessary.

For example, in teaching computational modelling based on semantic network and production system type techniques, a commonly favoured tool is the PROLOG programming language. In the early stages this language is relatively simple to learn and reasonably sophisticated projects can be attempted by undergraduates as Scott and Nicolson's (1991) text demonstrates. In addition, Eisenstadt and Brayshaw's (1990) 'Transparent Prolog Machine' environment deserves a mention as a very useful graphical tool to assist in the debugging and understanding of PROLOG programs. (The software for this together with a demo version of *MacPROLOG*, adequate for most undergraduate use, is available free from the Human Cognition Research Laboratory at the Open University.) At Southampton we have used these resources successfully in undergraduate laboratory classes. Hasemer (1992) has also described the successful use of *HyperCard* in this context, even to the point of providing it as an alternative to PROLOG.

Some departments have introduced POP-11 to undergraduates as their first programming language, and *Alphapop* makes good use of the facilities of the Mac in providing an acclaimed system. Stephen Payne (1988) describes it as coming 'close to providing an all-purpose Psychologist's programming system, that can be used for both modelling and for running experiments'. The positive features of this package are usability and flexibility. There are also two useful texts around which a course utilizing POP-11 could be based (namely, Burton and Shadbolt, 1987; and Sharples *et al.*, 1989).

Connectionism Another computational modelling technique, and an increasingly important one for psychology, is connectionism (also variously known as *connectionist networks, neural networks* or *parallel distributed processing models*). Some exposure to these ideas within the context of an undergraduate cognition or perception course is seen by many as essential (see, for example, Eysenck and Keane's popular textbook, 1990), and Orchard (1990) argues that some practical work in this area is crucial to bring the approach alive for students, while avoiding the underpinning mathematical sophistication of the subject matter. The difficulty is that much of the available software is either aimed at sophisticated users or is rather limited like the many low-level demonstration shareware and freeware programs now available. A good example of the former type of package is the handbook plus software (PC and Mac versions available) *Exploration in Parallel Distributed Processing* which McClelland and Rumelhart (1988a) produced to accompany their two volumes on parallel distributed processing (PDP) models of the microstructure of cognition. For those who want more information without commitment, a summary of the 'Explorations' package is available in a journal article by McClelland and Rumelhart (1988b).

While the 'Explorations' package would be suitable for a full-length course on PDP models for advanced undergraduates or postgraduates, Brown (1990) describes an ideal package, produced by Orchard and Phillips (1991), for the less specialized parts of the undergraduate curriculum. This is another combined handbook and software package (Acorn Archimedes, Mac and PC versions available), entitled *Neural Computation: A Beginner's Guide*, that really does offer a beginner's guide as its title suggests. The major network architectures are presented in the form of both demonstrations and interactive models that can be manipulated by the user. Clearly this would appear to be a cost effective way of building an intuitive understanding of connectionism into the psychology curriculum.

Expert Systems Another area of artificial intelligence applications that are finding their way into undergraduate psychology courses are expert systems (ES). As well as preparing psychology students with the information technology systems that they could be using or building after graduation, expert systems provide a view of decision-making and knowledge simulation that is both applied and formal. In the latter case, ESs can be used as a vehicle to discuss problem-solving behaviour.

Fully developed, advanced courses will continue to use professional expert systems shells, but an introductory shell which has many of the features of the full system is the Open University's *Micro Interpreter for Knowledge Engineering (MIKE)* available freely to the educational community from the Human Cognition Research Laboratory at the Open University (OU). This PROLOG-based expert system shell for the PC forms part of one of the OU's specialized short distance education courses. While *MIKE* is simple relative to commercial ES shells, in his review of it, Scott (1991) argues that this is a virtue, and since the package contains most of the essential elements for knowledge engineering, he suggests that it could be valuable in undergraduate psychology courses that involve the teaching of AI techniques.

MULTIMEDIA

In terms of educational technology, multimedia currently is the message, but so far there is limited evidence that it is being used to support psychology teaching in any major way, largely because the necessary resource materials have not yet been gathered together appropriately. However, the educational opportunity afforded by interactive multimedia technology is too great for us to ignore.

The progenitor of multimedia was interactive video (IV) which burst onto the education scene in the mid-80s with the release of the BBC's Domesday disc, and supported by the Phillips video disc player which was in turn controlled by the BBC Master microcomputer or by the RML Nimbus computer. This technology presents the user with an integrated package combining still and moving pictures, text, graphical representations and sound. It is interactive in that the users can select material as they choose but they can also operate on information held in the multimedia database. This integration of the means of presenting information and the high quality of the pictorial material were two reasons for educational interest in IV. A further perceived advantage is that use of IV encouraged a non-formal learning situation in which students navigate themselves through the subject matter held on the disc. However, the cost was very high and few educators got involved.

The technology has developed a long way since that time and costs have dropped considerably. Analog laser discs have tended to give way to digital video techniques that can be handled by fairly standard Macs and PCs using conventional hard disc or CD-ROM storage devices. Software developments like *QuickTime* on the Mac and the AVI extension to Microsoft Windows on PCs, allow the incorporation of real motion video in standard applications, and Kodak's PhotoCD provides a relatively low cost direct method of getting full photographic quality still images in monochrome or colour onto desktop computers. Macs can handle high quality audio material as standard, and PCs can be so equipped with some modestly priced add-on hardware. Still and animated graphics have, of course, been a feature of desktop computers for some time. To pull all these types of resources together, so-called 'authoring' software is used (see Darby, 1992a, for an excellent set of reviews of this type of software, and Darby, 1992b, for an informative set of articles about the uses and experiences of multimedia in higher education). The high-end commercial software of this type is often very expensive, but there is now a number of academic developments that promise more open multimedia environments (that is, available on all main desktop hardware platforms in a flexible and customizable form) for a more modest investment, such as the *Microcosm* multimedia system at the University of Southampton (for example, Davis *et al.*, 1993; Hall, 1993; Hutchings *et al.*, 1992).

The potential of this technology for education is enormous. An interesting though somewhat restricted example of using multimedia techniques to explain and explore a complex cognitive theory is described by Tweedie and Barnard (1992). In a wider context, consider the wealth of pictorial, graphical, animation, film and video material that could bring the teaching of psychology really alive for students. Many lecturers use some of these materials in their teaching already, and perhaps would like to use more. Collecting such material onto, probably several, CD-ROM or bar-coded laser discs with an easy to use authoring package to access and link the material (in either linear or non-linear, that is, 'hypertext' fashion), would provide a major resource for teaching staff to use for self-study sessions, in conventional tutorials, practical classes and even lectures. The flexibility of allowing the 'end-user' teaching staff to organize the material as they wish should avoid the 'not-invented-here' syndrome (for example, Laurillard *et al.*, 1992) from diluting interest in this resource. However, producing such multimedia materials is not a straightforward exercise with copyright issues and how to select material clouding an otherwise bright prospect. In addition, the easy and appropriate use of such multimedia systems by students should not be taken for granted and we are only now starting to understand some of the necessary characteristics of learning with such technology (see, for example, Hutchings *et al.*, 1993).

Nevertheless, the current centrally-funded Teaching and Learning Technology Programme (TLTP), set up to fund deliverable technology-supported solutions to improve the learning experience and cope with student expansion in higher education, may well result in at least some of the wishes expressed above being realized. A consortium of psychology departments is involved in a TLTP project to develop a range of teaching materials and learning resources for introductory psychology courses (see *The CTISS File*, *15*, April 1993, p.57). At the time of writing this project has been running for less than a year and so it is too early to get a feel for the likely outcome, but a valuable set of resources and guidelines for using computers in psychology would seem on the cards, at the very least.

LEARNING TOOLS

The term *learning tools* is usually applied to software applications designed specifically to support learning according to some specific theoretical view of that process (see, for example, Kommers *et al.*, 1992). However, one might extend this definition to include all those general purpose applications to which students are introduced to support their academic work, for example, wordprocessors, spreadsheets, databases, drawing and painting programs, communications programs. It is very common now for psychology students (and of course most other disciplines as well) to be introduced to such a range of applications early in their course so that they can more easily produce reports and course assessments, and use the computer to obtain and manage the information they need from the various CD-ROM-based and on-line bibliographic databases, electronic mailing lists, bulletin board systems and information servers that are readily accessible via the academic networks. (See Colbourn, 1989, for an extended overview of academic/professional usage of computers in psychology.)

The *PsycLIT* CD-ROM database, essentially an electronic version of the well-known journal *Psychological Abstracts*, makes literature searches much more efficient. It has been enthusiastically received by staff and students alike (for example, Lewis, 1990) and provides a valuable resource for all psychologists. A very useful *HyperCard*-based utility called *LitStack* is now available which helps you manage your output from *PsycLIT* and could also be used to maintain your own personal bibliographic database. Another important bibliographic service is the Bath Information and Data Services (BIDS) facility, available using remote terminal access via JANET, the UK academic network. This offers an on-line version of the Institute for Scientific Information's (ISI) citation indices (covering social science, science and the humanities). Each of these bibliographic services has slightly different facilities and slightly different coverage of the literature so they should not be considered alternatives to each other. However, they are very expensive services and usually funded at an institutional level. At Southampton, undergraduates regularly make use of these facilities when engaged on their third-year projects, dissertations and other specialist courses.

The problem that we encounter is that the literature uncovered is often beyond the scope of our university library, requiring inter-library loan requests with the consequent delays (and costs). Some US-based university libraries offer similar on-line bibliographic databases but with the facility to have a copy of a required article faxed to you. Currently this is a very expensive service but possibly a direction that libraries will move in.

There is an increasing number of electronic documents (text, graphics, digital video and software) available on the academic networks worldwide. Now that many academic sites in the UK are connected, either directly or indirectly, to the Internet (the US-based network of networks that now provides truly global connections, see, for example, Quarterman, 1990), these 'global network' resources can be searched using new personal computer software tools that have become freely available. For example, electronic documents either titled with or containing particular user-specified keywords can be located and subsequently downloaded to your own desktop machine using an application known as 'gopher'. Essentially the gopher program on your desktop machine, known as the 'client' version, interacts transparently with similar 'server' versions of the program on remote computers holding electronic archives. There are various forms of these types of network navigation program, some with strange names like 'archie', 'veronica', 'ftp', etc. Unfortunately, there is no space here to cover this topic in detail and in any case it is in a state of rapid development with much of the documentation being maintained electronically rather than in hardcopy. If available, your own local computer services should be able to help you explore this topic further, and information relevant to psychologists on the subject is often published in *Psychology Software News*.

Access to networks also offers the crucial facilities of electronic communication. Electronic mail (email), computer conferencing, news groups and bulletin boards are now widely used by academics for scholarly discussion and information exchange, the latter being commonly related to the use of computers in psychology. Such electronic communication is efficient, by virtue of its speed and asynchronous nature, and also very cost effective. There are a number of electronic mailing lists, electronic newsletters and even electronic journals relevant to psychologists. The use of some of these facilities in undergraduate psychology teaching, at least on a local basis, has been found valuable in some circumstances and is certainly considered an area for expansion (see Colbourn, 1991c; Crook, 1988, 1990). For a general overview of this area see Darby (1991).

Cognitive Tools Finally, some mention must be made of a type of software tool that is aimed at supporting learning more directly and is based upon the cognitive view of learning as an active process (Mayes, 1992). These so-called 'cognitive' or, more specifically, 'concept-mapping' tools, offer facilities for the user to create explicit semantic networks of their knowledge about a topic. Essentially this means representing information as a collection of nodes interlinked by relations in a multi-dimensional space. A popular example of such a tool is *SemNet* (Fisher, 1992), which we have introduced to undergraduate students studying a cognitive psychology course at Southampton. *SemNet*, a Mac application, allows the user to represent concepts via the structure of relations between the elements of their knowledge. We used it both as a 'working model' of the semantic network form of internal representation, a topic on the course, and as a tool to assist students evaluate and develop their own knowledge of the wider course material. A somewhat complex user interface made it hard for quite a few of our students to be successful in the latter task, although it was successful as a 'model'. Intellimation's *Learning Tool* (Kozma, 1992) is a similar Mac application for concept mapping, though it is based on a note-card approach with a limited range of relation types. Trapp and Hammond (1991a) report some success in using these applications with third year undergraduates.

FURTHER INFORMATION

It should be very clear that not all of the software mentioned here has been used personally by the author. Part of the reason for this is that it would be a full-time occupation doing so, and in addition there is often reluctance by software producers to let potential users try their products before purchasing them. Even in my capacity as Computer Column Editor of *The Psychologist* it is commonly difficult to obtain review versions of software and hardware.

Updates on new releases of software for psychologists and evaluations of software packages can be found in *Psychology Software News* (published by the CTI Centre for Psychology at the University of York), in the 'Computer Column' of *The Psychologist*, and also in *Behavior Research Methods, Instruments, and Computers*, and in *Computers in Human Behavior*. Statistical software is regularly reviewed in the *British Journal of Mathematical and Statistical Psychology*. *Behavior Research Methods, Instruments, and Computers* also publishes articles by psychologists who are sometimes prepared to make their programs generally available. It is also worth mentioning the more general CTI publication, *The CTISS File* (available free to anyone working in UK higher education) which often contains articles and information relevant to anyone using computers in teaching. An extensive and invaluable catalogue of currently available software, with brief descriptions, which can be used in psychology teaching has been prepared by Trapp and Hammond (1991b). This catalogue also comes from the CTI Centre, which, as mentioned previously, provides a software information service and holds regular open days when you can try out any of the software in their extensive library.

Finally, a further mention should be made of the various on-line sources of information and other techniques in psychology teaching (and research, of course) which are now accessible to a large part of the academic community (for example, mailing lists like CTIPSYCH, IPCT-L, MACPSYCH, PSYCOLOQUY, TIPS, etc.). These are regularly publicized in *Psychology Software News*, and are often well worth the effort to use.

Acknowledgements

Thanks are due to the many colleagues and students with whom I have discussed, questioned, researched and taught the use of computers in psychology over the not inconsiderable number of years I have been involved with this topic. I particularly wish to mention Wendy Hall, Nick Hammond, Tony Hasemer, Gerard Hutchings, Paul Light, Cliff McKnight, and Tony Roberts. Finally I wish to thank Geoffrey and Jean Underwood for producing such a sound chapter to update for this edition.

REFERENCES

BARRETT, P. (1991) Your flexible friend – a review of SYS TAT 5.0 for DOS. *The Psychologist, 4,* 438.

BATES, T.C. (1991) A Macintosh II psychophysiology system. *Behavior Research Methods, Instruments, and Computers, 23,* 395–402.

BROWN, G.D.A. (1990) Review of Neural Computation: A Beginner's Guide. *Psychology Software News, 2,* 26–28.

BUCKLEY, P. and GREEN, M. (1993) Review of Micro Experimental Laboratory (MEL) version 1.0. *The Psychologist, 6,* 271–272.

BURTON, M. and SHADBOLT, N. (1987) POP-11 *Programming for Artificial Intelligence.* Wokingham: Addison-Wesley.

BUSHNELL, I.W.R. and MULLIN, J.T. (1987) *Experimental Psychology: A Computerized Laboratory Course* and *Cognitive Psychology: A Computerized Laboratory Course.* Hove: Lawrence Erlbaum Associates

CHAMBERS, W.V. and GRICE, J.W. (1986) Circumgrids: a repertory grid package for personal computers. *Behavior Research Methods, Instruments, and Computers, 18,* 468.

COLBOURN, C.J. (1989) Using computers. In G. Parry and F.N. Watts (Eds) *Behavioural and Mental Health Research: A Handbook of Skills and Methods.* Hove: Lawrence Erlbaum.

COLBOURN, C.J. (1991a) A view through Windows. *The Psychologist, 4,* 33.

COLBOURN, C.J. (1991b) Issues in the selection and support of a microcomputer system. In A. Ager (Ed.) *Microcomputers and Clinical Psychology: Issues, Applications, and Future Developments*. Chichester: Wiley.

COLBOURN, C.J. (1991c) Local area networks (LANs): Southampton's choice. *The CTISS File*, No. 11, March 1991, pp.19–20.

COLBOURN, C.J. (1992a) Review of Eye Lines. *Psychology Software News, 3,* 9–11.

COLBOURN, C.J. (1992b) Repertory grids revisited. *The Psychologist, 5,* 465.

COLLIS, G. (1991) Review of Experiments in Cognitive Psychology. *Psychology Software News, 2,* 48–49.

COOK, R.D. (1987) Review of MacSpin. *The American Statistician, 41,* 233–236.

COULOURIS, G. and THIMBLEBY, H. (1993) *HyperProgramming: Building Interactive Programs with HyperCard.* Wokingham: Addison-Wesley.

COX, R., HULME, C. and BROWN, G.D.A. (1992) STM experimenter: Using HyperCard and MacRecorder in short-term memory experiments. *Behavior Research Methods, Instruments, and Computers, 24,* 575–579.

CROOK, C. (1990) Networks. *Psychology Software News, 1,* 22–23.

CROOK, C.K. (1988) Electronic media for communications in an undergraduate teaching department. In D. Smith (Ed.) *New Technologies and Professional Communication in Education*. London: National Council for Educational Technology.

DARBY, J. (Ed.) (1991) Theme issue: Networks and communications. *The CTISS File*, No. 11, March 1991.

DARBY, J. (Ed.) (1992a) Theme issue: Authoring systems for courseware development. *The CTISS File*, No. 13, April 1992.

DARBY, J. (Ed.) (1992b) Theme issue: Multimedia. *The CTISS File*, No. 14, October 1992.

DAVIS, H.C., HUTCHINGS, G.A. and HALL, W. (1993) *A Framework for Delivering Large Scale Hypermedia Learning Materials*. In Proceedings of the ED-MEDIA '93 Conference, Orlando, Florida, June 1993.

DOENIAS, J.M., LANGLAND, S.E. and REISBERG, D. (1992) A versatile, user-friendly tachistoscope for the Macintosh. *Behavior Research Methods, Instruments, and Computers, 24,* 434–438.

DRAT (Directory of Research into Automated Testing) (1988) S.L. Wilson (compiler) London: The Royal Hospital and Home.

ECCLESTON, C. (1992) Review of SuperLab. *Psychology Software News, 3,* 51–52.

EISENSTADT, M. and BRAYSHAW, M. (1990) A fine-grained account of Prolog execution for teaching and debugging. *Instructional Science, 19,* 407–436.

EYSENCK, M.W. and KEANE, M.T. (1990) *Cognitive Psychology: A Student's Handbook*. Hove: Lawrence Erlbaum Associates.

FIELDING, N. (1991) Qualitative data analysis packages in teaching. *Psychology Software News, 2,* 74–76.

FISHER, K.M. (1992) SemNet: A tool for personal knowledge construction. In P.A.M. Kommers, D.H. Jonassen and J.T. Mayes (Eds) *Cognitive Tools for Learning*. Berlin: Springer-Verlag.

GLENDON, I. (1991) Short review of CIRCUMGRIDS III. *Psychology Software News, 2,* 88.

HALL, G. (1992) Review of Laboratory in Classical Conditioning. *Psychology Software News, 3,* 93.

HALL, W. (1993) A campus-wide structure for multimedia learning. *The CTISS File*, No. 15, April 1993, p.33.

HAMMOND, N.V. and TRAPP, A.L. (1989) Where, what and why – the results of our initial survey. *Psychology Software News, 1,* 6–7.

HAMMOND, N.V. and TRAPP, A.L. (1992) Psychology. In *Computers in University Teaching: Core Tools for Core Activities. A Report from the Computers in Teaching Initiative*. Oxford: CTISS Publications.

HASEMER, T. (1992) Teaching psychology with animated transparencies. *Psychology Software News, 3,* 46–47.

HAUSSMANN, R.E. (1992) Tachistoscopic presentation and millisecond timing on the IBM PC/XT/AT and PS/2: A Turbo Pascal unit to provide general-purpose routines for CGA, Hercules, EGA, and VGA monitors. *Behavior Research Methods, Instruments, and Computers, 24,* 303–310.

HAY, D. (1989) Review of SAMP survey sampling. *The Psychologist, 2,* 75.

HEARD, P. (1991) Review of Active Eye. *Psychology Software News, 2,* 17–20.

HEARD, P. (1992) Review of MindScope. *Psychology Software News, 3,* 48–50.

HINDE, J. (1988) Review of MacSpin. *Applied Statistics, 37,* 124–126.

HOOGLAND, A. (1993) A teaching tool for research methods and experimental design. *Psychology Software News, 3,* 81–82.

HOWARD, L. and BINKS, M. (1990) Micro-Experimental Laboratory: short review. *Psychology Software News, 1,* 56–57.

HUFF, C. and SOBILOFF, B. (1993) MacPsych: An electronic discussion list and archive for psychology concerning the Macintosh computer. *Behavior Research Methods, Instruments, and Computers, 25,* 60–64.

HUTCHINGS, G.A., CARR, L.A. and HALL, W. (1992) StackMaker: An environment for creating hypermedia learning material. *Hypermedia, 4,* 197–212.

HUTCHINGS, G.A., HALL, W. and COLBOURN, C.J. (1993) Patterns of students' interactions with a hypermedia system. *Interacting with Computers, 5*, (in press).

JANKOWICZ, A.D. (1990) Review of Repgrid. *The Psychologist, 3*, 307.

JOHNSON, C. (1988a) Review of Test Plus. *The Psychologist, 1*, 150.

JOHNSON, C. (1988b) Review of Spectrum-1. *The Psychologist, 1*, 413.

KINNEAR, P.R. and GRAY, C.D. (1992) *SPSS/PC+ Made Simple*. Hove: Lawrence Erlbaum Associates.

KOMMERS, P.A.M., JONASSEN, D.H. and MAYES, J.T. (Eds) (1992) *Cognitive Tools for Learning*. Berlin: Springer-Verlag.

KORNBROT, D. (1991) Review of SuperANOVA. *Psychology Software News, 2*, 50–52.

KORNBROT, D. (1992) Review of MINITAB Release 8.1 for the Mac. *British Journal of Mathematical and Statistical Psychology, 45*, 166–169.

KOZMA, R.B. (1992) Constructing knowledge with Learning Tool. In P.A.M. Kommers, D.H. Jonassen and J.T. Mayes (Eds) *Cognitive Tools for Learning*. Berlin: Springer-Verlag.

LAURILLARD, D., SWIFT, B. and DARBY, J. (1992) Probing the Not Invented Here syndrome. *The CTISS File*, No. 14, October 1992, p.54.

LEHMAN, R.S. (1986) Macintosh statistical packages. *Behavior Research Methods, Instruments, and Computers, 18*, 177–187.

LEWIS, M. (1990) PsycLIT CD-ROM at the University of Sussex: An optical disc for the literature of psychology. *The CTISS File*, No. 10, September 1990, pp.18–20. (This paper is reprinted in *Psychology Software News, 1*, 46–48.)

LOCKSHIN, S.B. and HARRISON, K. (1991) Computer-assisted assessment of psychological problems. In A. Ager (Ed.) *Microcomputers and Clinical Psychology: Issues, Applications, and Future Developments*. Chichester: Wiley.

LOVIE, A.D. and LOVIE, P. (1991) Graphical methods for exploring data. In P. Lovie and A.D. Lovie (Eds) *New Developments in Statistics for Psychology and the Social Sciences*. Leicester: BPS Books and Routledge.

LOVIE, P. (1988a) Statistical software for microcomputers – A new review section. *British Journal of Mathematical and Statistical Psychology, 41*, 151–154.

LOVIE, P. (1988b) Review of NCSS version 5. *British Journal of Mathematical and Statistical Psychology, 41*, 289–290.

LOVIE, P. (1990) Review of MINITAB Release 7 for DOS. *British Journal of Mathematical and Statistical Psychology, 43*, 168–169.

LOVIE, P. (1991a) Review of DOS SYSTAT 5.0. *British Journal of Mathematical and Statistical Psychology, 44*, 240–243.

LOVIE, P. (1991b) Review of Mac SYSTAT 5.1. *British Journal of Mathematical and Statistical Psychology, 44*, 422–425.

LOVIE, P. (1992) Review of MINITAB Release 8 for DOS. *British Journal of Mathematical and Statistical Psychology, 45*, 337–338.

MACLEOD, H., HUTTON, P. and COX, R. (1991) HyperCard in the psychology practical class. *Psychology Software News*, 2, 41–43.

MARCHAK, F.M. and ZULAGER, D.D. (1992) A review of scientific visualization software for the Macintosh computer. *Behavior Research Methods, Instruments, and Computers*, 24, 328–335.

MAYES, J.T. (1992) Cognitive tools: A suitable case for learning. In P.A.M. Kommers, D.H. Jonassen and J.T. Mayes (Eds) *Cognitive Tools for Learning*. Berlin: Springer-Verlag.

McCLELLAND, J. L. and RUMELHART, D. E. (1988a) *Explorations in Parallel Distributed Processing: A Handbook of Models, Programs and Exercises*. Cambridge, Mass.: MIT Press.

McCLELLAND, J.L. and RUMELHART, D.E. (1988b) A simulation-based tutorial system for exploring parallel distributed processing. *Behavior Research Methods, Instruments, and Computers*, 20, 263–275.

MILLS, M.I. and SCHIFF, W. (1988) *The Active Eye Stack Guidebook*. Hillsdale, N.J.: Lawrence Erlbaum Associates.

NARBOROUGH-HALL, C.S. and BRENNAN, S.D. (1992) Challenge your brain? A review of IQ-Plus Vol.1 Platonic Solids. *The Psychologist*, 5, 123.

O'CARROLL, P., BROOKS, P., HARROP, A. and SHELTON, A. (1993) Testing times: A demonstration of a computer-assisted tutorial for the undergraduate teaching of psychometrics. *Psychology Software News*, 3, 86–87.

ORCHARD, G.A. (1990) Teaching neural computation. *Psychology Software News*, 2, 24–25.

ORCHARD, G.A. and PHILLIPS, W.A. (1991) *Neural Computation: A Beginner's Guide*. Hove: Lawrence Erlbaum Associates (handbook and software package).

PAYNE, S. (1988) Alphapop. *The Psychologist*, 1, 454–455.

PICKLES, A. and BATTAGLIA, M. (1992) SPSS/PC+; Producer's Response. *Applied Statistics*, 41, 438–442.

QUARTERMAN, J.S. (1990) *The Matrix: Computer Networks and Conferencing Systems Worldwide*. Bedford, Mass.: Digital Press.

SCOTT, P.J. (1991) Review of Knowledge Engineering (Open University course including a Prolog-based expert systems toolkit MIKE). *Psychology Software News*, 2, 80–82.

SCOTT, P. and NICOLSON, R. (1991) *Cognitive Science Projects in Prolog*. Hove: Lawrence Erlbaum Associates.

SHARPLES, M., HOGG, D., HUTCHINSON, C., TORRANCE, S. and YOUNG, D. (1989) *Computers and Thought: A Practical Introduction to Artificial Intelligence*. Cambridge, Mass.: MIT Press.

SHROUT, P.E. (1987) Review of DataDesk. *The American Statistician*, 41, 314–317.

SMITH, P.T. (1990) Review of laboratory in cognition and perception. *Psychology Software News*, 1, 51–53.

St JAMES, J.D. (1989) The MEL Library in the undergraduate research methods course. *Behavior Research Methods*,

Instruments, and Computers, 21, 245–247.

TESCH, R. (1990) *Qualitative Research: Analysis Types and Software Tools.* London and Philadelphia: The Falmer Press.

THOMPSON, P. (1992) Review of Insight. *Psychology Software News, 3*, 53–55.

TRAPP, A. and HAMMOND, N. (1991a) Concept mapping tools: A different approach. *Psychology Software News, 2,* 10–11.

TRAPP, A. and HAMMOND, N. (1991b) *The CTI Directory of Psychology Software,* 2nd ed. York: CTI Centre for Psychology.

TUFTE, E.R. (1983) *The Visual Display of Quantitative Information.* Cheshire, Connecticut: Graphics Press.

TWEEDIE, L. and BARNARD, P. (1992) The interactive talk: A new tool for presenting complex theory. *Psychology Software News, 3,* 43–45.

UNDERWOOD, G. (1989) Review of Experimental Psychology: A Computerized Laboratory Course and Cognitive Psychology: A Computerized Laboratory Course. *The Psychologist, 2,* 254–255.

WEST, R. (1991) *Computing for Psychologists: Statistical Analysis using SPSS and Minitab.* Switzerland: Harwood Academic Publishers.

WEXLER, S. (1990) Computerized psychological assessment. In D. Baskin (Ed.) *Computer Applications in Psychiatry and Psychology.* New York: Brunner/Mazel.

WILSON, S.L. and McMILLAN, T.M. (1991) Microcomputers in psychometric and neuropsychological assessment. In A. Ager (Ed.) *Microcomputers and Clinical Psychology: Issues, Applications, and Future Developments.* Chichester: Wiley.

Software Index

Distributors are given in brackets after each item, and their addresses listed in the following section. It is suggested that you contact your Combined Higher Education Software Team (CHEST) representative, should one be available, to establish if there are any special deals for the software you are interested in. Such deals are most likely for widely used software.

Active Eye (Capedia and Lawrence Erlbaum Associates Inc., USA)

Alphapop (Cognitive Applications)

Circumgrids (William V. Chambers and Stephen Morley)

Cognitive Psychology: A Computerized Laboratory Course (Lawrence Erlbaum Associates Ltd)

DataDesk (MacLine)

DataDesk (Student Edition) (W.H. Freeman & Co. Ltd)

Experimental Psychology: A Computerized Laboratory Course (Lawrence Erlbaum Associates Ltd)

Experiments in Cognitive Psychology (Stanford University, USA)

Exploration in Parallel Distributed Processing (MIT Press)

Eye Lines (Capedia and Walter Beagley, USA)

HyperCard (Claris International, Inc.)

Insight (Capedia)

IQ-Plus (Far Communications)

Laboratory in Classical Conditioning (Conduit)

Laboratory in Cognition and Perception (Conduit)

LabVIEW (National Instruments)

Learning Tool (Capedia)

LitStack (Peter Richardson)

MacPROLOG (Logic Programming Associates Ltd)

MacSpin (Cherwell Scientific Publishing Ltd)

Micro-Experimental Laboratory (MEL) and *MELLAB* (Psychology Software Tools, Inc. and iec ProGAMMA)

Micro Interpreter for Knowledge Engineering (MIKE) (Human Cognition Research Laboratory)

MindScope (West Educational Publishing)

Minitab (CLECOM Ltd)

NCSS (NCSS, USA)

Neural Computation: A Beginner's Guide (Capedia and Lawrence Erlbaum Associates Ltd)

PsycLIT (SilverPlatter Information Ltd)

SAMP Survey Sampling (Park Lodge Associates and Conduit)

SemNet (SemNet Research Group)

Spectrum-1 (The Test Agency)

SPSS (including *SPSS/PC +* and *SPSS for Windows*) (SPSS UK Ltd)

StatView (Cherwell Scientific Publishing Ltd)

SuperANOVA (Cherwell Scientific Publishing Ltd)

SuperLab (Cedrus Corporation)

SYSTAT (including *SYGRAPH*) (SYSTAT UK Ltd)

Test Plus (The Test Agency)

ToolBook (Entec)

Transparent Prolog Machine (Human Cognition Research Laboratory)

UNISTAT (UNISTAT Ltd)

UK *Overseas Software Agents' and Suppliers' Addresses*

Campden Instruments Ltd
King Street
Sileby
Loughborough LE12 7LZ
tel. (0509) 814790
fax (0509) 816097

Capedia
FREEPOST 627
St Albans, Herts
tel./fax (0727) 869791

Cherwell Scientific Publishing Ltd
The Magdalen Centre
Oxford Science Park
Oxford OX4 4GA
tel. (0865) 784800
fax (0865) 784801

Claris International, Inc.
1 Roundwood Avenue
Stockley Park
Uxbridge
Middx UB11 1BG
tel. (081) 756 0101
fax (081) 573 4477

CLECOM Ltd
The Research Park
Vincent Drive
Edgbaston
Birmingham B15 2SQ
tel. (021) 471 4199
fax (021) 471 5169

Cognitive Applications
4 Sillwood Terrace
Brighton
East Sussex BN1 2LR
tel. (0273) 821600
fax (0273) 728866
UK0025@applelink.apple.com

CTI Centre for Psychology
Department of Psychology
University of York
Heslington
York YO1 5DD
tel. (0904) 433156
fax (0904) 432917
CTIPSYCH@uk.ac.york

Lawrence Erlbaum Associates Ltd
27 Church Road
Hove
East Sussex BN3 2FA
tel. (0273) 748427
fax (0273) 205612

Electronic Developments
46 St James's Avenue
Hampton Hill
Middlesex TW12 1HN
tel./fax (081) 979 5047

Entec
Spirella Building
Bridge Road
Letchworth
Herts SG6 4ET
tel. (0462) 677744

Far Communications
5 Harcourt Estate
Kibworth
Leicestershire LE8 0NE
tel. (0533) 796166

W.H. Freeman & Co. Ltd
20 Beaumont Street
Oxford OX1 2NQ
tel. (0865) 726975
fax (0865) 790391

Human Cognition Research
  Laboratory
The Open University
Walton Hall
Milton Keynes MK7 6AA
tel. (0908) 653800
fax (0908) 653169
a_carson@uk.ac.open.acs.vax

Logic Programming Associates Ltd
Studio 4
Royal Vic. Patriotic Building
Trinity Road
London SW18 3SX
tel. (081) 871 2016
fax (081) 874 0449

MacLine
Mill House
Mill Lane, Carshalton
Surrey SM5 2WZ
tel. (081) 401 1111
fax (081) 401 1112

MIT Press
c/o John Wiley & Sons Ltd
Southern Cross Trading Estate
1 Oldlands Way
Bognor Regis PO22 9SA
tel. (0243) 829121
fax (0243) 820250

Stephen Morley
Department of Psychiatry
University of Leeds
15 Hyde Terrace
Leeds LS2 9LT
tel. (0532) 332733

National Instruments (UK) Corp
21 Kingfisher Court
Hambridge Road
Newbury
Berkshire RG14 5SJ
tel. (0635) 523545 or (0800) 289877
fax (0635) 523154

Park Lodge Associates
47 Four Oaks Road
Sutton Coldfield
Birmingham B74 2XU
tel. (021) 323 2282
fax (021) 323 2292

Peter Richardson
LitStack
65 Rosedale Road, Kingsthorpe
Northampton NN2 7QE

SilverPlatter Information Ltd
10 Barley Mow Passage
Chiswick
London W4 4PH
tel. (081) 995 8242
fax (081) 995 5159

SPSS (UK) Ltd
SPSS House
5 London Street
Chertsey
Surrey KT16 8AP
tel. (0932) 566262
fax (0932) 567020

SYSTAT UK Ltd
47 Hartfield Crescent
West Wickham
Kent BR4 9DW
tel. (081) 462 0093
fax (081) 462 0493

The Test Agency
Cournswood House
Clappins Lane
North Dean
High Wycombe
Bucks HP14 4NW
tel. NAPHILL (024024) 3384

UNISTAT Ltd
PO Box 383
Highgate
London N6 5UP
tel. (081) 883 7155
fax (081) 444 9512

Overseas Software Agents' and Suppliers' Addresses

Walter Beagley
Professor of Psychology
Department of Psychology
Alma College
Alma, MI 48801–1599
USA
tel. 010-1-517-463 7111
beagley@alma.edu

Cedrus Corporation
PO Box 8026
Silver Spring
Maryland 20907
USA
tel. 010-1-301-589-1828
superlab@cedrus.com

William V. Chambers
Department of Psychology
University of South Florida
8111 College Parkway
Fort Myers
Florida 33919
USA

Conduit
University of Iowa
Oakdale Campus
Iowa City
Iowa 52242
USA
tel. 010-1-319-335-4100

Lawrence Erlbaum Associates, Inc.
365 Broadway
Hillsdale
NJ 07642
USA
tel. 010-1-201-666 4110
fax 010-1-201-666 2394
lea@eies2.njit.edu

NCSS
329 North 1000 East
Kaysville
Utah 84037
USA
tel. 010-1-801-546 0445
fax 010-1-801-546 3907

iec ProGAMMA
Kraneweg 8
9718 JP Groningen
The Netherlands
Tel. +31 50 636900
Fax +31 50 636687
Email: gamma@rug.nl.bitnet

Psychology Software Tools Inc
511 Bevington Road
Pittsburgh
PA 15221
USA
tel. 010-1-412-244 1908

SemNet Research Group
1043 University Avenue Suite 215
San Diego
CA 92103–3392
USA
tel. 010-1-619-232 9334
kfisher@edu.sdsu.sciences

Stanford University
Office of Technology Licensing
Software Distribution Center
857 Serra Street
Stanford
CA 94305–6225
USA
tel. 010-1-415-723 0651
fax 010-1-415-725 7295

West Educational Publishing
620 Opperman Drive
PO Box 64779
St. Paul
MN 55164–0779
tel. 010-1-612-228 7151

MICROCOMPUTER USE AT PRE-DEGREE LEVELS

Geoff Haworth

❏ *hardware: which micro?* • *statistical packages* • *demonstrations and experiments*

Teachers of psychology at pre-degree levels do, I believe, face particular difficulties in respect of microcomputer use, and these are deserving of consideration. Findings from Haworth (1992) point to problems arising from a lack of availability of computer resources, budget limitations affecting both hardware and software purchase, as well as a general unfamiliarity with the whole area of microcomputer use for the teaching of psychology. Additionally, teachers may be dogged by the constraints upon their time imposed by the breadth and depth of the syllabuses often found at this level, as well as the general demands of teaching in the school and further education sectors. However, the inclusion of Artificial Intelligence (AI) on some syllabuses and the continuing spread of computer use across the curriculum (prompted in the past by TVEI and now encouraged by the National Curriculum Council as one of the cross-curricular dimensions), has meant an increase in interest in microcomputer applications in psychology teaching at pre-degree levels.

Over the past two years I have been co-ordinating information on micro use for the Association for the Teaching of Psychology (ATP). During that time I have received many enquiries from teachers of GCSE, BTEC, A/S and A-level psychology. Overall the nature of these enquiries does not appear to have changed – it continues to be dominated by requests for information on the availability of software and practical advice on which hardware to purchase. One noticeable drift, however, has been towards enquiries about IBM-compatible software and away from programs for the BBC machines (although these still remain popular in many schools). In this section I will seek to address this shift in emphasis and concentrate on those aspects of microcomputer use that I hope will be of interest and practical use to psychology teachers at the pre-degree levels.

HARDWARE: WHICH MICRO?

Underwood and Underwood (1990) suggest that there is no necessary advantage to be gained in looking at the electronic wizardry of the microcomputer. I agree – but those who wish to do so might care to look at McKnight (1984). However, whilst teachers at pre-degree levels do not need to be well versed in the finer points of how computers work or fluent in the jargon of the computer buff, there remains some useful information that is of value to anyone wishing to begin or increase the use of micros in their teaching programmes.

Some teachers may work in schools and colleges where policy decisions about the purchase of microcomputers are out of their hands. The question facing those who are given the opportunity to buy their own micros for psychology use is, of course, 'which micro?'. This decision is made more difficult if the teacher has little knowledge of microcomputer hardware and lacks the information necessary for an informed choice to be made. Initially it is worth talking to someone in the IT or computing department before rushing out to buy any machine. You may be able to pick up some useful tips as to the advantages and disadvantages of certain machines from others who are already using micros in their teaching. As always, be wary of 'special bargain offers' and High Street computer sales staff who may be motivated to sell you something that suits their profits rather than your teaching needs.

Basically, you will want a machine that can run the software that is suitable for psychology teaching now and in the future. Hence a word of caution about the BBC B and Master series: most schools and colleges have some BBC micros available, and because of their once popular status there is a good deal of software that will run on these machines, some of which is directly relevant to psychology teaching (for example, *UnderStat* and the ATP's *Psychology Experiments and Demonstrations*). However, these machines are fairly limited in their use because of their small memory capacities – some software is just too demanding of memory to run on them. You can tell the memory capacity of a micro by finding out how many K (kilobytes) it has. Most now have at least 512K (roughly half a megabyte) of Random Access Memory (RAM) – a sort of working memory – and it is not uncommon to see computers advertised as having two to four megabytes of RAM or even more (up to 38 megabytes depending on the machine). By contrast the BBC B has only 32K and the Master only 128K. Furthermore most BBCs will only store around 100K on floppy disc whereas modern PCs will hold up to one-and-a-half megabytes on floppy disc and may have a hard disc (which is permanently installed in the computer) which will hold 20 or 40 megabytes.

Although many teachers still report using BBC machines (Haworth, 1992), most are fairly old and/or well-used and may experience maintenance problems in the long term. It is still possible to buy a new BBC machine on very favourable terms (for example, see *Educational Computing and Technology*, November 1992) or get a good deal on a second-hand model. These machines will run some useful software for teaching psychology at pre-degree levels but you may wish to consider whether they will meet all of your current and future teaching needs.

It is not advisable to recommend a particular machine here, since different teachers will probably have their own individual requirements. However, most schools and colleges now seem to be standardizing on IBM machines or those that are IBM PC-compatible (for example, some RM Nimbus machines, Opus, Compaq and Amstrad – not the PCW8256/8512). In the 'Computers in Psychology Teaching Survey' (Haworth, 1992), about two-thirds of the centres surveyed reported using IBM PC-compatible machines. The big advantage with such micros is that they are all able to run the same software by virtue of the fact that they use the same operating system called MS-DOS (or simply DOS). However, this is not always the case (especially where programs use graphics) and before you buy any software you should always check that it will actually run on your machine, or better still, see it running before you pay for it. Some micros, for example Nimbus, have what is called a BBC Basic interpreter which will translate some programs written for BBC machines to run on that particular micro – but you should check the copyright before you do this. Most PCs will come complete with DOS 5 (the operating system) and Microsoft *Windows 3.1*. *Windows* is a graphical user interface (GUI) which is simply described as an environment for running programs based upon the use of windows which appear on the monitor and icons which you 'click on with the mouse' in order to execute certain actions. It is a very user-friendly and inexpensive way of running programs and many packages now run from within *Windows*.

An alternative to the IBM PC-compatible machine is the Apple Macintosh, and there is some evidence of Mac use in schools and colleges, but not on the scale of the PCs – about 13 per cent of centres have access to these machines (Haworth, 1992). Software for the Mac is typically user-friendly employing an environment similar to that described above for *Windows*. It is not, however, possible to run PC packages on the Mac (and vice-versa) directly, although there is software available to allow you to manage MS-DOS files on the Macintosh (for example, *AccessPC* and *DOS Mounter*). There is an increasing amount of Mac software for use in the teaching of psychology and Apple Computer UK Limited produce a useful Educational Software Catalogue. Many of the larger software producers are now offering PC and Mac versions of their packages.

Probably the best person to advise you on the purchase of a microcomputer is someone who is familiar with the software you wish to run. Many distributers will send you a demonstration disc of the software you require prior to purchase. This will enable you to run through the programs and make sure they are at the right level and suitable for your purposes before you part with any money. It is also worth reading up on software reviews, and an excellent directory of psychology software, together with a regular newsletter, is available to subscribers from the CTI Centre for Psychology at the University of York. The ATP also offers (non-professional) advice to teachers on issues related to computer use and software for psychology teaching. For help with running particular software packages, however, the best person to consult is usually the technician in the IT or computing department and it is well worth getting to know her or him.

Hardware is, of course, developing all the time and it may be that within the next few years we see the blossoming of interactive CD (CD-i) or some other new technology in schools and colleges.

The following sections will briefly review several pieces of software that are commercially available and aimed at pre-degree courses. These fall predominantly into two camps – statistical packages and experiments/demonstrations.

STATISTICAL PACKAGES

There are several powerful statistical packages that are available and widely used at both research and undergraduate level (for example, *SPSS PC+*, *Systat* and *Minitab*). There are others, however, that have been written specifically for the pre-degree level market and designed to run on a variety of machines. I will look at three of these in some detail and mention others that are available.

Concorde Informatics Ltd have produced *stATPak* – a statistics program designed with the analysis of results from A/S and A-level practicals in mind. The program offers seven significance tests including parametric and non-parametric tests for a comparison of means, correlation and a chi-square test of association – the basic tests that are needed by students at this level. *stATPak* will run on the Amstrad wordprocessor (PCW8265 and PCW8512) and IBM PC-compatible machines, which makes it particularly useful for those who do not have BBC machines. It costs a modest £20 and is available through the ATP (at a discounted price for members).

stATPak is fairly user-friendly, although a thorough reading of the rather sketchy accompanying literature and several trial runs will be needed for the uninitiated. In its Amstrad PCW guise, *stATPak* couldn't be simpler to load – just place the disc in the drive and away you go. In the IBM-compatible version, this operation is slightly more complicated since it runs from within MS-DOS.

Once loaded, *stATPak* offers the user the choice of entering data, running statistical tests or seeing what data files are available. The program conducts tests in three categories, depending on whether the data is from correlated samples, independent samples or is nominal data. One very useful feature is that the user can enter up to 20 sets of scores which are then stored on disc so that various statistical tests may be conducted without having to re-enter the data on each occasion. The user interacts with the program by responding to a series of questions, such as 'Which test do you want to use?' and this makes for ease of use. *stATPak* will test the significance of the results from the given sets of data, tell the user if the results are significant, and say whether the null hypothesis is to be accepted or rejected at pre-selected significance levels for 1- and 2-tailed hypotheses. There is also a print-out option that gives very useful step-by-step calculations of the particular statistic chosen. In fact, *stATPak* will do all the things that most students will require in terms of inferential statistics for A/S and A-level (or equivalent) work and is certainly cheap enough for some to want to buy their own.

TokSoft have developed *UnderStat* – a statistical package for the BBC (B and Master series) microcomputer which is specifically designed for students studying psychology at A/S and A-level (or equivalent). The disc comes complete with a user's guide that includes an introduction to experimentation and the use of statistics that is valuable as a text for student use in its own right and is worthy of a few comments here. Not so much a user's guide, the TokSoft literature gives a comprehensive 22-page introduction that covers more or less the basic areas needed at pre-degree levels. It deals with the question of why we need statistics, and introduces concepts such as sampling, variables, hypotheses, experimental design, levels of measurement, and significance testing, as well as offering guidance on choosing and using statistical tests. The User's Guide is available separately from the computer disc and costs £7.50. The software itself comprises programs for both descriptive and inferential statistics (14 different calculations in all), giving on-screen step-by-step calculation of results, plotting histograms and other graphs where appropriate, and offering a print-out option. Such sophistication is reflected in the price, which is nonetheless still targeted at the school/FE department budget, and is currently £50 (exclusive of VAT and p&p).

The *UnderStat* package is menu-driven and includes on-screen instructions and comprehensive supporting literature that make running the software a fairly simple operation. Data entry is straightforward and scores are stored in the computer's memory (not to disc as in *stATPak*) – making data temporarily available for use in a choice of tests without the need for it to be continually re-entered. Results can be seen on screen in tabular form and can easily be edited if mistakes have occurred. The software will use stored data to plot histograms and graphs (such as scattergrams for the correlation options) and will enable the user to obtain print-outs from the tables of results and graphs shown on the screen, provided that a suitable printer (such as the Epson FX or RX) is connected – this is vital for the smooth running of the programs and the production of hard-copy.

UnderStat will perform a variety of statistical tests on data-entries and these are chosen from the menu by the selection of an appropriate key. Having completed the calculations, *UnderStat* shows the result on the screen, but requires the user to check for significance and interpret its meaning – a valuable exercise at this level. The supporting literature gives clear guidance on how to do this and statistical tables are provided in the Guide for users to consult. For the BBC user, *UnderStat* will perform all the statistical calculations that are needed at pre-degree levels (and beyond) and provide hard-copy of tables and graphs for use in experimental write-ups. In addition, the Introduction to Statistics in the User's Guide is a valuable teaching and learning aid in support of the experimental and practical work of the A/S and A-level syllabus.

Stephen Fearnley from the Department of Psychology at Oxford Brookes University has produced a statistics package that is aimed at the A/S and A-level market as well as early undergraduate level work. *Alstats* is much more sophisticated than the two packages already described and runs on IBM PC-compatible machines. It currently costs £45 and comes complete with a user's manual which, unlike the one accompanying *UnderStat*, is not a tutorial text.

Alstats offers a comprehensive package of programs that will do a variety of calculations from simple descriptive statistics to regression and analysis of variance. It offers the user much more than is required at A/S and A-level, but includes all the tests that students will want to use for data analysis in their practical work. The user can choose from t-tests, chi-square, and a variety of non-parametric tests – including Kruskal-Wallis, Friedman, Page's trend test and Jonckheere's trend test – as well as being able to conduct tests of correlation.

The package is relatively user-friendly, but because of its nature it is much more difficult to use than *stATPak*, for example. *Alstats* is menu-driven and once familiar with the package, the less computer-shy student should have little difficulty entering data, selecting tests and printing out results. At the entry stage, data is given a title and the columns of data can also be named. Once this is done the user can select the options available by using the cursor keys. Any number of manipulations can be carried out without having to re-enter the data, and students can see their data set out graphically as a frequency distribution, for example. A certain familiarity with statistical procedures is required, however, and many students at pre-degree levels may need some initial guidance to ensure that they use the package successfully. For example, *Alstats* gives you a null hypothesis and requires you to select an appropriate 1- or 2-tailed hypothesis and state the level of significance required; only then will the calculations be completed. Both critical and table values are given for the chosen statistic and advice is given on rejecting the null hypothesis – which should make *Alstats* appealing to student users. Results can then be printed out and saved to disc for later use.

One example of how *Alstats* is friendly to the user can be seen in the chi-square option. Here a warning is given if low values appear when the expected frequencies are calculated and these account for more than 20 per cent of the cells. In such cases the Fisher exact test is offered for analysing the data. (For a more comprehensive account of the *Alstats* package, you might care to look at Sneddon's review in *Psychology Software News*, April 1992.)

If you require a statistics package at a similar level of sophistication as *Alstats*, you could consider Synthetic Software's *Supastat*. Whilst this is probably written with the undergraduate student in mind, it is nonetheless described as 'versatile' and 'easy to use' in a recent software review (Nott, 1992).

There are other statistics packages that are available for use at the pre-degree level including *Statistics for Psychology* by Geoff Haworth and Shelley Gooding. This is a user-friendly, menu-driven package written for the RML Nimbus machine. It will run on the 186 machine directly and the 386 with the aid of the RM Console Driver (which most machines have installed on the hard disc). It offers a choice of nine tests for descriptive and inferential statistics, together with a 'Help' option that guides unfamiliar users through the steps of choosing an appropriate statistic. Whilst *Statistics for Psychology* is easy to use and does all that is necessary for the basic analysis of experimental data, it doesn't save data in the computer's memory or to disc, unlike *UnderStat* and *stATPak* respectively, and doesn't go beyond the calculation of given statistics (the actual number-crunching). Users are left to check suitable tables for significance etc.

There is also a statistics disc with Psychology Software's *Experiment, Design and Statistics in Psychology*, which is designed to run on the BBC B and Master series. This is the second disc of the package and comes with some detailed, yet difficult, instructions and worked examples. It is designed more as a student-centred learning aid which takes the user through various menu options that include a look at several aspects of experimentation, such as: design, variables, hypotheses, etc. (together with some very useful self-assessment questions); samples, populations and the normal distribution (including some descriptive statistics); the concept of probability; and several options for the calculation of such inferential statistics as t-tests, correlation coefficients and 2x2 chi-square. The package offers itself as a 'computerised companion' to Robson's (1983) *Experiment, Design and Statistics in Psychology* text, and provides some guided examples and interesting graphics in relation to probability and significance testing. Consequently, the statistics disc has value as a tool for both classroom use and for distance learning but comes as a package together with the accompanying experiments disc (see below).

DEMONSTRATIONS AND EXPERIMENTS

The first two packages that are included here both run on the BBC B and Master series microcomputers. The remaining packages run on IBM PC-compatible machines. They offer some colourful and interesting graphics and provide the users with stimulating and useful visual demonstrations of psychological phenomena, and offer frameworks for students' own experimental work. They are easy to use and accessible to pre-degree level students (although I am sure they would also be of interest to undergraduates and their tutors alike).

Dr George Mather of Sussex University has edited the programs for the ATP's *Psychology Experiments and Demonstrations* disc, which is available at costs of between £17.50 and £20 depending on format – with discounts for ATP members. The package (described as a 'suite of programs') is easily loaded and is menu-driven with users initially selecting from the demonstrations or experiments options. In the former, Dr Mather has put together some ten visual demonstrations that include the Müller-Lyer illusion, the Hermann Grid, the Kanizsa Triangle and the Rubin Vase, and these are presented in sequence or individually selected by pressing the appropriate key. The illusions and other visual phenomena are ideal for presentation on the BBC machine and provide some fascinating material to show to students of psychology at all levels. Each demonstration is preceded by a short on-screen description and the user moves easily through the sequence by pressing identified keys. The inclusion of supporting literature within the programs has meant that the user booklet is kept to an absolute minimum of a couple of pages and is simply written and extremely easy to follow.

In the experiments option, six examples suitable for A/S and A-level or equivalent (and in some cases, GCSE) are presented. Users select from a menu of choices that include the Müller-Lyer illusion (with differing fin-angles from 15° to 75°), the Stroop effect, and the primacy-recency effect in memory (with immediate recall and delayed recall conditions). In each case, there is simple supporting literature offering references to source material and on-screen details and instructions. The joy of using this disc is in the ease of running the various options – even the most computer-terrified user has nothing to fear! It offers a variety of programs that are useful for simple classroom demonstration purposes and others that have far more interesting applications in experimental work.

By contrast, Psychology Software's *Experiment, Design and Statistics in Psychology* is accompanied by a weighty, well-documented 42-page User's Manual that supports some far more sophisticated software, which is reflected in the price of £99.50. The total package includes two discs: the statistics program discussed earlier and a set of 11 separate basic proposals for experiments. Access to these is achieved through selections from the main menu which includes some familiar ideas, such as the Müller-Lyer illusion and the Necker Cube, as well as some more obscure and interesting programs, such as congruency with self and visuo-spatial ability. Other selections include serial/parallel information processing, pitch and volume discrimination, memory tests, and experiments in conformity. Some of the procedures in the package are fairly complex and constant reference to the User's Manual is needed. Also contained in the Manual is some very useful background material for each experiment, with supporting references that would enable the user to refer to wider sources for any practical write-up.

BBC users might also be interested in the packages available through AVP, and which include *Psychology Lab, Visual Illusions* and *Behaviour*. These are generally suitable for students at pre-degree level and range in price from £25 to £34.

CMS Software have produced two excellent packages which are ideal for this level: *Psychology on a Disc* (POAD) and *Behaviour on a Disc* (BOAD). They are described as 'interactive activities for psychology' and differ from the software considered above in that they are designed for integration into teaching courses, enabling students to actively engage in psychology and not just read about the theory. With POAD, the idea is that students work through the programs on the disc as part of their introductory course in psychology and (in the United States) gain credits for completing the tasks required. Teachers in the UK could do the same and/or set assignments around the tasks demanded of the students by POAD. Because POAD is designed for students to purchase their own copy it is affordable ($11.95) and requires no prior computer experience. It runs on IBM PC-compatible machines with 3.5" or 5.25" drives and comes complete with instructors' (that is, tutors') manual. If you adopt the disc you are covered by the licence to replace any student discs if they are damaged. Don't be put off by the fact that POAD comes from the US. Orders are despatched very quickly (mine came in about three weeks) and if you are unsure about how it will work, CMS Software offer to send you a user's manual before you purchase the software. The language employed is American English, but this is not a problem for the user, and there are few words, if any, that will not be immediately recognized.

POAD is menu-driven and runs from a single command which is typed at the prompt sign in MS-DOS. The package offers a series of 'standard' programs which include visual illusions, guilt detection, behaviour shaping, STM and making interpersonal judgements; as well as more advanced options comprising the neural basis of a visual illusion, developing a psychological test, and scatterplots and correlation. Additionally there is a progress update option which provides details of the items that users have completed together with the date – and since each disc is initially accessed by typing in a name – and code number, teachers can be sure that students are using their own disc. Each program is entered by simply typing in the appropriate key, and from then on the tasks are self-explanatory and require no additional operating instructions.

It is not possible here to run through each menu option, but I have selected a few which might be useful at the pre-degree levels. In the visual illusion program, users are given background information on illusions and presented with the standard horizontal–vertical illusion. On separate trials, involving feedback and no feedback on accuracy, students can see how their performance on judging line length can improve. There are questions to answer about the illusion and how its effects are overcome, a graph of the data is given, and items for discussion are raised.

A similar procedure is followed in the other programs. In 'Guilt Detection' users play the part of someone who has committed a crime and reaction times on a word-association task for neutral and incriminating words are used to identify the guilty party. Students can also use behaviour shaping to condition a rat; investigate how we assign certain adjectives to others on the basis of their gender; as well as explore scattergrams and correlations. In this latter program, users are invited to plot their own scattergram on the screen, a line-of-best-fit is drawn by the computer, the correlation coefficient is shown, and the nature of the relationship between the two variables is described. It is then possible to add and remove scores and see immediately the effect this has upon the coefficient and the relationship. On each program, users are given background information and the task is followed by a discussion of salient points that will have emerged in the course of completing the activity.

BOAD comes from the same stable and follows the same format and procedures. The programs, however, deal specifically with issues of learning and reinforcement. With this package, users are introduced not only to a bar-pressing rat, but also to JF (a student who can only study for a few minutes at a time), a discriminating mouse that pops up on screen when reinforcements are given, and a therapy client in need of positive feedback. In each case students will be exploring concepts such as shaping, goal-setting and discrimination, and the likely effects of reinforcements on different types of behaviour. Success on completing the tasks set by BOAD is itself reinforcing and student users are actively doing psychology in an exciting and educationally useful way. As with POAD, the package is intended for purchase by students and consequently the costs are low, only $8.95.

Similarly intended for student use, but very different in nature to the programs described above, is *Psytests* from Peter Mulligan. This package uses software from Question Mark Computing and offers computer-based tests in certain areas of psychology (for example, research methods, moral development, and learning theory) delivered in a variety of styles and designed to maintain student motivation and interest. *Psytests* runs from MS-DOS on an IBM PC-compatible machine with a 3.5" drive. It is very user-friendly with commands appearing on screen and requiring keyed responses. It is accessed through an initial menu offering tests in six areas of psychology which can only be entered by using the given password. Users then respond to the questions in the required style (for example, multiple choice, true/false, etc.) and are given a score together with comments on performance at the end of each test. Questions range in difficulty and level of obscurity and these are interrupted occasionally by amusing and interesting asides of the 'did you know...?' type. The package is presented as being of benefit for consolidating student learning at the end of a taught topic and for revision purposes. *Psytests* costs £29.99 for the single user version or £49.99 for the Network version. It is, however, limited to the preprogrammed questions of the author. Teachers might be interested in the original *Question Mark* software (costing £199 plus VAT and £3 p&p) which allows the user to write any number of their own tests using different question styles. This option is, of course, a little more complicated than simply running *Psytests* but still very accessible.

PYM Software have just released *Experiments in Cognitive Psychology*: a suite of programs that offer student-run experiments in several areas of cognitive psychology, including investigation of the primacy-recency effect, interference in memory, the capacity of short-term memory, and the Stroop effect, amongst others. This software has been specifically written for students at pre-degree levels and consequently is very easy to use and competitively priced for the school/FE college budget. The programs are menu-driven and are selected by using the keyboard or mouse. Comprehensive instructions appear on screen and guide the user through any operations necessary to run the experiments, conduct practice trials, or consult the tutorial text that accompanies each program option. The software also uses quite a sophisticated means of storing the experimental data which is extremely useful for students' practical work at A/S and A-level, for example.

In addition to the software considered above, there is an increasing amount of shareware becoming available and which may be of interest to teachers of psychology. Such shareware is usually free or available at minimal cost, and details appear in publishers' and distributors' catalogues (for example, the *Products and Services Information Pack* from Park Lodge Associates) or can be found in the CTI *Directory of Psychology Software*. A good deal of the software in use in the psychology departments of schools and FE colleges has been produced in-house. In some respects this has the advantage over software that is bought-in since it is usually tailor-made to suit the needs of the teacher concerned and her/his students – and so tends to be unsophisticated and simple to use. There is probably a good deal of psychology software being produced and used but which is not commercially available to others. Not only that, there are possibly many teachers struggling to write software for their courses when someone else in another college has already done the same thing or something similar. Because of this, the ATP is acting as a collector and disseminator of information concerning the uses of microcomputers for psychology teaching and, in so doing, is trying to stimulate the production and use of psychology software in schools and colleges where there appears to be scope for development.

REFERENCES

HAWORTH, G.T. (1992) Computers in Psychology Teaching 1992. Research project in progress, funded by Canterbury Christ Church College and the Association for the Teaching of Psychology.

McKNIGHT, C. (1984) Microcomputers in psychology teaching. In D. Rose and J. Radford (Eds) *Teaching Psychology: Information and Resources*. Leicester: BPS Books (The British Psychological Society).

NOTT, K. (1992) Software review: Supastat statistical package. *Psychology Software News, 1* (3), 14–16.

ROBSON, C. (1983) *Experiment, Design and Statistics in Psychology*. Harmondsworth: Penguin Books.

SNEDDON, P. (1992) Software review: Alstats. *Psychology Software News, 1* (3) 16–17.

UNDERWOOD, G. and UNDERWOOD, J.D.M. (1990) Microcomputers: courseware and software. In D. Rose and J. Radford (Eds) *Teaching Psychology: A Handbook of Resources*. Leicester: BPS Books (The British Psychological Society).

Software Suppliers

ATP
c/o BPS
St Andrews House
48 Princess Road East
Leicester LE1 7DR

AVP
School Hill Centre
Chepstow
Gwent NP6 5PH

CLE COM Ltd
The Research Park
Vincent Drive
Edgbaston
Birmingham B15 2SQ

CMS Software
PO Box 1514
Columbia
MD 21044–0514
USA

Computers Unlimited
2 The Business Centre
Colindeep Lane
London NW9 6DU

Eurostat Ltd
Icknield House
Eastcheap
Letchworth
Herts S96 3DF

Stephen Fearnley
Department of Psychology
Oxford Brookes University
Oxford OX3 0BD

Geoff Haworth
Canterbury Christ Church College
Canterbury CT1 1QU

Microsoft Corporation
1 Microsoft Way
Redmond
WA 98052–6399
USA

Peter Mulligan
Monkwearmouth College
Redcar Road
Sunderland SR5 5DB

Park Lodge Associates
47 Four Oaks Road
Sutton Coldfield
Birmingham B74 2XU

Principal Distribution Ltd
Todd Hall Road
Carrs Industrial Estate
Haslingden
Lancs BB4 5HU

Psychology Software
c/o Andy Bell
Department of Psychology
Manchester Metropolitan University
Oxford Road
Manchester M15 6BH

PYM Software
c/o Geoff Haworth

Question Mark Computing
41b Brecknock Road
London N7 0BT

SPSS UK Ltd
SPSS House
5 London Street
Chertsey
Surrey KT16 8AP

Synthetic Software
36 Green Lane
Hove Edge
Brighouse
West Yorkshire HD6 2PP

TokSoft
20 Heatherdale Road
Camberley
Surrey GU15 2LT

Software Index

AccessPC (Principal Distribution Ltd)

Alstats (Stephen Fearnley)

Behaviour (AVP)

Behaviour on a Disc (CMS Software)

DOS Mounter (Computers Unlimited)

Experiment, Design and Statistics in Psychology
   (Psychology Software)

Experiments in Cognitive Psychology (PYM Software)

Maze (AVP)

Microsoft Windows (Microsoft Corporation)

Minitab (CLE COM Ltd)

Psychology Experiments and Demonstrations (ATP)

Psychology Lab (AVP)

Psychology on a Disc (CMS Software)

Psytests (Peter Mulligan)

Question Mark (Question Mark Computing)

SPSS PC+ (SPSS UK Ltd)

Statistics for Psychology (Geoff Haworth)

stATPak (ATP)

Supastat (Synthetic Software)

Systat (Eurostat Ltd)

UnderStat (TokSoft)

Visual Illusions (AVP)

Useful Addresses

Apple Computer UK Limited
6 Roundwood Avenue
Stockley Park
Uxbridge
Middlesex UB11 1BB

CTI Centre for Psychology
University of York
York YO1 5DD

PSYCHOLOGY LABORATORY EQUIPMENT

Rosemary Westley

❏ *further information sources • purpose built equipment • standard psychological laboratory equipment • electrophysiological equipment • recording equipment • suppliers' addresses*

Experimental work in psychology makes use of a very wide range of equipment and materials. This chapter covers equipment most commonly found in psychology teaching laboratories other than computers (which are covered in the chapter on microcomputers in this volume). It provides a guide to commercially available equipment together with a list of suppliers to contact for further information on specific items.

The suppliers are all based in the UK, but the listed equipment is manufactured both here and abroad. A complete list of their addresses and telephone numbers is provided at the end of the chapter.

The chapter covers traditional psychology laboratory equipment such as tachistoscopes, mirror-drawing equipment and reaction time apparatus, electrophysiology equipment and a range of recording and monitoring devices.

Not included in this chapter are:
1. *Tape recorders and accessories* – suppliers of tape recorders are so numerous that it is impossible to list them. Your local *Yellow Pages* or *Thomson Directory* will provide a list of dealers in your area that will give you a wide choice to meet your needs and price range.

2. *Video equipment* – lists of suppliers, reviews of equipment and services can be obtained from:
Audio Visual Directory (published annually by EMAP McClaren Publishing) – contains details of equipment, dealers by region and production services.
Yellow Pages (British Telecom).
University Audiovisual Units – The staff of these units are experts in video equipment requirements for teaching and are usually willing to give advice. They will also have up-to-date suppliers' catalogues of the full range of video equipment.

FURTHER INFORMATION SOURCES

Apart from the manufacturers and suppliers listed in the following pages, information, equipment and services can also be obtained from the following sources:

1. *Local education authorities* buy in large quantities a wide variety of educational equipment such as scientific apparatus, audiovisual equipment, video equipment and stationery. They will quite often supply other educational establishments with goods at very low prices.

2. *Large teaching psychology departments* employ technical staff who are usually very helpful in providing information concerning equipment, and are often prepared to lend apparatus for the occasional demonstration or for a class.

3. *Purchasing groups* Many educational establishments now belong to purchasing groups to obtain the best prices for equipment and services. These groups are likely to tender through the European Community Supplies Directive. If your school is party to such contracts you will legally be obliged to use their supplier if the items you require are included in the contract. You should contact your purchasing or finance department before placing an order.

4. *Trade directories*
Kelly's Manufacturers and Merchants Directory has details of thousands of British companies and importers, listed under trade, product and service headings.
   Kompass has two volumes. Volume I lists producers and services while Volume II carries the names and addresses of British companies together with company information both alphabetically and by county.
   The directories may be found in your local library or central purchasing department. The publishers' addresses are also listed at the end of this chapter.

PURPOSE BUILT EQUIPMENT

Not all apparatus can be bought 'off the shelf', and you may need something special built. If you do not have access to technical assistance the problem can be approached as follows:

1. *Existing suppliers* – it is worth asking the companies listed in the following pages whether they are prepared to produce equipment to your specifications. They will often make adaptations or additions to equipment they already manufacture.

2. *Technical staff* – in large psychology departments a great deal of 'one-off' apparatus is built. They may have what you want and be prepared to lend it to you. They can also advise you on what manufactured equipment could be adapted to meet your purpose.

3. *Consultancies* – there are many small engineering firms that caⁿ build equipment for you. However they may require drawings and Martock Design will turn your ideas into a set of engineering drawings. Weylec also have a design and drawing service for electronic equipment. They are also battery consultants, and can provide useful advice on power supplies when designing portable equipment.

SECTION 1: STANDARD PSYCHOLOGICAL LABORATORY EQUIPMENT

The standard equipment covered in this section has been used in GCSE, A-level, and undergraduate courses for many years, but only a few companies now produce it. This type of equipment is very robust and does last for years. Also included is a list of less common items that have either been designed for teaching or may be relevant for project work. Items are in alphabetical order.

Aesthesiometer ➤ Used to measure sensitivity to touch.
1. Von Frey – consists of either a hypodermic-type tube and horse hair that can be varied in length, or a disc on which graduated nylon bristles extend.
2. Caliper – sliding caliper with two pointers and a scale calibrated in millimetres. (See also the chapter in this book on DIY laboratory equipment.)

Audiometer ➤ Used to test hearing and may be used where hearing defects can affect the experiment, for example musical perception.
Models are available that test air conduction, bone conduction and pure tone for thresholds in each frequency zone. Output can be selected for left or right ear or both.

Biofeedback equipment See Section 2

Colour mixer ➤ Used to demonstrate a variety of perception phenomena.
The equipment consists of a variable speed motor in a cabinet with a circular disc mounted on the front. Stimulus materials such as black and white discs can be fixed to the front and spun at low speed to produce subjective colour effects (Benhams tops), or coloured discs can be spun at high speed for colour-mixing experiments.

Depth perception apparatus ➤ For judgement of distance and perspective.
The subject, seated 20 feet from the apparatus, manipulates pull cords to align the moveable vertical rod with a stationary rod. Progression, overshoot and absolute accuracy can thus be determined and recorded.

Dispensers   ➤ For reinforcement of subjects.
Electromechanical device for dispensing peanuts or Smarties
to subjects as a reward.

Discrimination   ➤ Used to test ability to discriminate between small weight
weights   differences.
The weights are identical in colour, size and texture.
1. Light series –12 weights from 75 to 125 grams.
2. Heavy series – 12 weights from 175 to 225 grams.

Dynamometer   ➤ For measuring grip/pressures for strength of handedness
(hand)   experiments.
1. Steel frame design – when frame is compressed by hand
the pressure is indicated on a scale. Not very accurate.
2. Lever design – with scale that can measure maximum energy and fatigue rates. Measurement range 0 to 100kg.

Flicker fusion   ➤ Used to measure the point at which a rapidly flashing light
apparatus   stimulus is perceived as a constant light.
The apparatus consists of a lamp and control unit which can
present flickering light at either ascending or descending
rates.

GSR meter   See Section 2

Maze   ➤ Used for learning experiments.
1. Pencil maze – stencil of aluminium placed over paper to
produce a permanent record of subject's performance.
2. Automatic tally maze – designed to be attached to an
impulse counter or stopclock to save time in scoring the subject's performance.
3. Electronic maze – an experimenter's panel is also provided
with the maze to record errors.

Memory drum   ➤ Can be used for numerous learning experiments.
A variety of stimuli can be presented: words, word groups,
figures, pictures or symbols. Stimuli are attached to a cylin-
drical drum mounted in a box with a viewing slit. The drum
can be rotated to provide various exposure times between
0.25 and 8 seconds.

Mirror-drawing   ➤ Used for skill learning tasks or to demonstrate cerebral
apparatus   dominance.
1. Standard – paper patterns are attached to a board and
traced from visual cues reversed and inverted in a mirror.
(See also the chapter on DIY laboratory equipment in this
book.)
2. Automatic scoring – metal base with non-conducting pattern flush with surface. Plate and tracing stylus can be
connected to a battery and timer counter. Contact is made if
the subject traces outside the pattern and a score is recorded
on the counter.

Perimeter   ➤ Apparatus for mapping the colour-sensitive areas of the
retina.

Standard models consist of an arc approximately 80cm wide with a 33cm radius, which can be rotated 100 degrees in each direction. Test stimulus which is projected onto the arc can be varied by size, colour (white, red, green, blue) and brightness. Measurements are recorded on charts which are supplied in pads of 100.

Phi phenomenon apparatus
➤ This apparatus demonstrates the phenomenon of apparent movement from one light to another.
The equipment has two individual light sources which are alternately illuminated; cycle times are variable.

Photic stimulator
➤ For experiments on perception, attention, vigilance etc.
This is basically a low-powered stroboscope.

Pursuit rotor
➤ For tests of speed and accuracy.
The equipment comprises of a variable speed turntable with a target which the subject has to hit with a stylus as it rotates. There are also photoelectric versions which eliminate the necessity for any physical contact.

Reaction timer
➤ To measure the reaction time to a visual or auditory stimulus.
The equipment consists of a timer, a controller to activate the stimulus and start the timer simultaneously and a response key for the subject. Apparatus is available with either a single light or auditory stimulus or with up to eight visual stimuli (multiple-choice reaction) and one to four response keys.

Rod and frame apparatus
➤ Designed for both teaching and research, applications include testing the subject's ability to perceive the orientation of his or her body in relation to a hypothetical axis of gravity. The apparatus consists of an adjustable rod which the subject alters until it is apparently parallel to the true upright axis under conditions of reduced environmental cues.

Steadiness tester
➤ Used to measure psychomotor control.
The equipment comprises a block with nine holes of varying diameters, to which the subject is required to insert an electrical contact-making stylus without touching the sides. The apparatus is wired to a battery and counter.

Sound-attenuating chamber
➤ Although this type of equipment is very expensive, you may require a sound-attenuating chamber when external noise affects experimental procedures.

Tachistoscope
➤ Can be used for investigating figural after-effects, recognition thresholds, perceptual defence and visual acuity.
A tachistoscope displays a visual stimulus for brief periods. It may be a one, two or more field unit and use cards or slides to display stimuli.
1. Optical tachistoscopes have stimuli mounted on cards seen through a viewing hood. The field illumination and exposure times can be varied electronically. For more complex exercises, a sophisticated range of three, four, and

six-field tachistoscopes is available and a pack tachistoscope for three-dimensional stimuli.
2. Projection tachistoscopes (projectors fitted with shutters and controllers) use photographic slides to display the stimuli. These are better for some tasks, for example group presentations. One to four- field versions are available.
(See the chapter on microcomputers in this book for software for computer version.)

Tapping board   ➤ Used to measure motor skills and fatigue rates.
This apparatus is a wooden board with metal plates at each end. The subject uses an electrical contact stylus to tap successively on the plates as rapidly as possible. Hits are recorded on a counter.

Timers, counters, tally counters, event recorders, frequency counters   See Section 3

Tone generator   ➤ For presenting audio stimuli.
The generator can present separate tones on a wide range of frequencies.

Visual illusions   See Table 3

White noise generator   ➤ Used to mask out external noises or as a distraction device.

Table 1. Standard Laboratory Equipment and Supplier References

Equipment	Supplier references*
aesthesiometer	
Von Frey	6
caliper	6
audiometer	6, 20
biofeedback equipment *see* Section 2	
colour mixer	
machine	6, 9
discs	6, 9
depth perception apparatus	6
dispensers	
peanut	6 made to order
Smartie	6 " " "
discrimination weights	6
dynamometer	6, 20
flicker fusion apparatus	6, 9
maze	6
memory drum	12
mirror-drawing/ mirror-tracing apparatus	
equipment	6, 14
stars	6, 14
perimeter	6, 15, 20
phi phenomenon apparatus	6, 9
photic stimulator	27
pursuit rotor	6, 9, 14
reaction timer	6, 9, 14, 20
rod and frame apparatus	20
steadiness tester	6
sound-attenuating chamber	1, 7
tachistoscopes	
single-field	6
two-field	6, 9, 14, 20
three-field	9
six-field binocular	9
projection	
single-field	6, 20
two-field	6, 9, 14
three-field	9, 14
four-field	14
accessories	6, 9, 14, 20
tapping board	6, 20
timers *see* Table 7	
tone generator	6
visual illusions *see* Table 3	
white noise generator	6

* The numbers given in the righthand column of this table and the six that follow refer to the relevant equipment suppliers, whose names and addresses are listed at the end of the chapter.

Table 2. Standard Laboratory Equipment Accessories and Supplier References

These accessories allow apparatus to perform more than one task and create more choice for experimental investigation. The items listed are only an indication of what can be obtained.

Equipment	Supplier references*
automatic card changer (for 3-field tachistoscope)	9
blindfold goggles	6
computer interface (for the control of equipment)	6, 9, 14
counter (impulse)	6
double-pulse generator (for 2-field tachistoscope)	14
electronic shutter (for converting projector into tachistoscope)	6, 9, 14
footswitch or switch mats (for time reactions)	6, 14
four-field tachistoscope adapter (converts 2 X 2-field tachistoscopes to 4-field)	9
headphones*	
interconnection cables	9, 14
microphones*	
reaction time controller (simultaneously initiates tachistoscope display and reaction timer)	9
reed relay unit (adds to tachistoscope timer to provide central changeover for control of other experiments)	9
response keys (for time reaction)	6, 9
shutter driver, two channel (drives a pair of electromagnetic shutters)	9, 14
spare lens	6, 9, 14
spare probes for pursuit rotor	6, 14
tachistoscope stands	14
tape/slide synchronizer	9
viewing hoods (for tachistoscopes)	9
voice-key/voice-activated relay (triggers equipment by a verbal signal)	6, 9
zoom lens (for projection tachistoscopes)	9, 14

Items marked * can be obtained more cheaply in high street shops than from specialized suppliers.

Table 3. Visual Perception Equipment and Supplier References

Experiments on the visual system are generally the most frequent in experimental psychology courses up to first degree level. Table 3 contains an additional selection of equipment and materials which you may find useful for experiments on visual perception.

Equipment	Supplier references
binocular vision tests	15
city university colour vision test	15
eye movement tracking equipment	20
eye test charts	15
Fletcher simplified colour vision test	15
Ishihara cards (for revealing colour blindness)	6, 15
light discrimination apparatus	6
Müller-Lyer	6
optical illusions (set includes rotating unit for trapezoid window and a set of traditional illusions such as spirals and reversing figures)	6
visual acuity tests	15
visual field testing equipment	15
visual perception unit (both flicker fusion and phi phenomenon)	6
vision tester	6, 31

Table 4. Unusual Equipment and Supplier References

A list of less usual items of equipment that can be purchased and which psychology teachers may wish to include in their laboratory courses. This type of equipment can also be useful for project work.

Equipment	Supplier references
back and leg dynamometer	6
bicycle ergometer	20
bug-in-the-ear (a wireless ear bug receiver for communications between teacher and student)	2, 31
card sorting box	6
communication aids for rehabilitation and education (various lever switches, sound operated switch, mercury tilt switch, see-saw switch, suck-blow switch, pressure switch, also communicators, page turners, speech synthesizers, dice thrower)	23
finger tapper	6
foot tapper	6
linear movement apparatus (used for motor learning tasks and assessment of temporal or spacial memory)	6
peg board (tests complex visual-motor co-ordination)	6
sensitivity kit (measures sensitivity to heat/cold, touch and pressure)	6
speech delayer	31
two-arm co-ordination test (a test of the co-ordination of both arms working together to move a stylus around a six-pointed star)	6

SECTION 2: ELECTROPHYSIOLOGICAL RECORDING AND MEASURING EQUIPMENT

Non-invasive physiological measurements are frequently used in psychology experiments to relate psychological and physiological variables. It is not likely that a complete physiological laboratory will be set up for teaching purposes. Table 5 lists the range of equipment that exists in this field from the very sophisticated evoked potential measuring equipment to single-channel recorders and meters. Recent interest in health education and advances in electronics have produced a range of cheaper devices that can be useful to students of psychology in their experimental work. Different manufacturers tend to use different names to describe their version of the same equipment, for example, equipment to measure heart rate or pulse is variously called: heart-rate monitor, pulsemeter, pulse-rate monitor and electronic stethoscope. Table 6 contains a list of these devices arranged under function and suppliers' references.

Table 5. Electrophysiological Recording and Measuring Equipment and Supplier References

Equipment	Supplier references
accessories	
chart paper	27, 28
electrodes	6, 27, 28
electrode gel	6, 27, 28
transducers	6, 20, 28
ambulatory monitoring equipment	2, 5, 27
biofeedback systems	2, 5, 6, 29
biotelemetry systems	20, 27
evoked potential measuring equipment	8, 27, 28
oscillographs and preamplifiers	
(1, 2, and multi-channel for measuring)	
blood pressure	6, 20, 27, 28
ECG	2, 6, 20, 27, 28
EEG	5, 6, 20, 27, 28
EMG	2, 6, 20, 27, 28
heart rate	2, 6, 20, 27, 28
respiration	6, 20, 28
skin resistance	6, 9, 20, 28
temperature	2, 6, 20, 28
stimulators	
auditory	8
pattern reversal	8, 28
photic and click	27, 28

Table 6. Single-Channel Physiological Monitors and Meters
and Supplier References

Equipment	Supplier references
blood pressure	
blood pressure monitor	6, 26
electronic/digital sphygmomanometer	6, 29
sphygmomanometer	6
carbon monoxide	
smokerlyser	4
EEG	
alpha sensor	2
EMG	
EMG feedback monitor	6
EMG training system	6
myoelectric instruments	2
myotrac EMG monitor	6
GSR	
biofeedback relaxation system	6
galvanic skin response meter	6
relaxometer	2
skin conductance meter/monitor	6, 9
pulse/heart rate	
heart-rate monitor	6, 29
heart-rate feedback monitor	6
pulsemeter	29
pulse-rate monitor	26, 29
pulse stick	26
electronic stethoscope	29
wristwatch pulse monitor	6, 26, 29
respiration	
respiration feedback	2
spirometer	6
peak flow meter	6
temperature	
clinical thermometers (digital/electronic)	6, 26, 29
skin temperature meter	9
temperature feedback	2, 6

SECTION 3: RECORDING EQUIPMENT

Table 7 covers a range of recording equipment that is often used with the apparatus mentioned in previous sections. Of course microcomputers are also very good recording devices (see chapter in this book on microcomputers). Also included in the list is equipment for the measurement of environmental variables such as noise levels, humidity, room temperature and light levels. This kind of information is necessary when carrying out experimental procedures such as physiological recording where levels of light, temperature and noise can affect the results.

Table 7. Recording Equipment and Supplier References

Equipment	Supplier references
balances	13, 19, 21, 22, 26
counters	
talley (hand operated 4-digit, reset single or multiple units)	12, 13, 21, 22, 25, 26
frequency	11, 12, 24, 25, 26, 30
timers	
Birkbeck	14
clocks	13, 22, 26
interval	13, 19, 24
stopclock	13, 19, 21, 22
stopwatch	13, 19, 21, 22, 26
timer/counters	11, 12, 24, 25, 26, 30
recorders	
chart	11, 12, 13, 19, 21, 22
X/Y	11, 25
physiological (*see* Tables 5 and 6)	
environmental monitoring	
electrostatic meter	19
humidity recorder	13, 21, 26
hygrograph	13, 21
hygrometer	12, 13, 19, 21, 22
light meter	12, 13, 19, 25, 26
pH meter	12, 13, 22, 26
sound level meter	12, 13, 19, 21, 25, 26
temperature recorder	19, 21
thermohygrograph	13, 22
thermometer	
electronic	11, 12, 19, 22, 25, 26
max - min	13, 19, 26
wall	13, 25, 26
oscilloscopes	11, 12, 25, 16, 30

Suppliers' Addresses

1. Acoustic & Vibration
   Control Ltd
   Box 33
   United Road
   Old Trafford
   Manchester
   M16 0RG
   tel. (061) 8766093

2. Aleph One Ltd
   The Old Courthouse
   High Street
   Bottisham
   Cambridge CB5 9BA
   tel. (0223) 811679
   (agents for Farrell Instruments)

3. Ashby Technical Products Ltd
   Instrument Division
   5 Market Street
   Ashby-de-la-Zouch
   Leics LE6 5YF
   tel. (0530) 416876

4. Bedfont Technical
   Instruments Ltd
   Bedfont House
   Holywell Lane
   Upchurch
   Sittingbourne
   Kent ME9 7HN
   tel. (0634) 375614

5. Biodata
   10 Stocks Street
   Manchester M8 8QG
   tel. (061) 8346688

6. Campden Instruments Ltd
   Kings Street
   Sileby
   Loughborough
   Leics LE12 7LZ
   tel. (0509) 814790
   (agents for Lafayette
   Instruments)

7. Designed for Sound Ltd
   12 Rectory Road
   Wivenhoe
   Colchester CO5 9ES
   tel. (0206) 827171

8. Digitimer Ltd
   14 Tewin Court
   Welwyn Garden City
   Herts AL7 1AF
   tel. (0707) 328347

9. Electronic Developments Ltd
   16 St James Avenue
   Hampton Hill
   Middx TW12 1HN
   tel. (081) 9795047

10. EMAP McClaren Ltd
    PO Box 109
    19 Scarbrook Road
    Croydon
    Surrey CR9 1QH
    tel. (081) 6887788

11. ESD Electronic Services
    Head Office
    Edinburgh Way
    Harlow
    Essex CM20 2DF
    tel. (0279) 441 687

    10th floor
    Colston Centre
    Colston Street
    Bristol BS1 4XE
    tel. (0272) 264079

    20 Gatwich Road
    Crawley
    West Sussex RH10 2RU
    tel. (0293) 5223568

    8th Floor
    St John's House
    East Street
    Leicester LE1 6NA
    tel. (0533) 548704

    3rd Floor
    Macintosh House
    Market Place
    Manchester M4 3AF
    tel. (061) 8323768

    54A High Street
    Paisley
    Renfrewshire PA1 2DJ
    tel. (041) 8876162

12. Farnell Electronic
    Components Ltd
    Canal Road
    Leeds
    West Yorkshire LS12 2TU
    tel. (0532) 636311

13. Fisons Scientific Equipment
    Bishops Meadow Road
    Loughborough
    Leicestershire
    tel. (0509) 231166

14. Forth Psychology Instruments Ltd
    14 Brewster Square
    Brucefield Industrial Estate
    Livingston
    Lothian EH54 9BJ
    tel. (0506) 418500

15. Keelers Instruments Ltd
    Clewer Hill Road
    Windsor
    Berks SL4 4AA
    tel. (07538) 57177

16. Kelly's Directories
    Windsor Court
    East Grinstead House
    East Grinstead
    West Sussex RH19 1XA
    tel. (0342) 26972

17. Kompass Publishers Ltd
    Windsor Court
    East Grinstead House
    East Grinstead
    West Sussex RH19 1XA
    tel. (0342) 26972

18. Martock Design
    The Old Doctors House
    Water Street
    Martock
    Somerset TA1 26IN
    tel. (0935) 822870

19. Merck Ltd
    Head Office
    Merck House
    Poole
    Dorset BH15 1TD
    tel. (0202) 669700

Hunters Boulevard
Magna Park, Lutterworth
Leics LE17 4XN
tel. (0800) 223344

Burnfield Avenue
Thornleebank
Glasgow G46 7TP
tel. (041) 6372333

20. Overseas Medical Supplies Ltd
    Cumberland Business Park
    32 Cumberland Ave
    London NW10 7RT
    tel. (081) 9659711
    (importers of overseas
    psychology equipment)

21. Patterson Scientific
    Unit 2 Brookside
    Colne Way
    Watford
    Herts WD2 4QJ
    tel. (0923) 56177

22. Philip Harris
    Head Office
    Lynn Lane
    Shenstone, Lichfield
    Staffs WS14 0EE
    tel. (0543) 480077

    Unit 39, Nottingham
    South Industrial Estate
    Wilford, Nottingham
    NG11 7EP
    tel. (0602) 455226

    Sainsbury Way
    Hessle, North Humberside
    HU13 9NX
    tel. (0482) 572436

    Unit 4
    Parkway Four, Trafford Park
    Manchester M17 1SN
    tel. (061) 8488800

    35 North Avenue
    Clydebank Business Park
    Clydebank, Glasgow
    G81 2DR
    tel. (041) 9529538

36 Western Avenue
Park Royal
London W3 0TE
tel. (081) 9925555

23. Quest Educational Designs Ltd
Prince Alfred Street
Gosport, Hants
PO12 1QH
tel. (0329) 828444

24. Racal Recorders
Hardley Industrial Estate
Hythe
Southampton SO4 6ZH
tel. (0703) 843265

25. RS Components
National:
PO Box 99, Corby
Northants NN17 9RS
tel. (0536) 201201

London only:
tel. (081) 3608600

Trade Counters:
Duddeston Mill Industrial Estate
Birmingham
B8 1BQ
tel. (021) 3594900

Lammas Road
Weldon Industrial Estate
Corby
Northamptonshire NN17 9RS
tel. (0536) 201201

40 Baird Street
Glasgow G4 0ED
tel. (041) 552444

PO Box 12
Kennedy Way
Greenlane Industrial Estate
Stockport
Cheshire SK4 2JT
tel. (061) 4778400

Old Ford Trading Centre
Maverton Road
London E3 2JE
tel. (081) 9806513

The Fairway Estate
Green Lane
Hounslow
Middx TW4 6BU
tel. (081) 5724225

26. Solexpress
Unit 25
Swannington Road
Cottage Lane Industrial Estate
Broughton Astley
Leics LE9 6TU
tel. (0455) 383486

27. Specialized Lab Equipment
43 Seldon Road
South Croydon
CR2 6PL
tel. (081) 6811414

28. Stag Instruments
46 Monument Industrial Park
Chalgrove
Oxon OX44 7RW
tel. (0865) 891116

29. Surgicon Ltd
Northern Depot and Head Office
48 Wakefield Road
Brighouse
West Yorks HD6 1QL
tel. (0484) 712147

Midland Southern Depot
Unit 7
Birkdale Avenue
Healey Road
Selly Oak
Birmingham B29 6UB
tel. (021) 4727171

30. Tektronic UK Ltd
Fourth Avenue
Globe Park
Marlow
Bucks SL7 1YD
tel. (0628) 474799

31. Warwick-Evans Optical
51 Palace Road
Bounds Green Road
London N11 2PS
tel. (081) 8880051

32. Weylec
53 Guildown Road
Guildford
Surrey GU2 5EW
tel. (0483) 67287

DO-IT-YOURSELF LABORATORY EQUIPMENT

David Westley and Rosemary Westley

❑ creating card materials • developing apparatus from existing resources • building your own equipment • practicals using inexpensive materials

*T*he previous chapter dealt with manufactured equipment and materials available for teaching. However, such equipment can be very expensive especially as the size of classes is now increasing rapidly. Also many classes say at GCSE, A/S or A-level do not have specialist laboratories where such equipment can be set up. There is in any case a lot of equipment and materials that cannot be purchased.

The range of equipment and materials that can be used for psychological investigations is vast. Any equipment acquired must be flexible so that it can be used in many different studies. Creating your own has advantages because it can be specially designed to meet your needs and can be easily adapted.

To encourage students to be original and adventurous in their experimental work, teachers need to use their imagination in providing materials and equipment.

This chapter offers practical advice on the creation and acquisition of apparatus and materials that can be used for very little cost. It is intended to help teachers make the most out of whatever resources they may have.

SECTION 1: CREATING CARD MATERIALS

The materials for many experiments can be created out of paper and card. Students quite often create their own materials for investigation and it is a good idea to collect the efforts of the more artistic students, such as line drawings of everyday objects, which can be difficult to find in books and magazines and impossible to create if you cannot draw, for use in next year's courses. Supplies of index cards, sheets of card, glue or staples and felt-tip pens are essential, as is sticky back plastic or spray coating to preserve all the creative efforts. Many textbooks carry examples of materials which can be copied, such as the following visual illusions.

Two versions of the Ponzo illusion

A variation of the Herring illusion

Archimedes spiral   *Poggendorff illusion*

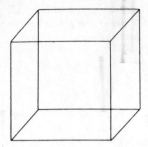

Necker cube

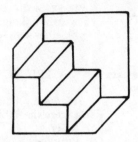

Reversing figure staircase illusion

Two ambiguous figures

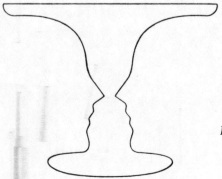

Rubin's vase

Müller-Lyer illusion and Stroop effect cards are amongst those card materials that are used repeatedly, and are well worth making. Full instructions for these are given below, together with some ideas for other materials.

Müller-Lyer Illusion

MATERIALS:

1 large sheet thin white card
1 large sheet thick white card
Ruler
Protractor
Black felt-tip pen
Glue
Scissors or sharp knife
Graph paper

INSTRUCTIONS:
1. Cut a piece of thick card 220mm long and 40mm wide (card A).
2. Cut a piece of thin card 150mm long and 125mm wide (card B).
3. Place card A lengthways down the middle of card B.
4. Fold over edges of card B and glue to form a sheath (see Figure 1a).
5. Pull out card B and lay A and B end to end on a flat surface.
6. With a ruler draw a 90mm line lengthways along card A and a 130mm line lengthways along card B, making sure that the lines are aligned. Using the protractor, draw two arrowheads (see Figure 1b).
7. Glue the back of card B onto some graph paper to provide a handy measure.
8. Now card A can be inserted into card B and then slid in and out to make the 'combined' line shorter or longer.
9. Repeat instructions four more times using different angle fins (see Figure 1c).

See practical in Section 4

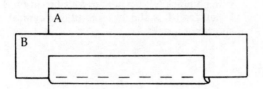

Figure 1a. Müller-Lyer illusion

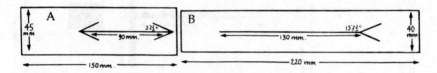

Figure 1b

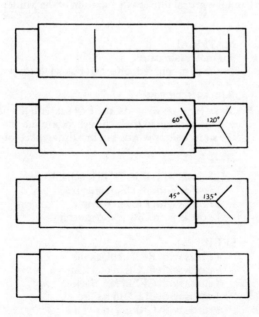

Figure 1c

Other experimental material can be created in a similar way to the Müller-Lyer, such as the horizontal–vertical illusion (see Figure 2). Cut a narrow slit in the centre of card A and, using a black felt-tip pen, mark a broad black strip on card B. When card B is slid in and out, the central line will become shorter or longer.

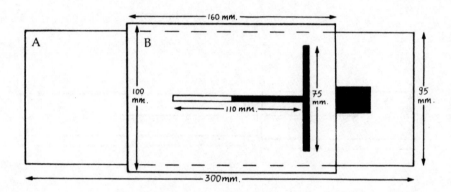

Figure 2.   Horizontal–vertical illusion (a variation of the Müller-Lyer)

Stroop Cards

MATERIALS:
96 small plain cards
1 each of green, red, blue and black felt-tip pens or pencils

INSTRUCTIONS:
Make two sets of cards, the first set with the names of the four colours written in their correct colour and the second set with the same colour words but in a different colour, as follows:

SET I
    12 cards with BLACK in black ink
    12 cards with BLUE in blue ink
    12 cards with RED in red ink
    12 cards with GREEN in green ink

SET II
    4 cards with RED in black ink
    4 cards with BLUE in black ink
    4 cards with GREEN in black ink
    4 cards with BLUE in red ink
    4 cards with GREEN in red ink
    4 cards with BLACK in red ink

4 cards with RED in blue ink
4 cards with GREEN in blue ink
4 cards with BLACK in blue ink
4 cards with RED in green ink
4 cards with BLUE in green ink
4 cards with BLACK in green ink

See practical in Section 4

Bruner or
Concept Cards
Concept cards are also easy to make. They consist of 81 individually different cards which feature symbols in red, green and black. The symbols are a cross, a circle or a square. There are one, two and three symbols. Each card has in black a one-, two- or three-line border. The 27 cards with black symbols are shown in Figure 3. Repeat for red crosses; red squares; red circles; green crosses; green squares; green circles.

See practical in Section 4

cont. ....

cont. ....

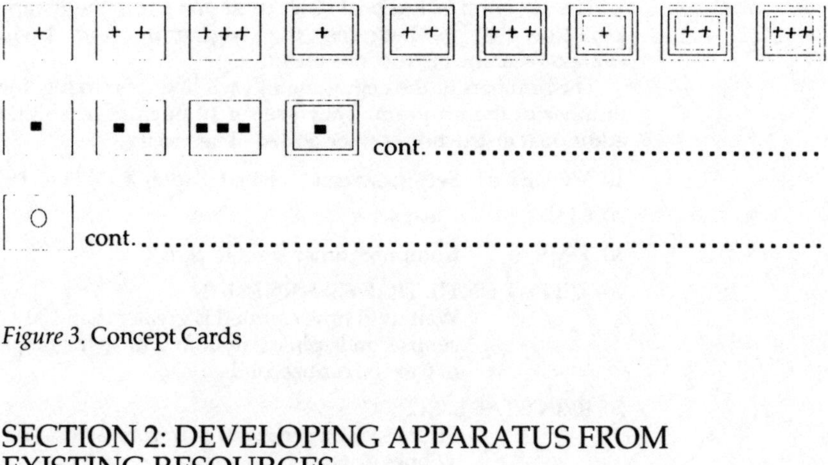

Figure 3. Concept Cards

SECTION 2: DEVELOPING APPARATUS FROM EXISTING RESOURCES

In most institutions, departments other than psychology will use equipment that can be useful for psychology experiments.

Microcomputers are now widely used in psychology and colleges quite often set up computing laboratories to meet the teaching needs of all departments. If you have programming skills, a microcomputer can be turned into a reaction timer, tachistoscope, memory drum, pursuit rotor and used for statistical analyses. However, for those who find programming a little difficult you might like to use the following simple reaction time program to get you underway.

Reaction Time Program

The program is in BBC Basic, and enables you to measure reaction times to the nearest 10 milliseconds. Type in the following instructions:

```
10 MODE7
20 CLS
30 TIME=0
40 REPEAT UNTIL TIME>100+RND(100)
50 PRINT TAB (20,12);"*"
60 *FX 15,0
70 TIME=0
80 r=GET
90 rt=TIME
100 CLS
110 PRINT "Reaction time was   ";rt*10;" milliseconds"
120 TIME=0
130 REPEAT UNTIL TIME>200
140 GOTO 20
```

Now check that you have not made any typing errors, as they will alter the program. To start the program type RUN. A star will appear in the centre of the screen and remain there until any key is pressed. A reaction time will then be displayed.

The program will repeat itself until you press the Escape key. Now that you have seen the program in action, I will explain what the instructions mean.

The numbers at the beginning of each line refer to the line number of the program. They are set 10 lines apart so that additional instructions can be added if necessary.

10 MODE 7   Sets up screen (Teletext display 40 X 25 text)

20 CLS   Clear screen

30 TIME=0   Computer timer is set to zero

40 REPEAT UNTIL TIME>100+RND(100)
                   Wait until time counted is greater than 100
                   centiseconds plus a random time in the range
                   of 0 to 100 centiseconds

50 PRINT TAB (20,12);"*"
                   Print a star on screen 20 characters across and
                   12 lines down

60 *FX 15,0   Clears keyboard buffer to prevent early
                   response

70 TIME=0   Computer timing is now set to zero

80 r=GET   Waits until a key is pressed

90 rt=TIME   Reaction time is stored

100 CLS   Clear screen

110 PRINT   "Reaction time was   ";rt*10" milliseconds"
                   Prints statement in quotes and the reaction
                   time in centiseconds (milliseconds X 10)

```
120 TIME=0    Computer timer set to zero
130 REPEAT UNTIL TIME>200
              Wait until time counted is greater than 200
              centiseconds
140 GOTO 20   Go to line 20 and repeat program.
```

This program can easily be altered to suit your needs; for example, waiting times can be increased or decreased by changing the values in line 40 or 130 or the position of the star can be altered by changing the tab setting in line 50. You could also add an extra line 55 to display a second character.

Here are some additional instructions you could use as well:

```
5 DIM REAC(10)
7 FORI=1 TO 10
42 X=RND(40)
44 Y=RND(25)
50 PRINT TAB (X,Y)"*"
90 REAC(I)=TIME
110 PRINT "Reaction time was ";REAC(I)*10;"
140 NEXTI
145 CLS
147 T=0
150 FORJ=1 TO 10
160 PRINT"TRIAL";J"RT=";REAC(J)*10
170 T=T+REAC(J)
180 NEXTJ
190 PRINT " Average for ten trials  " T*10/2 " ms"
```

The position of the stimulus (star) will now be displayed randomly and the program will run 10 trials, store the data, display the reaction times and calculate the average.

There is, of course, a number of other pieces of equipment that are often used in biology, physics, chemistry, physical education, design and technology and audiovisual departments which you may be able to use. Table 1 provides a few ideas.

Table 1. Other Departments' Resources

Equipment	Department	Used for
pulsemeters	PE; Biology	heart-rate monitoring
Ishihara cards	Biology	measuring colour blindness
signal generator and headphones or speaker	Physics; Audiovisual	generating tones
radio or television	Audiovisual	tuned to hiss between stations for white noise
tape recorder	Audiovisual	to record tones, white noise, word lists, stories or interviews
projector and shutter	Audiovisual; Physics	a single field projection tachistoscope that can be used for single or group studies
dividers or calipers	Mathematics; Physics	aesthesiometers
record player	Audiovisual	rotating illusion demonstrator, or with a mirror spiral after effects (see Section1 for Archimedes spiral)
stroboscope	Physics; Design & Technology	a) greaseproof paper fitted over the lamp to reduce glare – photo stimulator b) with black card with small aperture fitted over lamp – flicker fusion
mirror, bosses, clamps and stands	Physics; Chemistry	mirror-drawing equipment
timer/counter, wire and keys or switches	Physics	to measure reaction times
metre rule	Physics; Works Department	time reaction ruler (see following section for instructions for use)
sound level meter light meter	Works/Estates Departments; Physics	to measure environmental conditions

You will see on Table 1 that there are two other methods that can be used to measure reaction times. Table 2 can be used for measuring reaction times using a ruler and the circuit diagram (Figure 4) if you wish to use a counter timer.

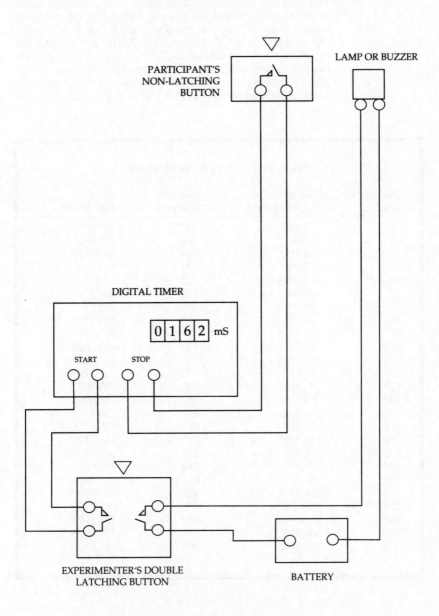

Figure 4. Equipment and wiring for measurement of simple reaction time

Reaction Time
Ruler

MATERIALS:
A metre rule

INSTRUCTIONS:
The subject is asked to hold the thum.   .orefinger about
one and a half inches apart at waist height. The experimenter
holds the metre rule with the 0 mm mark exactly level with
the subject's thumb and forefinger. At the given signal the
experimenter drops the rule and the subject responds by clos-
ing the thumb and finger to stop the fall. The table below
gives a read off of reaction time (to the nearest 10 milliseconds) measured to the point at which the subject stops the
rule.

Table 2. Converting distance into time

Reaction time(ms)	Distance travelled (mm)	Reaction time (ms)	Distance travelled (mm)
10	0.4905	260	331.578
20	1.962	270	357.5745
30	4.415	280	384.552
40	7.848	290	412.5105
50	12.2625	300	441.45
60	17.658	310	471.3705
70	24.0345	320	502.272
80	31.392	330	534.1545
90	39.7305	340	567.018
100	49.05	350	600.8625
110	59.3505	360	635.688
120	70.632	370	671.4945
130	82.8945	380	708.282
140	96.138	390	746.0505
150	110.3625	400	784.8
160	125.568	410	825.5305
170	141.7545	420	865.242
180	158.922	430	906.9345
190	177.0705	440	949.608
200	196.2	450	993.2625
210	216.3105	460	1037.898
220	237.402	470	1083.5145
230	259.4745	480	1130.112
240	282.528	490	1177.6905
250	306.5625	500	1226.25

SECTION 3: BUILDING YOUR OWN EQUIPMENT

Maze   There are several methods of creating a finger or pencil maze. Figure 5 illustrates a typical branch maze but the following instructions allow for any design to be made.

MATERIALS 1
Thick card
Scissors or sharp knife

INSTRUCTIONS 1
Cut out track wide enough to insert pencil. Place a sheet of paper under the maze to record errors made.

MATERIALS 2
As number 1

INSTRUCTIONS 2
Cut slot wider so that the subject is able to follow track with their finger.

MATERIALS 3
Plywood
Beading
Glue

INSTRUCTIONS 3
Glue beading to track to form a slot that can be followed with a finger.

See practical in Section 4

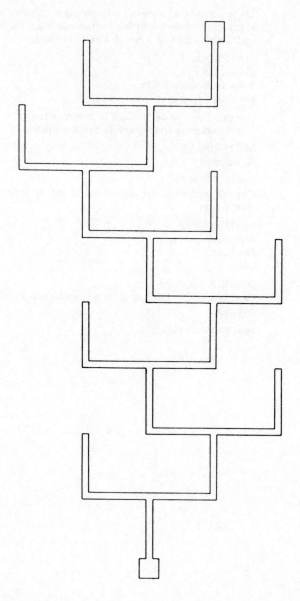

Figure 5. Maze

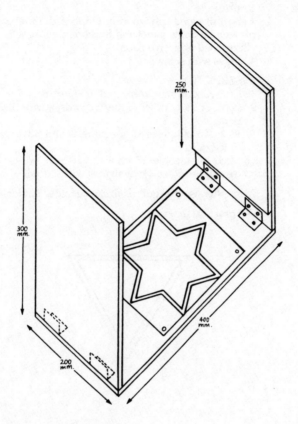

Figure 6a. Mirror-drawing apparatus

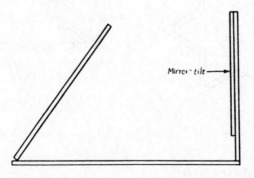

Figure 6b. Side view

Mirror-drawing MATERIALS:
Apparatus   1 mirror tile
1 sheet of wood (plywood or chipboard, fibreboard – ideally plywood for side panel and fibreboard for base)
Glue or self-adhesive pads
4 hinges with screws

INSTRUCTIONS:
1. Cut wood to sizes indicated in Figure 6a.
2. Glue, or fix with self-adhesive pads, mirror tile to side panel B.
3. Fit a pair of hinges to side panel A and side panel B then fit to board C.
4. Make photocopies of a five- or six- pointed star (see Figure 6c) or other shapes with a double border.

Note: After use the equipment can be folded flat for easy storage.

See practical in Section 4

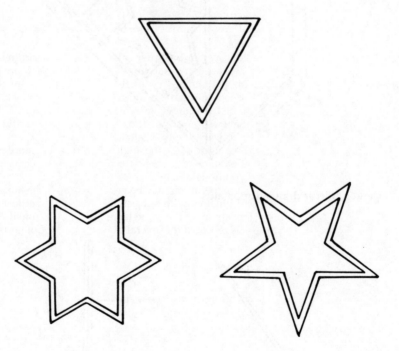

Figure 6c. Mirror-drawing shapes

SECTION 4: PRACTICALS USING INEXPENSIVE MATERIALS

This final section provides a few ideas for running laboratory-based practicals using some of the materials outlined in the previous sections as well as other everyday inexpensive items. These examples will hopefully serve to help teachers with a limited equipment budget to get a program of laboratory classes underway.

The practicals outlined are intended to give a brief idea of the broad range of practicals that can be used to demonstrate various phenomena from those areas of psychology which have traditionally been studied in the laboratory. The only limitation on the number and variety of practicals that can be conducted by the class is the imagination and ingenuity of teachers and students.

Perception Practicals

1. VISUAL ILLUSIONS

Materials
Müller-Lyer illusion (see Section 1)
Horizontal– vertical illusion (see Section 1)

Experiments
The Müller-Lyer apparatus can be used to examine the effects of fin angle on the size of the illusion. Subjects are presented with five Müller-Lyer cards each with fins at different angles and asked to adjust the cards so that the black line appears to be the same length on the two halves of the illusion. The actual length of the lines is measured and the difference between the two calculated. Typically, the results show that the more acute the angle of the fins, the more inaccurate the judgement as predicted by Gregory's Constancy Scaling Hypothesis (1963).

A similar experiment may be performed with the horizontal–vertical illusion, with subjects adjusting the vertical line until it appears to be the same length as the horizontal. This procedure is repeated for several different lengths of horizontal line.

2. THE STROOP EFFECT

Materials
Stopwatch, Stroop cards (see Section 1)

Experiment
A simple demonstration of the Stroop effect can be performed by presenting subjects with the two sets of cards (which should have been shuffled). Subjects are timed while they sort each set into piles corresponding to the colour of the ink (not the name). Typically it takes subjects longer to sort set II (those cards where the name and colour of the ink are different), as the name of the colour interferes with the processing of the ink colour. An explanation of this effect is given in Lindsay and Norman (1977).

3. PATTERN RECOGNITION

Materials

Ten to 20 lists of letters arranged in vertical columns 20 to 30 characters in length. Half of these lists should be composed of letters which contain no curved lines (for example L,M,N); the other half should be made up from letters which include curved lines (for example C,O,G). All lists should contain the same target letter, either 'X ' or 'K'. The position of the target letter should be varied within the two conditions (curved letters and straight-lined letters) for each list, but kept constant across the conditions (in order to permit a comparison of location times of the target letter for both list types). For example 'list 1' in the curved letter condition might contain the target letter seven characters down the list and, thus, there should be a corresponding list composed of straight-lined letters with the target letter in the same position.
A stopwatch or reaction timer (see Section 2)

Experiment

One way of investigating pattern recognition is to use the visual search technique originally employed by Neisser (1964). Subjects are instructed that when they are ready, a list will be uncovered and they should search through it as quickly as possible from top to bottom and say 'now' when the target letter has been located (or press the key on the reaction timer). The experimenter should start the stopwatch or reaction timer immediately as the list is uncovered and stop it as soon as the subject indicates that they have located the target, making a record of the time. This procedure should be repeated for all the lists which should be given in a different randomized order to each subject.

Typically, the results should indicate that the subjects take longer to locate the target in a visually similar context (that is, lists which contain no curved lines) than the visually dissimilar context (lists which include curved lines). Such a finding lends support to 'feature detection' theories of pattern recognition (see Eysenck and Keane, 1990, Lindsay and Norman, 1977, and Wilding, 1982, for discussion of these theories).

Memory Practicals

1. FREE RECALL

Materials

Slide or overhead projector or tape recorder
20 slides or overheads each showing one monosyllabic word

Experiment

Subjects are shown 20 words in succession either on a slide or overhead projector. (Alternatively the words may be spoken aloud by an experimenter or recorded onto cassette tape.) Subjects are told to begin recall of the words, in any order that they choose, immediately after the last word has been presented.

Typical results are that items presented at the beginning of the list and at the end of the list are generally recalled more easily than items in the middle of the list. The superior recall of earlier list items (the primacy effect) is interpreted as retrieval of those words from a longer term memory store, and high recall of later items (the recency effect) is often interpreted as retrieval from a short-term memory store.

If delay is introduced (20 to 25 seconds) between the final word and recall, during which subjects perform some interim task (such as counting backwards in threes), the recency effect should be reduced or eliminated.

Cognition Practicals

1. CONCEPT ATTAINMENT

Materials
1 set of Bruner/concept cards (see Section 1)

Experiment
Subjects are shown one concept card from the set which corresponds to a concept/rule that the experimenter has chosen. The experimenter may choose various concepts/rules, based on the design of the cards; for example, cards with one figure, cards with green symbols, cards with a circle, etc. The subject's task is to discern the chosen concept by asking whether other cards (which are all on view) are also instances of the rule. This procedure was originally used by Bruner, Goodnow and Austin (1956) to discern strategies used by their subjects to attain concepts from the cards. A description of the strategies of concept attainment that Bruner *et al.* identified can be found in Turner (1975).

If it is possible to negotiate access to a group of children, the same procedure may be used to investigate concept attainment in younger people.

Skill Acquisition Practicals

1. MIRROR-DRAWING EXPERIMENTS

Materials
Mirror-drawing apparatus (see Section 3)

Experiment
The subject, seated facing the mirror, draws round the star shape, between its double border, whilst looking at the star reflected in the mirror. The panel at the front prevents the subject from seeing his/her hand directly.

This basic procedure may be used to investigate the acquisition of a visual motor skill on a number of variables such as massed versus distributed practice or learning by observation. It can also be used to investigate transfer of training from left to right hand.

2. MAZE TRACING EXPERIMENTS

Materials

Finger or pencil maze (see Section 3)

Experiment

Subjects trace the maze blindfolded. This apparatus can be used to investigate learning under a variety of different conditions: for example, active versus passive practice, massed versus distributed practice, and transfer of practice from one hand to the other. Other variables such as age, sex and handedness of the subject can also be investigated with this equipment.

Social Psychology Practicals

1. CONFORMITY/SOCIAL FACILITATION

Materials

A jar filled with beans, pebbles, marbles, etc.

Experiment

This experiment is based on an early study of social facilitation originally performed by Jenness (1932). Subjects individually write down their estimate of the number of beans, etc. in a glass jar. Then in groups of four to eight people, they discuss their estimates and agree on a group estimate. Finally subjects make another individual estimate. The results might be expected to indicate a shift in the second individual estimate relative to the first estimate. The findings are relevant to the study of both conformity and social facilitation.

2. INTERPERSONAL ATTRACTION

Materials

Photographs of married or long-term couples cut in half to separate the partners.

Experiment

Photographs of couples may be used to investigate the role of physical attractiveness in long-term intimate relationships. Students individually rate each partner for attractiveness without knowing which couple they belong to. Overall scores for each picture are then calculated in order to see whether partners from the same couples are rated similarly for physical attractiveness.

3. GROUP VERSUS INDIVIDUAL PERFORMANCE

Materials

Various

Experiments

Group versus individual performance can be measured on an almost limitless range of inexpensive and easily obtainable materials. Tasks for this type of study could include: solving word puzzles; arithmetic tests; finding the concept from Bruner cards; estimating the number of beans in a jar.

Developmental Practicals

1. CONSERVATION

Materials
Various

Experiment
Many aspects of cognitive development may be examined using everyday items. Perhaps the simplest aspect of cognitive development to investigate is performance on conservation tasks. Number conservation can be investigated using coins, counters, or buttons; substance conservation using plasticine; and conservation of continuous quantities with cups or glasses of equal volume but different shapes. Typically very young children (ages two to six) are unable to solve any of these conservation problems correctly. Slightly older children (five to seven) are able to solve number conservation tasks and later able to understand substance and continuous quantity conservation.

2. EGOCENTRISM

Materials
Lego

Experiment
It is possible to examine egocentrism in young children using a lego space station as an alternative to the 'three mountain task' (Piaget and Inhelder, 1956).

The child is allowed to view the lego model from all sides. The child then sits facing one side of the model while a lego figure is placed at another location on the 'space station'. The child is asked to describe what the lego figure is able to 'see' from where it is standing. Typically, the majority of young children (three to four years and under) are unable to perform this task accurately, describing instead, what they themselves can see.

Interestingly, though, young children often perform this task using a lego space station more accurately than they did in the original 'three mountain task'.

Testing and Assessment

Materials
Questionnaires
These materials are very expensive to purchase. However many textbooks contain questionnaires which you may be able to copy with the permission of the author or publishers. Recently NFER-Nelson have published *Assessment: A Mental Health Portfolio* which contains 20 tests. After you have purchased the portfolio you may photocopy the masters and use them within your organization an unlimited number of times without incurring further cost.

Experiments
Questionnaires can be used to investigate a wide range of topics, for example, attitudes to women, race and religion; social issues; fears; thinking styles and personality types.

The *Mental Health Portfolio* provides tests for the measurement of distress, anxiety, depression, interpersonal difficulties, habit disorders, psychological adjustment to illness and stress, coping and social support. Certain tests should only be used with the proper training (see chapter on psychological tests).

OTHER SOURCES FOR PRACTICAL IDEAS

There are other sources that provide information on inexpensive, do-it-yourself apparatus such as the *Association for the Teaching of Psychology Newsletter* and their journal *Psychology Teaching*. The textbook for GCSE, *Psychology: An Introduction* by Nicky Hayes and Sue Orrell, contains many useful ideas.

The British Psychological Society has published two books on practicals: *Doing Social Psychology: Laboratory and Field Exercises* (1988) edited by Glynis Breakwell, Hugh Foot and Robin Gilmour, and the *BPS Manual of Psychology Practicals* (1992) compiled by Rob McIlveen, Louise Higgins, Alison Wadeley and Paul Humphreys. This book provides a collection of well-proven laboratory experiments with instructions for data analysis and the interpretation of results.

REFERENCES

ASSOCIATION FOR THE TEACHING OF PSYCHOLOGY *Psychology Teaching*. Association for the Teaching of Psychology, c/o The British Psychological Society, St Andrews House, 48 Princess Road East, Leicester LE1 7DR.

BRUNER, J.S., GOODNOW, J.S. and AUSTIN, G.A. (1956) *A Study of Thinking*. New York: John Wiley.

EYSENCK, M.W. and KEANE, M.T. (1990) *Cognitive Psychology: A Students Handbook*. Hove, East Sussex: Lawrence Erlbaum.

GREGORY, R.L. (1963) Distortion of visual space as inappropriate constancy scaling. *Nature, 99*, 678–680.

HAYES, N. and ORRELL, S. (1987) *Psychology: An Introduction*. Harlow: Longman.

JENNESS, A. (1932) The role of discussion in changing opinion regarding matter of fact. *Journal of Abnormal and Social Psychology, 27*, 279–296.

LINDSAY, P.H. and NORMAN, D.A. (1977) *Human Information Processing: An Introduction to Psychology*, 2nd ed. London: Academic Press, 453–455.

NEISSER, U. (1964) Visual Search. *Scientific American, 210 (June)*, 94–102.

PIAGET, J. and INHELDER, B. (1956) *The Child"s Conception of Space*. London: RKP.

STROOP, J.R. (1935) Studies of interference in serial verbal reactions. *Journal of Experimental Psychology, 18*, 643–662.

TURNER, J. (1975) *Cognitive Development*. London: Methuen.

WILDING, J.M. (1982) *Perception: From Sense to Object*. London: Hutchinson.

CAREERS AND COURSES

Ben Ball

❏ *careers for psychology graduates • courses in psychology • guidance resources*

The aim of this chapter is to provide an introductory overview of the main sources of information available to present and prospective students of psychology. It focuses primarily on the principal training and qualification routes and ends with a summary description of the career and educational guidance services provided for students in secondary, further and higher education. For a more detailed analysis, readers can refer to titles suggested in the references and further reading sections.

CAREERS FOR PSYCHOLOGY GRADUATES

Career Choices in Psychology (Higgins, 1988, published by BPS Books) gives a clear account of the main avenues in professional psychology in the UK. Qualification and training routes, the opportunities for career development, sample diaries of job holders are provided for each of the main specialisms: educational, occupational, clinical, criminological and legal, and teaching and research. A further source of information is provided by the range of booklets produced by the Association of Graduate Careers Advisory Services (AGCAS) which cover similar ground but link the work of psychologists with other professionals. Clinical psychology, for example, appears in 'Health Care in the Public Sector'.

It is perhaps important to point out that competition for training in the main specialist areas can be severe. This is particularly true in the case of clinical psychology. In 1992 there were 3,644 applicants for 223 training places and it is now the norm for candidates to have a IIi degree and at least a year's pre-entry experience prior to training.

The process of education and professional training may also be protracted. In the case of educational psychology, for instance, it takes at least seven years from the start of a first degree in psychology to the completion of a masters course in educational psychology, because of the additional need to achieve qualified teacher status.

A postgraduate qualification is becoming increasingly important for anyone intending to work as a professional psychologist, as is chartered status of The British Psychological Society (BPS). The *Appointments Memorandum* of the BPS provides details of immediate job vacancies for professional psychologists.

Options for Psychology Graduates

So what happens to those who qualify at first degree level and and who do not undertake professional training? A number of studies have pointed to the difficulties sometimes faced by psychology graduates in finding related employment and the diverse range of alternative options available to them. In an early study, Rose and Radford (1986) estimated that over 75 per cent of psychology graduates were unlikely to qualify as professional psychologists, either because of the lack of suitable training opportunities or because of a wish to use their degree in other ways. Other studies have pointed to the employment difficulties experienced by psychology graduates in finding permanent employment. The CNAA's report, *Social Science Graduates: Degree Result and First Employment Destinations* (1988), using statistical data for the period 1982–5, pointed to the higher than average unemployment rates for graduates in psychology from all UK degree courses. However, recent surveys by Careers Advisory Services for 1990 and 1991 reveal an employment pattern for psychology graduates which corresponds more to the norm for all subjects.

Given that over 30 per cent of graduate job vacancies are open to graduates of any discipline, a key question is how psychology students are perceived by employers in a nonspecialist job market. Fletcher *et al.* (1991) assessed employer's ratings of graduates in psychology in comparison with those of other subject groups and showed that on a range of factors, notably those involving interpersonal skills, psychologists were given higher ratings. They concluded, however, that more needed to be done to promote to employers the benefits of employing psychology graduates.

One important first step to improve the ability of psychology graduates to find professional level work is to help them identify the personal skills and competencies that accrue from their degree course programmes. As Hayes (1989) has pointed out, there are a range of transferable skills to be derived from studying psychology, and making these manifest will increase graduates' confidence in their search for work relevant to their needs.

Careers Using Psychology

So what are the options open to psychology graduates who do not want to work as professional psychologists, but who would like to apply some or all of their specialist knowledge? In terms of career planning and development, much will depend on an individual's personal skills, values and interests, and the extent of their previous experience, but the following provides a summary of some of the more obvious career routes.

Commercial applications. For those who like working in a commercial environment there are obvious applications of psychology in the field of advertising and market research. Consumer research – the planning of large scale attitude surveys, carrying out in-depth studies of reaction to different products – provides an obvious example. But there are many other examples of the way graduates with statistical and data-handling skills can find an appropriate outlet in a commercial or industrial environment.

Working with people. Students are often drawn to psychology because of a basic interest in people and many graduates will enter work which requires a wide range of interpersonal and helping skills. Counselling in educational settings or in statutory or voluntary agencies; careers guidance in schools and colleges; social work in its variety of specialist forms; teaching, particularly in special education, are obvious examples of areas in which psychology graduates will extend their professional training and be able to develop skills of diagnosis and person-centred intervention.

Research. For those graduates interested in developing their research skills there are a range of opportunities in industry as well as in higher education. Ergonomists, working on the human–machine interface, psychologists working in human factors research for the Ministry of Defence, can apply the methods of experimental psychology. But there are other kinds of research activity, for example, labour market research and manpower planning, which can take place in independent research consultancies and which rely on data-handling and problem-solving skills.

A review of the options open to those graduating in psychology is provided in *How about Psychology?* (Higgins, 1989) and in the various publications written by careers advisers that are listed in the further reading section.

Opportunities Overseas

Opportunities for both training and employment for psychology graduates exist overseas but the situation naturally varies widely from country to country.

Opportunities overseas are advertised in the general educational press, and on occasion in The British Psychological Society's *Appointments Memorandum*. Information may also be available through the British Council. It may be worthwhile enquiring of the cultural attaché of a country in which one is interested.

The USA is most likely to be of interest, being English-speaking and having far the largest psychological profession. The *APA Monitor*, published by the American Psychological Association, carries vacancies. The American Psychological Association also publishes *Graduate Study in Psychology and Associated Fields*, which annually covers some 600 programmes.

General advice is given in the following publications: *Scholarships Abroad* (British Council, annual); *The Directory of Jobs and Careers Abroad* (Lipinski, 1989); and *Working Overseas* (AGCAS, 1992).

COURSES IN PSYCHOLOGY

The following notes will give an idea of the range of courses in psychology and serve as a guide to the sources of information available. They are illustrative rather than definitive.

GCSE, A/S and A-level Courses and Exams　Most A-level psychology courses are offered by colleges of further education. In schools the amount of psychology teaching continues to increase, largely in the form of courses in child development, but there is comparatively little teaching at A-level. At present it is not possible to study psychology as an examination subject for Scottish Highers or indeed for lower level qualifications in Scotland. Further information about the extent of psychology teaching in schools and colleges of further education may be obtained from the Association for the Teaching of Psychology (ATP). The BPS Group of Teachers of Psychology is concerned largely with the teaching of psychology in higher education settings.

Two examining boards, the Joint Matriculation Board (JMB) and the Associated Examining Board (AEB) offer psychology at A-level. The AEB also offers A/S-level psychology, while the Northern Examining Group (NEA), the Midlands Examining Group (MEG) and the Southern Examining Group (SEG) all offer psychology examinations at GCSE-level in child development. There is also a 'higher level' psychology exam organized by the International Baccalaureate for students aged 16 to 18. (See useful addresses section for the boards' addresses.) To give just one example of the increasing popularity of psychology courses, the numbers of candidates for the AEB's A-level exam have doubled in the last four years. In 1988 there were over 6,000 and in 1992, 12,848. An estimated 20,000 candidates will sit the exam in 1993.

Details of all college course centres in the UK can be found in the *Directory of Further Education* and from individual local education authorities.

First Degree and Other Professional Courses

Recent evidence from the relevant admissions clearing houses reveals that psychology remains a popular subject of study. The ratio of applications to available places continues to exceed the average for all subjects and this has, in turn, led to an increase in the number of students of psychology in the higher education system.

Degree course information. The main sources of information concerning undergraduate programmes in psychology are obviously the prospectuses of individual institutions. However, there are four separate compendia which list all courses in the principle sectors of higher education, and enable prospective students to compare the entry qualification required, length of course and so on. *University Entrance: The Official Guide* provides information on all universities, their degree courses and precise details of entry requirements. *The Colleges and Institutes of Higher Education Guide* describes the small number of colleges which have psychology as a component in modular and social science degrees.

A detailed summary of existing psychology courses in the UK is found in the *Degree Course Guide for Psychology* (CRAC), which is updated every two years. This contrasts course content, selection procedures, assessment methods, recruitment numbers and departmental research interests. As well as single-honours programmes it also provides some information on joint-honours programmes or modular courses in which psychology may play a large part. *Which Psychology Degree Course?* (Gale, 1993) also provides essential reading for prospective psychology undergraduates.

A range of other publications are available for the intending student – alternative prospectuses, 'good' university guides and so on. Existing students and staff provide an immediate source of information and, when attending for interviews or open days, applicants need to make use of these 'primary sources'. Applicants may also want to check whether a particular degree programme gives the Graduate Basis for Registration as a Chartered Psychologist.

There are of course a range of study options in which psychology forms a major part. It is possible, for example, to complete an undergraduate programme with the Open University (OU). To obtain Graduate Membership of the BPS students must undertake a range of full credit courses: social psychology, cognitive psychology and introduction to psychology as well as a selection from a range of other courses which include personality theory, development and learning, research methods in education and the social sciences.

Many vocational first degree courses, which form the basis of professional training, will also contain a significant psychology component. Programmes in education, nursing, social work, speech therapy and training for other paramedical careers are obvious examples.

Postgraduate Courses

The Compendium of Postgraduate Studies in Psychology in the UK and Ireland is compiled biennially by the Department of Psychology at the University of Surrey. It comprises information supplied by departments of psychology on opportunities for research or graduate training. This usually includes a list of staff and their research interests. It does not necessarily include all courses in which psychology graduates may be interested and should be used in conjunction with *Graduate Studies*.

Graduate Studies is published yearly by Hobsons Press. It lists degrees by research and by taught course, and certificate and diploma courses by subject, with institutions listed alphabetically within subject. Entry qualifications and content are specified for many of the courses. It aims to provide a comprehensive listing of postgraduate courses, representing all sectors of the higher education system. A range of freely available publications for undergraduates also summarize the main taught courses.

For those wanting to qualify in clinical psychology, the *Clearing House Handbook* covers all aspects of admission to the relevant postgraduate training courses. It is also worth remembering that a small number of postgraduate diploma courses provide a conversion course for graduates who have studied a first degree with a major psychology component. Successful completion of these courses enables students to apply for graduate membership of the BPS.

For anyone interested in teaching, *The NATFHE Handbook* is essential reading since it lists all forms of initial teacher training. It is perhaps worth noting that it is not possible to use psychology as a main subject specialization for the Postgraduate Certificate in Education.

The Postgraduate Bulletin published three times a year by the Central Services Unit lists immediate vacancies for graduate study, research and training across the entire range of disciplines.

For many students wishing to study further, the main problem is one of finding finance. All students are advised to read the relevant Research Council booklets, available in their Careers Advisory Services.

Other Specialist Courses

In addition to full-time courses lasting a year or more, there are other short, intensive courses which can be grouped under two broad headings. Firstly those concerned with *professional updating*, for example, short courses of introduction to new psychometric tests for occupational psychologists, workshops on counselling skills and approaches for those in the helping professions are examples of the vast range of short course provision.

There are also numerous *general interest* courses run under the auspices of university extramural departments or local authority adult education programmes which may provide a basic introduction to general psychology for people who have not studied the subject before.

A range of courses also exist under the OU's associate student programme, providing shorter professional updating courses and those designed to develop personal interests. Courses include: Introduction to Psychology, Biology, Brain and Behaviour, Cognitive Psychology.

GUIDANCE RESOURCES

Students about to complete their courses will want to make use of the guidance resources available to them in order to clarify their future educational or occupational decisions. In secondary schools the careers teacher will be the main focus for guidance activity, with possibly the additional involvement of the Head of Sixth Form. Local Education Authority careers officers will be closely involved in school-based guidance activity and, in particular, in one-to-one advisory interviews with pupils. In colleges of further education, there may be full or part-time careers tutors to fulfil a careers guidance role. Once again, students will have access to their Local Education Authority Careers Service, whose careers officers will be trained in careers guidance, many of whom will have studied psychology at undergraduate level. In universities and colleges of higher education there will be institution-based careers advisory services staffed by small teams of careers advisers. They tend to operate on a self-referral basis – students and graduates use the services as and when they wish, but contact tends to be concentrated in a student's final year.

An overview of careers guidance services in higher education is provided by Ball (1987). Careers advisers work on a counselling/advisory and information-giving model. Typically, students are offered counselling interviews, followed by an introduction to the information resources available to them. This may occasionally be supplemented with the results of psychometric test data, although this is not generally the pattern. Instead, many careers services will offer a programme of seminars by representatives of particular occupations, or provide workshops designed to improve students' job search skills. In some institutions, careers advisers have an educational role, and contribute to various courses of study on the subject of career and professional development. Careers advisers also maintain links with the graduate recruiters and engage in placement activity.

Computer-Based Guidance Systems Computer-assisted career guidance systems (CAGS) are now increasingly used in the UK and the United States. In schools and some colleges, the most widely used are CASCAID and JIIG-CAL. Both encourage 'self-assessment' by finding a match between students' interests and occupational titles. The system most widely used in commercial and industrial settings is CAREER BUILDER which has a career-planning rationale, providing self-appraisal on the basis of personal skills, values and interests. The most comprehensive system to date, PROSPECT, has been designed initially for use in higher education, and funded largely by the Department for Education. Users have the choice of completing one of four linked modules concerned with:

- self-assessment – appraising abilities, skills, interests and values;
- identifying options – searching and analysing occupations and employers;
- a decision aid to evaluate options;
- planning for entry and self-marketing.

While based on a career planning rationale, PROSPECT nevertheless retains a matching orientation – user profiles of skills and values, for example, are matched against over 200 graduate-level occupations.

Diagnostic Guidance and Vocational Guidance Agencies

A different model of guidance practice is provided by the private vocational guidance agencies. Here the emphasis is on diagnostic guidance based on assessment. Psychometric test data from interest, aptitude and personality tests are assembled prior to a one-to-one consultation and form the basis of a written summary or report. Differential fee rates may be changed according to the kind of service offered. Initial career guidance, for example, may attract a lower rate of fee than a career review for those in mid-career. Some employing organizations now provide career guidance for employees, particularly at managerial level by using the services of external consultants. In particular, outplacement counselling for redundant executives is now provided by a number of consultancies, using psychometric testing, group discussion and/or individual counselling. For the majority of adults in the UK, there has been, however, no freely available national careers guidance provision since the closure of the Occupational Guidance Units in the early 1980s, although this situation may change with the activities of the Training and Enterprise Councils.

Educational Guidance

In the field of educational guidance for adults, a number of educational guidance units, offering advice and information about education and training routes have been established in LEAs in England and Wales. They have made a distinctive contribution in offering information, advice and counselling to a wide range of adult clients about learning opportunities at all levels. In particular they have been able to co-ordinate the efforts of a range of agencies to promote educational opportunities at a local level. Cuts in LEA funding have resulted in the closure of a number of Educational Guidance Services for Adults and, again, it seems likely that the Training and Enterprise Councils may be involved in the delivery of this kind of service provision.

REFERENCES

AMERICAN PSYCHOLOGICAL ASSOCIATION (APA) (annual) *Graduate Study in Psychology and Associated Fields.* Washington DC: APA.

ASSOCIATION OF COMMONWEALTH UNIVERSITIES (ACU) (1992) *University Entrance: The Official Guide.* London: ACU.

ASSOCIATION OF GRADUATE CAREERS ADVISORY SERVICES (1991) *Guidance, Counselling and Advisory Work.* Manchester: Central Services Unit.

ASSOCIATION OF GRADUATE CAREERS ADVISORY SERVICES (1991) *Health Care in Private Practice.* Manchester: Central Services Unit.

ASSOCIATION OF GRADUATE CAREERS ADVISORY SERVICES (1991) *Health Care in the Public Sector.* Manchester: Central Services Unit.

ASSOCIATION OF GRADUATE CAREERS ADVISORY SERVICES (1992) *Personnel Work.* Manchester: Central Services Unit.

ASSOCIATION OF GRADUATE CAREERS ADVISORY SERVICES (1992) *Working Overseas.* Manchester: Central Services Unit.

BALL, B. (1987) Graduates and careers guidance. *Guidance and Assessment Review, 3,* no. 3.

BRITISH COUNCIL (annual) *Scholarships Abroad.* London: British Council.

CANTER, D. (Ed.) (biennial) *Compendium of Postgraduate Studies in Psychology in the UK and Ireland.* Leicester: The British Psychological Society.

CAREERS RESEARCH AND ADVISORY CENTRE (CRAC) (1993/4) *The Degree Course Guide for Psychology.* Cambridge: CRAC/Hobsons Press.

CAREERS RESEARCH AND ADVISORY CENTRE (CRAC) (annual) *The Directory of Further Education.* Cambridge: CRAC/Hobsons Press.

CAREERS RESEARCH AND ADVISORY CENTRE (CRAC) (annual) *Graduate Studies.* Cambridge: CRAC/Hobsons Press.

CENTRAL SERVICES UNIT (triannual) *Postgraduate Bulletin.* Manchester: Central Services Unit.

CLEARING HOUSE FOR POSTGRADUATE COURSES IN CLINICAL PSYCHOLOGY(annual) *Clearing House Handbook.* Leeds: Clearing House for Postgraduate Courses in Clinical Psychology.

Colleges and Institutes of Higher Education see Standing Conference of Principals.

COUNCIL FOR NATIONAL ACADEMIC AWARDS (CNAA) (1988) Social Science graduates: Degree results and first employment destinations. *CNAA Information Services Outcomes, Paper 1,* July.

Directory of Further Education see Career Research and Advisory Centre.

FLETCHER, C., ROSE, D. and RADFORD, J. (1991) Employers' perceptions of psychology graduates. *The Psychologist*, October, 434 – 437.

GALE, A. (1993) *Which Psychology Degree Course?* Leicester: BPS Books.

Graduate Study in Psychology and Associated Fields see American Psychological Association.

Graduate Studies see Careers Research and Advisory Centre.

HAYES, N. (1989) The skills acquired in psychology degrees. *The Psychologist*, June, 238 – 239.

HIGGINS, L.T. (1989) *How about Psychology?* rev. ed. Leicester: BPS Books (The British Psychological Society).

HIGGINS, L.T. (1988) *Career Choices in Psychology*. Leicester: BPS Books (The British Psychological Society).

LIPINSKI, A. (1989) *The Directory of Jobs and Careers Abroad*. Oxford: Vacation Work.

NATIONAL ASSOCIATION OF TEACHERS IN FURTHER AND HIGHER EDUCATION (NATFHE) (annual) *The NATFHE Handbook: The Handbook of Initial Teacher Training* London: NATFHE.

NEWSTEAD, S., MILLER, M. and FARMER, E. (1989) *Putting Psychology to Work*. Leicester: BPS Books (The British Psychological Society).

Postgraduate Bulletin see Central Services Unit.

ROSE, D. and RADFORD, J. (1986) The unemployment of psychology graduates. *Bulletin of The British Psychological Society*, 39, 451 – 456.

Scholarships Abroad see British Council.

STANDING CONFERENCE OF PRINCIPALS (SCIP) (annual) *Colleges and Institutes of Higher Education*. Ormskirk: SCIP.

University Entrance: The Official Guide see Association of Commonwealth Universities.

FURTHER READING

BALL, B. (1989) *Manage Your Own Career: A Self-Help Guide to Career Choice and Change.* Leicester: BPS Books and Kogan Page.

CANTER, S. and CANTER, D. (Eds) (1982) *Psychology in Practice.* Chichester: Wiley.

CAREERS RESEARCH AND ADVISORY CENTRE (CRAC) (annual) *Graduate Employment and Training.* Cambridge: CRAC/Hobsons Press.

CENTRAL SERVICES UNIT (CSU) (annual) *Register of Graduate Employment and Training.* Manchester: CSU.

DAUNCEY, G. and MOUNTAIN, J. (1987) *The New Unemployment Handbook.* Cambridge: National Extension College. [A practical handbook with chapters on time use and survival strategies as well as job hunting.]

MARZILLIER, J.S. and HALL, J. (Eds) (1987) *What is Clinical Psychology?* Milton Keynes: OU Press.

NEWPOINT PUBLISHING (annual) *Graduate Opportunities.* London: Newpoint Publishing.

NEWPOINT PUBLISHING (annual) *Which Degree?* London: Newpoint Publishing. [Provides information on all university and college of higher education first-degree courses.]

PATES, A. and GOOD, M. (1986) *Second Chances: The Guide to Adult Education and Training Opportunities.* Sheffield: Careers and Occupational Information Centre.

256

USEFUL ADDRESSES

American Psychological Association
750 First Street, NE
Washington DC 20002–4242
USA

Associated Examining Board
Staghill House
Guildford
Surrey GU2 5XJ
tel. (0483) 506506

Association of Graduate Careers Advisory
Services
c/o Central Services Unit

Association of Heads of Psychology
Departments
c/o Prof R. Bull
Department of Psychology
Portsmouth University
King Charles Street
Portsmouth PO1 2ER
tel. (0705) 827681

Association for the Teaching of
Psychology (ATP)
c/o The British Psychological Society

British Association for the Advancement
of Science
Fortress House
23 Saville Row
London W1A 1AA
tel. (071) 4943326

BBC Resources for Training
White City
London W12 7TS
tel. (081) 7461111

The British Psychological Society
St Andrews House
48 Princess Road East
Leicester LE1 7DR
tel. (0533) 549568

Business and Technician Education
Council
Central House
Upper Woburn Place
London WC1H 0HH
tel. (071) 4138400

Careers Research and Advisory Centre
2nd Floor, Sheraton House
Castle Park
Cambridge CB3 0AX
tel. (0223) 460277

Central Services Unit: The Graduate
Employment Service
Crawford House
Precinct Centre
Manchester M13 9EP
tel. (061) 2734233

Council on the Public Understanding of
Science (COPUS)
c/o The Royal Society

Department for Education
Sanctuary Buildings
Great Smith Street
Westminister SW1P 3BT
tel. (071) 9255000

Economic and Social Research Council
Polaris House
North Star Avenue
Swindon SN2 1UJ
tel. (0793) 413000

International Baccalaureate Organization
Pascal Close
St Mellons
Cardiff
South Glamorgan CF3 0YP
tel. (0222) 770770

Library of The British Psychological
Society
University of London
Senate House
Malet Street
London WC1E 7HU

Medical Research Council
20 Park Crescent
London W1N 4AL
tel. (071) 6365422

Midland Examining Group
c/o Oxford and Cambridge Schools
Examination Board
Purbeck House
Purbeck Road
Cambridge CB2 2PU
tel. (0223) 411211

National Foundation for Educational
Research
The Mere
Upton Park
Slough SL1 2DQ
tel. (0753) 574123

Northern Examinations and Assessment
Board
Devas Street
Manchester M15 6EX
tel. (061) 9531180

Office of Science and Technology
Office of Public Service and Science
Albany House
84–86 Petty France
London SW1H 9ST
tel. (071) 2701234

Open University Educational Enterprises
The Open University
Walton Hall
Milton Keynes MK7 6AA
tel. (0908) 274066

Research Defence Society
58 Great Marlborough Street
London W1V 1DD
tel. (071) 2872818

The Royal Society
6 Carlton House Terrace
London SW1Y 5AG
tel. (071) 8395561

Science and Engineering Research Council
Polaris House
North Star Avenue
Swindon SN2 1ET
tel. (0793) 411000

Scottish Education Department
New St Andrew's House
St James Centre
Edinburgh EH1 3TB
tel. (031) 5568400

Society for Research into Higher
Education
344–354 Gray's Inn Road
London WC1X 8BP
tel. (071) 8377880

Southern Examining Group
Central Administration Office
Stag Hill House
Guildford
Surrey GU2 5XJ
tel. (0483) 503123

Special Group of Teachers of Psychology
c/o The British Psychological Society

University and Colleges Admissions
Service
PO Box 28
Cheltenham
Glos. GL50 35A
tel. (0242) 222444

INDEX

Introduction to
PSYCHOLOGY
Eleventh Edition
Rita L. Atkinson, Richard C. Atkinson, Edward E. Smith & Daryl J. Bem

A Continuing Academic Tradition....

Introduction to Psychology celebrates its 40th anniversary with the publication of the eleventh edition. Long considered a classic, the new edition continues in the tradition of the most respected introductory textbooks on the market by consistently and cohesively covering the most recent developments as well as established theories. This focus earns *Introduction to Psychology* the position as the most popular psychology textbook in Europe.

...of Timely Coverage

- The eleventh edition includes neural net (connectionist) models of cognition, providing a readable account of this major new theoretical breakthrough.
- The chapter on stress and coping has been completely revised to reflect the growth of health psychology.
- Discusses the latest research on genetic and biological contributions to mental disorders.
- Includes a new section on precognition emotions and the latest research on cross-cultural research on emotional expression.
- Covers brain imaging techniques which locate specific areas for cognition, emotions and language.

...and Innovation

- *Introduction to Psychology's* unique interdisciplinary viewpoint uses five perspectives in psychology (behavioural, biological, cognitive, psychoanalytical and phenomenological) to describe different approaches to the field.
- The eleventh edition now covers evolutionary psychology and ethological approaches to learning.
- The life-span approach to personality now includes a major discussion of how genetic, environmental and cultural factors interact to determine personality.

ISBN: 0-15-500914-1, January 1993, Paperback, £16.95

HARCOURT BRACE   *Harcourt Brace & Company, Publishers*
24-28 Oval Road, London NW1 7DX   Tel: 071 267-4466

Artesian Books

Publishers of The British Journal of Psychotherapy

BRITISH JOURNAL OF PSYCHOTHERAPY

Editor: Dr R D Hinshelwood
St Bernard's Hospital, Southall, Middlesex, England.

This journal takes articles on clinical and theoretical topics relevant to the psychotherapist practising privately or in institutions. The emphasis is on papers which concern the practice of ANALYTICAL PSYCHOTHERAPY; or which concern the APPLICATION of psychotherapeutic practice and theory to institutions, society and other settings.

The profession of psychotherapy is splintered by internal divisions. This journal is intended as a forum for discussion and debate, for the profession as a whole. It has the backing of the majority of the analytically orientated psychotherapy organisations but is not solely aligned with any one of them.

SUBSCRIPTIONS Volume 10 (Autumn '93–Summer '94): **£23 for individuals, £45 to libraries and institutions (outside UK £30 and £52).** Order from:

Artesian Books, 18 Artesian Road, London W2 5AR

MANUSCRIPTS: 5 copies of manuscripts, with references in the style of the Journal, should be submitted to the Editor.

HarperCollinsCollege Division

TEXTS FOR 1993...

PSYCHOLOGY 3/E
Wade & Tavris
February 1993, £16.95
0-06-501641-6 HB

PSYCHOLOGY 4/E
Crider et al
February 1993, £16.95
0-673-46835-6 HB

PSYCHOLOGY AND LIFE 13/E
Zimbardo
1992, £16.95
0-673-46509-8 HB

INTRODUCTION TO PSYCHOLOGY
Weber
1992, £7.95
0-06-467103-8 PB

EXPLORING ABNORMAL PSYCHOLOGY
Perrotto & Culkin
January 1993, £14.95
0-673-46413-X PB

ABNORMAL PSYCHOLOGY AND MODERN LIFE 9/E
Carson & Butcher
1992, £22.00
0-673-46488-1 HB

ABNORMAL PSYCHOLOGY
Costello
1992, £7.95
0-06-467121-6 PB

SOCIAL PSYCHOLOGY
Weber
1992, £7.95
0-06-467157-7 PB

THE DEVELOPING CHILD 6/E
Bee
1992, £13.95
0-06-501364-6 HB

CHILD DEVELOPMENT
Cunningham
March 1993, £7.95
0-06-467149-6 PB

... AND MANY MORE!

Please call our Sales and Marketing office on 081 307 4555/4750 for a copy of our complete Psychology 1993 catalogue and details of our 'On Inspection' service to lecturers.